The Role of Reflection in Managerial Learning

The Role of Reflection in Managerial Learning

Theory, Research, and Practice

Kent W. Seibert
and Marilyn W. Daudelin

Quorum

Westport, Connecticut • London

Library of Congress Cataloging-in-Publication Data

Seibert, Kent W., 1957-
    The role of reflection in managerial learning : theory, research, and
practice / Kent W. Seibert, Marilyn W. Daudelin.
      p.   cm.
    Includes bibliographical references and index.
    ISBN 1-56720-259-4 (alk. paper)
    1. Management—Research. 2. Organizational learning.
I. Daudelin, Marilyn W., 1953- . II. Title.
HD30.4.S433   1999
658—DC21   99-17995

British Library Cataloguing in Publication Data is available.

Library of Congress Catalog Card Number: 99-17995
ISBN: 1-56720-259-4

First published in 1999

Quorum Books, 88 Post Road West, Westport, CT 06881
An imprint of Greenwood Publishing Group, Inc.
www.quorumbooks.com

Printed in the United States of America

The paper used in this book complies with the
Permanent Paper Standard issued by the National
Information Standards Organization (Z39.48-1984)

10 9 8 7 6 5 4 3 2 1

For Mother and Father
(K.W.S.)

For Dennis
(M.W.D.)

Contents

Illustrations

Tables

Preface

It has become a truism to say that continual learning is necessary in today's workplace. The only constant really is change, and responding effectively to change almost always requires learning. Although much has been written about this issue, empirically and theoretically grounded information is sparse, especially relating to the role of reflection in managerial learning. Indeed, reflection and management are often thought to be as compatible as oil and water. Our work suggests otherwise, indicating that not only are reflection and management compatible, but their blending is essential to productive learning in business organizations.

The impetus for our interest in this issue was the Center for Creative Leadership's landmark study of how successful executives develop on the job (McCall, Lombardo, and Morrison, 1988). That research identifies the types of experiences most conducive to management development as well as the lessons those experiences provide. It masterfully describes experiences and lessons but gives much less attention to the specific processes by which lessons are derived from experience. Drawing on existing experiential learning theory, we contend that reflection is the key mechanism in translating experience into learning. Simply put, reflection is the cognitive activity of attempting to make sense of experiences. Thus we set out to study the reflection of managers undergoing developmental experiences of the type identified by the Center for Creative Leadership. Although our initial research was of high-potential managers, it has become increasingly clear to us that virtually all managers in today's marketplace need to be able to learn from experience.

The purpose of this book is to provide a comprehensive discussion of current scholarly thinking on the role of reflection in how business managers learn from experience. By integrating previous work on reflection from the fields of management and education with the Center for Creative Leadership's "lessons of experience" research, we will share our original research on the role of reflection in managerial learning. We have found that understanding the role of reflection in learning requires examination of the relationship between the *internal* cognitive process of how managers reflect and the *external* forces that affect managers' ability to reflect. A complete understanding of managerial reflection is possible only when it is examined in this holistic manner.

A unique aspect of the book is that it includes both quantitative experimental data and qualitative interview data. We each studied reflection in very different ways and thus can describe what are really two related yet distinctly different modes of reflection: *proactive* and *active*. The quantitative study reported here represents the first experimental test of the relative effects of three proactive reflection techniques with a managerial sample. The qualitative study provides the first in-depth description of the active reflection of a sample of managers, including the first description of the effects of work environments on managerial reflection during developmental job experiences.

Two additional contributions of the book are the proposal of a holistic model of reflection integrating the two modes as well as consideration of what our work implies for practice. We are committed to research that informs both practice and scholarship, believing that in applied fields like management and education, the best research is that which bridges the theory–praxis divide. Managers and organizations need help in learning from experience, and our findings provide specific recommendations for facilitating workplace learning. Our intent, then, is to write to both the scholarly and management communities. Our emphasis is certainly the book's contribution to theory and research, but those contributions have clear and direct implications for practitioners. And while we have attempted to write with scholarly rigor, we have also tried to use a style that will be readily accessible to human resource development professionals and practicing managers.

Without the assistance of many people, this book would not have been possible. We are deeply indebted to our academic mentors at Boston University: Tim Hall, Kathy Kram, Bill Kahn, Tim Weaver, and Alan Gaynor. Their service as scholarly role models who effectively integrate theory and practice has contributed not only to this book but to our professional development as well. The Executive Development Roundtable of Boston University provided funding for the first author's research as well as encouragement and substantive input to both authors' studies. A primary objective of the roundtable is to support research in executive development, and this book represents one tangible output of their support.

Special thanks go to the three companies—Food Corp., Health Co., and Tech Inc.—and their seventy-two managers, without whom none of this would have been possible. The managers' willingness to share their time as well as important and sometimes intimate aspects of their lives at work is deeply appreciated. We are especially grateful for their interest in managerial reflection and their receptivity to our research.

Several people at Wheaton College (IL) provided important logistical support for the development of the book. To Bruce Howard, Pat Unander, Kelley MacKerron, and Nalleli Lopez, we give a heartfelt thanks. We could not have done it without you.

Last to be mentioned but most deserving of appreciation are our families: Donna, Sarah, Christine, Dad and Mom; and Dennis. Your encouragement, support, and love have surrounded us at all stages of this undertaking. Yours is a debt that can never be repaid. We appreciate you, but most of all we love you deeply.

Introduction

**REFLECTION IN MANAGERIAL LEARNING:
THE NEED AND A NEW APPROACH**

Learning is widely accepted as an essential skill for success in the postindustrial world. As noted management expert Chris Argyris has said, "Success in the marketplace increasingly depends on learning, yet most people don't know how to learn" (1991, p. 99). The importance of individual learning in business organizations cannot be overstated. A company's ability to learn will be only as strong as the learning abilities of the individuals it comprises (Hall and Seibert, 1992).

Given that individual learning is so important, what is known about how learning happens in organizations? There is empirical support for two basic assertions. First, people really do learn from experience, as has long been asserted by leading management theorists (Lewin, 1951; Mintzberg, 1973). This assertion was thoroughly described by McCall, Lombardo, and Morrison (1988) based on extensive interviews with nearly 200 executives. One of the most important findings of McCall et al. speaks to the second general assertion: not all experiences are equally conducive to learning. Thus, mere exposure to new job content (as happens in conventional approaches to job rotation) does not necessarily promote significant learning. The key to whether an experience produces learning is the presence or absence of challenge; experiences that promote learning and development stretch people well beyond their current capabilities.

These challenging experiences are assumed to produce learning, but simply having one of these experiences does not guarantee that learning will occur. Experience merely provides raw data, which can be a source of learning but is not the learning itself. Our research shows learning results only after managers attribute meaning to an experience, that is, after they understand the raw data of the experience. Thus, managers learn from the meaning they give to experience, not from experience itself, and they give meaning to experience by *reflecting*.

Although its importance is beginning to be recognized in the business world (Hammer and Stanton, 1997; Sherman, 1994), the role of reflection in learning from experience in business is still not well understood. Reflection has received less attention than has the "action" component of the learning cycle. Studies of experiential learning have emphasized the active engagement of experience (Kolb, 1984) as opposed to the more detached process of reflection, since active involvement is at the very core of what it means to learn by doing. This focus is understandable, but the resulting inattention to reflection has produced an incomplete picture of learning. There is a critical need to understand more thoroughly the role that reflection plays in learning from experience in business organizations.

This book is designed to address this need. It provides (1) a comprehensive review of scholarly thinking on reflection in managerial learning, (2) discussion of inductive and deductive approaches to studying managerial reflection, (3) results of two studies of 72 managers at three leading companies, (4) a new, holistic model that integrates past and current research findings on managerial reflection, and (5) practical consideration of the implications of this model for enhancing managerial reflection and learning.

The current state of thinking about managerial learning in organizations will be briefly reviewed below, followed by consideration of the importance of reflection to managerial learning. This introduction will then conclude with an overview of the content and structure of this book.

MANAGERIAL LEARNING IN ORGANIZATIONS

The issues of how managers learn and how that learning can be maximized have taken on such significance during the last decade that a subfield of management devoted entirely to managerial learning is emerging. The first comprehensive and integrative description of this emerging field is given in a recent book edited by Burgoyne and Reynolds (1997), who frame managerial learning broadly to encompass both formal management training and development activities as well as informal managerial learning that occurs naturally on the job. They conclude their book with the recommendation "to enrich the theoretical debate without detaching theory from practice" (Burgoyne and Reynolds, 1997, p. 332). That is precisely the approach taken here. We attempt to make a significant theoretical contribution to the literature on reflection in managerial learning, yet that theory is derived from and designed to contribute directly to the practical concerns of managers and their organizations.

The term *managerial learning* has a more specific meaning here than that given by Burgoyne and Reynolds (1997). Its use here refers to the learning that managers naturally acquire while performing on the job. The following list gives basic definitions of this and other key terms that appear throughout this book. If managerial learning is about learning that happens through the normal course of responding to management challenges, learning is about the creation of meaning. Much of the literature defines learning in terms of the creation of symbols or clues from events that lead to patterns or meanings that can be used to guide future action.

BASIC DEFINITIONS OF KEY TERMS

Learning—The creation of meaning from past or current events that serves as a guide for future behavior.

Managerial learning—Learning that managers naturally acquire while performing on the job.

Developmental experience—A challenging on-the-job experience that stretches managers beyond the limits of their current capabilities, thereby providing the opportunity for learning and growth.

Managerial reflection—The cognitive activity managers engage in to make sense of an experience, both actively and proactively (as defined below).

Active reflection—An activity that contributes to learning *during* a developmental experience. An internal dialogue involving moments of inquiry and interpretation intended to produce increased insight into experience.

Proactive reflection—An activity that contributes to learning *from* a developmental experience. The process of stepping back from an experience to carefully and persistently ponder its meaning to the self.

Internal processes—The cognitive, psychological processes that managers experience when they are reflecting.

External forces—Outside forces impinging upon managers that affect their inclination to reflect.

Bandura states that "learning is largely an information-processing activity in which information about the structure of behavior and about environmental events is transformed into symbolic representations that serve as guides for action" (Bandura, 1986, p. 51). Bandura examined the role of cognitive factors in human learning and found that by reviewing the pattern of outcomes they experienced, people were able to arrive at key concepts and rules of behavior to guide future action. Knapp (1992) believes that one has learned when one can recover a body of information some time after acquiring it to apply to a new situation. Many attribute this view of learning—the discovery of symbols, clues, and patterns that guide future action—to Thorndike, whose research changed the view of how the brain functions in the learning process from a muscle to be exercised through rote repetition and nonevaluative recall to the association of activities to outcomes (Eichelberger, 1989).

It is from these ideas that we have derived our definition of learning. Learning is ultimately about creating meaning that is intended to impact future behavior.

So how do managers learn? As stated earlier, they learn primarily from the meaning they give to experience. The focus of this book is learning from experience, because the evidence that managers learn the most from experience—as opposed to formal training and education—is now overwhelming.

Empirical Evidence for the Power of Learning From Experience

Berlew and Hall (1966) and Hall (1976) demonstrated some time ago the importance of the job to the development of managerial abilities. Mintzberg concluded his classic study of the nature of managerial work by praising learning from experience: "But no other learning environment—classroom, executive development program, peer feedback session—can surpass the job itself, provided the manager knows how to learn from his own experience" (Mintzberg, 1973, p. 193).

Two of the earliest studies explicitly aimed at managerial learning found that learning occurred when a manager was required to construct new skills and capacities in a situation that demanded previously undeveloped abilities. According to Davies and Easterby-Smith (1984), on-the-job experiences, particularly active engagement of new experiences (e.g., a new job or changing circumstances in an existing job), are the primary source of managerial learning. In studying the learning of 43 managers, Kelleher, Finestone, and Lowy (1986) confirmed that daily on-the-job learning is a central part of managers' learning and development. The authors identified four key factors as contributors to managerial learning: demands of managing a staff, responding to change, exerting upward influence, and personal style.

A frequently quoted study of natural managerial learning sought to formally partition the contribution of the various sources of managerial learning. This research was conducted by the corporate human resource development group at Honeywell to determine how successful Honeywell managers learned to manage (Zemke, 1985). The relative contributions of job experiences/assignments, personal relationships (especially with superiors and subordinates), and formal training were determined to be 50 percent, 30 percent, and 20 percent, respectively. More recently, Robinson and Wick (1992) found that about 70 percent of managers' learning and development came through on-the-job experiences, with formal training providing less than 10 percent of managers' development.

Hoberman and Mailick (1992) distinguish between two types of experiences that provide learning: what they term "synthetic experiential" approaches, such as simulations, role plays, and case studies, and "natural" approaches, which involve on-the-job learning. In their study of both types of experiences as they occur in corporations, Hoberman and Mailick discovered that natural experiential learning is more effective than synthetic experiential learning, especially when the learner is assisted with the process.

The most thorough investigation of learning from experience was conducted by the Center for Creative Leadership (McCall et al., 1988). Extensive interviews were conducted with 191 high-performing executives from six large corporations. This work uncovered three primary sources of managerial learning: job assignments, other people, and hardships. It also fleshed out the specific characteristics of experiences that are most conducive to learning and development.

Types of Experiences Most Conducive to Managerial Learning

According to the findings of McCall et al. (1988), five types of job assignments have the greatest potential to produce learning: project/task force (a temporary assignment to address a specific issue), line-to-staff switches (moving from line operations to a staff role), start-ups (building something from nothing), fix-its/turnarounds (stabilizing a failing operation), and leaps in scope of responsibility (significant increase in the number of people, dollars, or functions to manage). The assignments taught managers confidence, toughness, and independence.

"Other people" and hardships also contributed significantly to managerial learning. The other people who provided the most learning for managers were their supervisors. Other research corroborates the important role of supervisors in managers' development (Lindholm, 1988) as well as the significant role of other relationships such as with mentors (Kram, 1988) and peers (Kram and Isabella, 1985). Finally, hardships such as career setbacks (demotions, missed promotions), business failures and mistakes, and having to address subordinate performance problems also contributed to learning. Success in coping with hardships resulted from managers turning inward and taking an intense look at themselves. Hardships provided managers with an opportunity to gain humility as a tempering agent to the confidence acquired from successful job assignments.

The basic finding of the Center for Creative Leadership research is that naturally occurring job experiences are the most potent source of individual learning. Furthermore, it is what a manager faces in a job that produces learning, not the job per se. Thus, exposure to job content, including new things, is less the issue than what the manager has to do while being exposed to that content: respond to challenge. Challenge—being stretched beyond the limits of one's current knowledge and skills—is at the core of all discussions of the primary source of managerial learning. Such learning is stimulating, expanding, and potentially even exhilarating.

Work at the Center for Creative Leadership has continued more recently with investigations of the impact of stress and coping on experiential learning (Bunker and Webb, 1992) and identification of the learning tactics managers employ when confronting challenging experiences (Dalton, 1998). There has also been considerable recent work attempting to apply our increasing understanding of managerial learning to improve managers' learning. Numerous examples of firms consciously using challenging job experiences to facilitate their managers' learning now exist (Dotlich and Noel, 1998; Saari, Johnson, Mclaughlin, and Zimmerle, 1988; Seibert, Hall, and Kram, 1995; Vicere, 1996).

For example, Seibert et al. (1995) describe how 3M assigns key managers to head its European business centers to expand the company's business overseas and to help the managers learn how to manage across the distinct yet interconnected countries of the European Union. They also describe Motorola's use of an increasingly common approach—action learning teams—designed to simultaneously develop managers and implement strategic business objectives. This approach traces its roots to Revans's (1982) work on "action learning," in which he developed a technique that promotes learning through the use of on-going small teams of managers who meet over a period of months to solve real business problems.

However, as all of the above writers recognize, current efforts to promote managers' experiential learning are far from fully effective. This is largely due to the incomplete state of knowledge about learning from experience in organizations and especially the role of reflection in experiential learning.

THE ROLE OF REFLECTION IN MANAGERIAL LEARNING

Reflection involves the mental activity of taking an experience from outside a person, bringing it inside the mind, filtering it through past experiences, examining it, and trying to understand it. When this activity is effective, individuals develop inferences about potential ways to respond to the demands they face in their experience. In doing this, they learn.

The central role of reflection in learning is well documented (Argyris, 1982; Bandura, 1986; Boyd and Fales, 1983; Dewey, 1910; Hall, 1979; Isaacs, 1992; Knapp, 1992; Kolb, 1984; Mezirow, 1991; Revans, 1982; Schön, 1983; Senge, 1990). According to Boyd and Fales, "The process of reflection is the core difference between whether a person repeats the same experience several times, becoming highly proficient at one behavior, or learns from experience in such a way that he or she is cognitively or affectively changed" (Boyd and Fales, 1983, p. 100). Osterman reports, "While experience may serve as the stimulus for learning, reflection is the essential part of the process that makes it possible to learn from experience" (Osterman, 1990, p. 135).

Marsick and Watkins (1997) have proposed and tested a theory of informal managerial learning. They define informal learning as unstructured and incidental learning controlled by the learner that occurs beyond a classroom. Their theory involves a cycle with multiple phases including experiencing challenges, reflecting, and planning next steps. Reflection is presented as a major component of their theory. Indeed, they claim, "Reflection is the primary tool to trigger learning from experience" (Marsick and Watkins, 1997, p. 304). Their empirical validation of the theory lends credence to it and reinforces the pivotal role of reflection in learning from experience.

Managerial reflection is here defined as the mental activity managers engage in to try to make sense of experience. This general definition incorporates the two types of reflection explored in our research: active and proactive reflection. Discussion of the differences between these two forms of reflection as well as ways they can be integrated constitutes the essence of this book. It will be shown that the two equally important types of reflection are distinct yet complementary.

Active reflection happens spontaneously to managers as they engage in developmental experiences. Those experiences put managers' minds in an active mode such that they cannot help but consciously think about their experiences. Through active reflection, managers come to not only develop a basic understanding of their experience but appreciate the learning required to successfully handle the situation. In contrast, proactive reflection happens only if managers are provided with the opportunity for it; it involves being removed from the experience in order to deliberately analyze the experience and what it means. Proactive reflection enables managers to surface and consolidate the learning that is inherent in their experience.

Marsick and Watkins conclude the discussion of their theory of informal learning by stating that "more studies are needed that focus on real-time reflection and the reflective learning/intervention relationship" (Marsick and Watkins, 1997, p. 308). This is precisely what the research reported in this book does. It examines in detail both real-time (active) reflection and the impact of reflection interventions (proactive reflection) on learning. We agree with Marsick and Watkins that these are the primary gaps in current understanding of the role of reflection in managerial learning.

These gaps are apparent in the two bodies of literature that are most relevant to managerial reflection: management and education. The primary emphasis of the management literature is on naturally occurring active reflection. However, that type of reflection is described only at a basic level, and scant attention is given to the organizational forces that impact it. Overall, reflection has received minimal attention in the field of management. Reflection has received much more attention in the education literature, having been recognized for many years as a key ingredient of learning. Even so, the effects of different methods for conducting proactive reflection have not been directly compared. Additionally, the use of proactive reflection with business managers has not been explored. These deficiencies in both bodies of literature will be addressed here.

Prior research has established the importance of reflection to learning from experience. This book will offer new insights into the applicability of active and proactive reflection to managerial learning. At the same time, it is important to emphasize that reflection is necessary but not sufficient for producing learning from experience. We fully recognize that reflection is only one piece, albeit a very important one, of the learning puzzle.

A NEW APPROACH TO MANAGERIAL REFLECTION

The approach taken here combines existing information from the two literatures relevant to managerial learning and integrates it with the findings of our own research to produce a holistic model of managerial reflection. The model produced has important implications for both theory and practice. A primary emphasis of the model is the need to give balanced attention to the two modes of reflection (active and proactive) as well as to the two factors most important to understanding managerial reflection: internal processes and external forces.

Internal processes refer to what goes on inside managers as they engage in active and proactive reflection; the focus here is the psychology of managerial reflection. External forces are those things outside managers that influence their reflection; the focus here is the ecology of managerial reflection. Particular attention is given to the conditions in managers' work environments that impact active reflection and to structured interventions that are designed to facilitate proactive reflection. Taken together, the two dimensions of (1) modes of reflection and (2) factors of reflection provide a complete and integrated framework for understanding the role of reflection in learning from experience in business organizations today.

In our own research, we discovered that active reflection and proactive reflection play different but equally important roles in promoting managerial learning. An inductive, theory-building study of active reflection resulted in a model that describes in detail this mode of reflection. Active reflection is described in relation to six dimensions: its process, outlook, orientation, timing, approach, and activity. Personal and emotional factors influencing active reflection are identified and discussed, and the types of work environments most conducive to active reflection are identified. Work environments characterized by ample amounts of autonomy and feedback, by three types of interactions with other people, and by two forms of pressure stimulate active reflection during developmental job experiences.

A deductive, experimental study of proactive reflection examined the relative effects on managerial learning of three different types of proactive reflection interventions: reflecting alone, with a tutor, and with a group of peers. Reflecting alone or with a tutor increased the amount of learning from experience by a statistically significant amount compared to a control group, whereas reflecting with a group of peers did not. The amount of learning was not affected by the type of developmental experience, length of experience, importance of experience, or negative or positive nature of the experience.

While the first study provides a theoretical model of active reflection and the conditions in organizations that enable it, the second study provides strong empirical evidence that certain forms of proactive reflection increase the amount of learning that managers obtain from experience.

OVERVIEW OF THE BOOK

This book is organized into four sections. The first section includes reviews of current thinking on reflection in experiential learning in the fields of management and education. The thinking in each field is reviewed separately for two reasons. First, the two studies reported here were grounded primarily in one of the two literatures, and second, the two literatures are quite distinct. Even though they occasionally address the same issue, there is minimal direct overlap between them. Because of this, they approach reflection in different ways. Part of what we hope to accomplish here is to provide a more integrated view of reflection than is currently apparent in each separate field.

Part I concludes with a discussion of the two different approaches to studying reflection taken here: induction and deduction. These approaches indicate the current state of knowledge of reflection in management and education as well as our personal orientations as researchers. This chapter discusses how two researchers looking at basically the same phenomenon can study it in very different ways.

Part II reports the inductive, theory-building research of the first author. It begins with a description of the specific methodology used in that study, followed by five chapters presenting and discussing the results. Chapters 5, 6, and 7 provide a detailed description of active reflection, while chapters 8 and 9 cover the conditions in organizations that influence the expression of active reflection. This is the longest section in the book because it reports qualitative data, which by its nature tends to be lengthy.

The deductive, experimental research of the second author is provided in part III. The specific methodology of that study is presented in chapter 10, followed by a discussion of the results in chapter 11. In addition to presenting two different types of reflection, parts II and III illustrate two contrasting ways to study a social–psychological phenomenon like reflection.

Part IV presents our integrated model of managerial reflection and considers the implications of that model for theory, research, and practice. In many ways, the initial impetus for both researchers' interest in reflection in managerial learning was the practical need to help managers learn and develop. It is fitting, then, that the book end with a discussion of how our findings and model can serve today's managers and businesses.

As with any book, this one can be read in a variety of ways. The chapters are arranged in logical sequence, as just described. However, readers whose primary interest is management may wish to focus on chapters 1 and 4 through 9, while readers interested in an educational perspective may want to read chapters 2, 10, and 11. Readers interested in methodological issues will find chapters 3, 4, and 10 most interesting.

Chapters 1 and 2 provide a thorough review of current thinking on reflection, whereas chapters 12 and 13 present the direction of future work in this area. These chapters are written primarily from a scholarly perspective. Finally, as indicated above, chapter 14 is most relevant to readers who are interested in how the material on managerial reflection presented here can be used with actual managers in real organizations. In addition to integrating management and educational perspectives on reflection, we have attempted to integrate theory and practice in ways that make contributions to both.

PART I

The Contributions and Limitations of Existing Perspectives of Reflection

Chapter 1

Reflection in Management

The term *reflection* conjures up several images. There is the scholar tucked away in a far corner of a musty library analyzing the intricacies of an obscure theory. Or there is the solitary monk quietly contemplating things spiritual while birds chirp overhead. There is even the vacationer reclining on a beach blanket, struggling to stay awake while pondering how to spend a week in paradise. None of these images are remotely similar to that of a manager closing a crucial deal or racing to meet a deadline. Does reflection have anything to do with management? It does, especially when a manager is involved in learning something new. The form that reflection takes may be different from that of a scholar or a monk, but it is reflection nevertheless.

After presenting an initial, working definition of reflection, this chapter will review previous empirical and theoretical work on reflection in management. The implications of that work for the theory, research, and practice of management will then be discussed, clarifying the relevance of reflection to management and the limited state of knowledge on this topic.

AN INITIAL DEFINITION OF REFLECTION

A comprehensive definition of reflection currently does not exist in the management literature. One of the purposes of the research reported here was to develop such a definition. The following provisional definition provides a starting point for research into managerial reflection. Reflection is defined initially as the cognitive examination of experience. People reflect when they take material from outside themselves and bring it into their minds to examine it. Defined this way, reflection is most logically understood as a form of managerial cognition. Managers' cognitive processes have long been of interest to management theorists, from March and Simon's (1958) identification of bounded rationality in decision making and Katz's (1974) study of the conceptual skill of administrators to more recent explorations of scripts and associated cognitive processes in organizations (Gioia and Poole, 1984; Weick, 1979).

Cognitive theory deals with the mental processes that mediate a person's responses to external stimuli. According to this theory, a general distinction can be made between two modes of processing information: schema-driven and stimulus-driven (Sims and Lorenzi, 1992). Schema-driven processing is relatively effortless, if not automatic, since it involves responding to a situation on the basis of an existing knowledge structure or mental model. In contrast, stimulus-driven processing requires active mental processing in response to a situation that cannot be easily fitted into an existing knowledge structure. The trigger for active cognition, thus, is an encounter with something novel. Such cognitive processing is slower, more effortful, and more consciously monitored.

In the context of a business organization, engagement in conscious thinking has been demonstrated by Louis (1980) as the natural "sensemaking" response of a firm's new members to being surprised by the unfamiliar. Similarly, heightened cognitive activity in response to a disruption in career routines has been presented by Hall (1986a) as a mechanism for fostering development at midcareer. The implication of these cognitive models is that active engagement in reflection should be an expected result of a manager's encounter with a challenging developmental experience, since this is precisely the type of event that elicits active cognition.

Although reflection is a form of cognition, the literature on organizational cognition makes virtually no reference to reflection, focusing instead on other forms of mental processing at work. Reflection has not been a part of research of managerial cognition and has received minimal attention from those directly studying managerial learning.

EMPIRICAL RESEARCH OF REFLECTION IN MANAGERIAL LEARNING

Hard data on how managers reflect while engaged in learning is almost nonexistent. In a phenomenological field study of natural managerial learning, Burgoyne and Hodgson (1983) found that managers learned at one of three levels: Level 1 involved the simple acquisition of new information that was of immediate use; Level 2 entailed something learned that was transferable to subsequent situations; and Level 3 consisted of managers becoming aware of their fundamental views of the world, how they were formed, and how they might change them. Five processes were apparent in the most common type of learning, Level 2, one process of which they called "reflective learning." Here managers learned by thinking about an incident or problem when not directly engaged with it. Burgoyne and Hodgson describe reflective learning as follows:

In some incidents, and their accompanying streams of events, critical insights, new ideas, approaches, etc. occur to managers in "reflective" moments, when they are thinking about the problem or incident but are not "in the thick of it." No particular external stimulus seems to be critical to this process other than just the time and "space" for it to occur. In some situations managers deliberately contrived to create the space for "reflective" learning to occur, and/or to delay decisions or actions until they had such an opportunity (Burgoyne and Hodgson, 1983, p. 395).

Although this is a meaningful finding, this is all Burgoyne and Hodgson have to say about reflection. They do not explain exactly how managers reflected or the extent to which it occurred.

An emerging source of data on reflection in management is corporate management development programs that include reflection as one of their objectives. The importance of reflection is gaining recognition among practitioners (Sherman, 1994). A survey study of "best practices" in executive development at 77 U.S. companies concluded that executives need to be encouraged to approach learning opportunities in a more conscious and reflective way (Mann and Staudenmier, 1991). Examples of applied, action-type research studies of reflection include Argyris (1991) and Robinson and Wick (1992).

Robinson and Wick's (1992) description of programs designed to help managers learn from experience at two leading companies illustrates this type of work. The three basic elements of these programs are planning prior to the experience, action learning during the experience involving a cycle of action and reflection/feedback, and structured reflection opportunities ("time-outs") after the experience. Critical reflection, critical thinking, and hypothesis testing are presented as three learning strategies that managers must employ to learn from experience.

Critical thinking enables managers to determine the extent to which a newly encountered situation is like or different from others they have encountered. If it is similar, they can appropriately apply past knowledge; if it is different, they can identify what needs to be learned. Robinson and Wick emphasize that critical reflection is not passive, contemplative thinking but is rather an active process of probing for and then challenging the assumptions, values, and beliefs that underlie actions.

The guiding principle for programs like these is that experience provides only the opportunity for learning to occur. For learning to actually happen, the manager must extract from experience the lessons it provides. Reflection is seen as the primary way to do this. Programs like those described by Robinson and Wick emphasize guided, structured reflection. While this approach to reflection is useful, there are limitations to viewing reflection exclusively in this way. One limitation is that removing reflection spatially and temporally from actual experience could lead managers and management development professionals to view reflection as just another classroom activity. Learning from experience could get artificially compartmentalized, with the action component occurring on the job and the reflective component occurring away from the "real world." Such an approach has potential to artificially dichotomize the behavioral and cognitive elements of learning from experience.

Action research of programs designed to enhance learning by facilitating reflection tends to be quite prescriptive. Suggestions for promoting reflection are usually made without a baseline understanding of managers' existing reflective processes and do not refer to a theoretical basis for recommendations. It should be clear from the previous review that rigorous empirical research of reflection in managerial learning is woefully inadequate.

RELEVANT THEORY ON REFLECTION

Some serious theoretical work on managerial reflection does exist in the literature, although much more is needed. Certainly the importance of reflection to managers and leaders has not escaped leading organizational theorists (Bennis, 1989; Katz, 1974; Tichy and Devanna, 1986). According to Mintzberg (1990), "Above all, the manager needs to be introspective in order to continue to learn on the job" (p. 175). Although many management scholars recognize the significance of reflection, there is still minimal theory dealing with this aspect of managerial functioning.

Related Theory

Half a century ago, Lewin (1951) wrote of reflection as that process which reinforces learned behavior and leads to new or higher level abstractions. Reflection, along with abstraction, concrete implication, experience, and observation–feedback, is posited as one of five elements in a cycle of learning from experience. Reflection is a central mechanism for producing new insights through examining experience. To Lewin, experience was the necessary ingredient for learning.

Kolb (1984) presents an elaborate theory of experiential learning that includes a form of reflection. The theory consists of a four-stage experiential learning cycle based on a synthesis of the theoretical work of Dewey (1910), Piaget (1968), and Lewin (1951). The four stages are concrete experience, reflective observation, abstract conceptualization, and active experimentation. The cycle describes how experience is translated into concepts, which in turn are used as guides in the choice of new experiences.

The four stages represent dialectically opposing forces: affect (concrete experience) versus cognition (abstract conceptualization) and perception (reflective observation) versus behavior (active experimentation). Learning requires the resolution of conflicts between these dialectically opposed modes of adaptation to the world. In other words, to learn from an experience, an individual must progress through all four stages of the learning cycle. Kolb refers to this as integrative competence. This is not as easy as it appears, since everyone demonstrates a preference for one of the four modes of learning. The existence of individual differences in learning styles, which Kolb has demonstrated empirically, is an important aspect of the theory.

Variations on Kolb's cycle exist. A well-known example is Honey and Mumford's (Mumford, 1990) learning cycle: having an experience, reviewing the experience, concluding from the experience, and planning the next steps. All these views have in common the belief that learning from experience involves the interaction of action and reflection, of engaging in an experience and then making sense of what is happening. Neither action without reflection nor reflection without action produces learning; rather, learning results when action and reflection are synthesized.

The two stages of Kolb's cycle that are relevant to this discussion are reflective observation and abstract conceptualization. We have defined reflection here as the cognitive examination of experience. Kolb uses the term *reflective observation* to refer to the perceptual dimension of experiential learning. Reflective observation entails examining situations by carefully watching and listening to what is happening. This involves viewing circumstances from different perspectives and searching for the meaning of things. There is an emphasis in this stage on deliberation as opposed to action, on giving observations personal meaning. In short, reflective observation is knowledge of experience.

Kolb uses the term *abstract conceptualization* to describe cognition in experiential learning. Abstract conceptualization involves formal hypothetico-deductive reasoning, with an emphasis on logic, ideas, concepts, and planning. The person is engaged in thinking—developing an intellectual understanding of a situation—as opposed to feeling. Relevant ideas and theories are generated and refined. In brief, abstract conceptualization is knowledge about experience.

Reflective observation and abstract conceptualization enable a person to make sense of a prior experience and then form concepts and generalizations to guide future action. These two stages encompass aspects of reflection as we define it, but they do not thoroughly describe the way managers engage in reflection when they encounter actual developmental experiences on the job. Kolb's contribution is the overall, formal theory of stages of experiential learning. However, the specifics of the reflective piece of the process of learning from experience remain underdeveloped in the theory. Moreover, Kolb's theory of experiential learning, including the validity of his Learning Style Inventory (Kolb, 1976), which was developed to assess learning styles, is not without its critics (Allinson and Hayes, 1988; Freedman and Stumpf, 1980; Kaskowitz, 1995).

Argyris and his colleagues have written extensively on learning in business organizations (Argyris, 1976; Argyris and Schön, 1978; Argyris, Putman, and Smith, 1985). Argyris has long held that experience is the ultimate teacher: "Self-insight and human skill in living can be learned only through living in, and learning from, the stream of 'life events' we call experience" (Argyris, 1957, p. 218). The primary contribution of this work is the distinction between what is called single-loop and double-loop learning.

Single-loop learning involves changes within the context of existing premises and assumptions. If goals are not being met, corrective action can be taken, but the goals and current operating procedures themselves are not questioned. Double-loop learning requires surfacing fundamental, underlying assumptions and beliefs and then challenging them to determine if they contribute to desired goals. Therefore, if goals are not being met, not only can corrective action be taken to meet them, but the goals themselves can be questioned. This allows for genuine learning to happen because it enables a person to generate valid information, think about it, and change behavior accordingly.

Exclusive reliance on single-loop learning actually inhibits more genuine learning (i.e., double-loop learning). Unfortunately, most managers and organizations tend strongly toward single-loop learning and have difficulty engaging in double-loop learning, even once they are made aware of it. A similar distinction between types of learning is made by Senge (1990), who distinguishes between adaptive learning, which is essentially about coping, and generative learning, which involves expanding one's capabilities and creating new ones. Generative and double-loop learning require systemic thinking, surfacing and testing mental models, and sharing a vision.

Argyris does not use the term *reflection* in his writings but clearly implies that cognition of the reflective sort is a prerequisite for the intense surfacing and questioning of fundamental, underlying assumptions involved in double-loop learning. Learning at this deep level requires deliberate mental effort and self-awareness. A major barrier to double-loop learning, and by implication to reflection, is defensive reasoning (Argyris, 1991).

Argyris claims that managers typically behave in ways to avoid embarrassment or threat as well as feelings of vulnerability or incompetence. This causes them to reason defensively, that is, to keep private and untested the premises, inferences, and conclusions that drive their behavior. Given this, the open inquiry implied by reflection could be perceived as intimidating by managers. Fear of not liking what they might uncover through such inquiry could hinder managers' reflection and ultimately could hinder double-loop learning. Although Argyris does not discuss reflection directly, his work highlights the importance of reflectionlike cognitive activity to deep learning. It also provides a reason why managers may find it difficult to learn reflectively.

While the previous theorists provide useful ideas that are relevant to reflection, none address the construct directly or in substantial detail.

Reflection in Professional Practice

Schön (1983, 1987) provides the most complete currently available theoretical treatment of reflection in a professional context. Schön's work is based on examining the way professionals (e.g., architects, psychotherapists, managers) practice their professions. It has had its greatest application in the training of teachers

(Sparks-Langer and Colton, 1991), but it also represents the most explicit investigation of managerial reflection to date.

Although Schön discusses different types of thought processes demonstrated by professionals, the centerpiece of his work is what he calls reflection-in-action, which is a process professionals use to address novel problems in their day-to-day work. It can be described most simply as thinking about what one is doing while one is doing it. The result of this is on-the-spot experimenting. Reflection-in-action occurs in situations of uncertainty, instability, uniqueness, or value conflict. Here the problem itself is not initially clear and there is no obvious fit between the characteristics of the situation and an existing body of knowledge and techniques. Reflection-in-action contrasts, thus, with what Schön calls technical rationality, which involves problem solving in familiar situations through an established process of rule-governed inquiry. Situations that invoke reflection-in-action are strikingly similar to the challenging situations described earlier that provide the opportunity for managerial learning.

Schön found that professionals in these types of situations reflect spontaneously and in an unstructured, natural way while performing their jobs. The process of reflection-in-action spirals through phases of appreciation, action, and reappreciation. It begins with a situation to which a person brings routinized responses that prove ineffective. This results in surprise, followed by conscious thought about the situation. This reflection then gives rise to rigorous on-the-spot experimenting. That is, the person thinks of, tries out, and considers new action intended to explore the situation and ultimately to change it in a desired direction. This experimenting may yield the intended results or it may produce new surprises that call for further reflection and experimentation.

One group of professionals Schön has studied are managers. Their reflection-in-action is essentially the same as the reflection-in-action of other professionals, but it also has special features of its own. The phenomena on which managers reflect-in-action are the phenomena of organizational life. The manager draws on an existing body of organizational knowledge (e.g., notions of mission and identity, facts about the task environment), adapting it to some present concern. The manager also serves as an agent of organizational learning, modifying, in her present inquiry, the body of knowledge that will be available for future inquiry by the organization. Additionally, within a business organization, the manager operates in a unique "learning system" that may promote or inhibit reflection-in-action.

According to Burgoyne and Hodgson (1983) (as described earlier), managers reflected by pausing in the midst of action to think about what was happening or what they thought about what had happened in a situation after the fact. Schön refers to this type of reflection as reflection-*on*-action, and he found this type of reflection to be much less characteristic of managers' behavior than was reflection-*in*-action. The idea that reflection-in-action occurs in real-time when it can still make a difference to the situation at hand is a distinguishing characteristic of reflection as described by Schön.

Schön's discussion of reflection-in-action and its relevance to managers is a very important contribution. Prior to the research reported here, his work represented the most thorough published investigation of managerial reflection. However, the relevance of his ideas to individual managerial reflection in the context of learning from experience is limited. He presents just four cases dealing with management, only one of which deals with an individual manager, and his overall focus is at more of a macro level of analysis, analyzing the interactions of various organizational units. One case, for example, deals with how the engineering, development, advertising, and manufacturing functions of a firm learn from their collaborative efforts in developing new products, while another considers how a marketing department interprets consumers' responses to its actions.

Schön's focus at the organizational versus individual level of analysis as well as the limited number of management cases he reports suggests that much could be gained from further exploration of the reflection of individual managers. Finally, even though Schön acknowledges the important role of context in reflection by referring to "organizational systems," his work is framed according to professions, not organizations. Reflection-in-action is by definition bound to the context from which it arises. Much more attention needs to be given to the immediate work environment within which managers' learning experiences occur if their reflection is to be more fully understood.

ANALYSIS AND IMPLICATIONS

Summary of Current Thinking on the Reflection Construct

The provisional definition of reflection—cognitive examination of experience—presented here is consistent with how the construct has been treated in the literature. Reflection is the process of making sense of what one is experiencing during a learning challenge. Through reflection, managers attempt to understand their experience. Reflecting on an experience can be contrasted with responding automatically, mechanically, or reflexively to an experience. Although reflection can be thought of as the opposite of the action component of learning from experience, it is not a passive activity. Reflection is very much an active mental process. It is at once distinct from taking action in an experience and yet it is inextricably bound to action. Indeed, reflection without experience can be thought of as form without substance, while experience without reflection is substance without form (Roth, 1989).

At its core, reflection involves exploring new things. Managers who reflect ask questions, of themselves and of the experiences in which they find themselves. Akin to Levinson, Darrow, Klein, Levinson, and McKee's (1978) "structure changing" periods of adult development, reflection entails questioning where one has been and evaluating where one wants to go. The reflective manager is an active explorer of the meaning of experience.

Schön (1983) and Kolb (1984) are responsible for the way reflection has been framed in the management literature. Reflection is seen primarily in its active mode; that is, as a cognitive activity that happens naturally as managers seek to respond to new and stretching experiences. Reflection is something managers engage in while they are in the midst of an experience to help them respond to and learn from that experience. The term *active reflection* is used here to describe this type of reflection. The existing management literature has also framed reflection as primarily an internal process. It involves what happens inside a manager's mind as he attempts to sort through novel and puzzling information. Although it is a mental process, reflection involves more than simple cognitive awareness or basic reasoning; it involves exploration that results in new discoveries and appreciations. It is at once different from acting on experience and yet it is woven through action, and through the weaving a cloth of learning is created.

The Importance of the Work Environment to Active Reflection

Management theorists have long emphasized the importance of organizational context to learning at work. Years ago McGregor (1960) proposed that agriculture provided a more accurate picture of managerial learning in business firms than did manufacturing, which was the prevailing metaphor. According to the manufacturing metaphor, organizations attempt to engineer programs and build the necessary machinery to "produce" managerial talent. McGregor's agriculture notion, in contrast, is based on the view that managers will learn and "grow" into what they are capable of becoming, provided the organization can create the proper conditions for growth. As in agriculture, where the emphasis is on influencing the climate and fertility of the soil and on methods of cultivation, what become central to learning are the characteristics, policies, and practices of the company.

The farmer cannot "make" anything grow, but can try to provide the best possible conditions for growth (adequate water, nutrients, etc.) and then let nature take its course. Likewise, managers will learn and develop into what they are capable of becoming, provided the organization creates the proper conditions for growth. McGregor believed that the manager's supervisor, the manager's on-the-job experiences, and the degree of organizational support for learning were the primary organizational conditions affecting growth. Subsequent research has confirmed that an organization's culture, policies, structure, and reward systems as well as the behavior of an employee's immediate supervisor impact learning and development (Barrett, 1995; Hall and Fukami, 1979; Kelleher et al., 1986; Wexley, 1984).

If the work context within an organization is critical to the overall process of managerial learning, then it should also be an important influence on reflection. Indeed, as indicated previously, active reflection—the kind of reflection that occurs in the midst of responding to a challenging experience—is by definition context-bound. It is impossible to separate active reflection from the setting in which it occurs; in fact, it is a direct function of what is happening in that setting. Schön (1983) pointed out the importance of contextual forces on reflection-in-action, referring to the unique "learning system" within which managers operate and the way that can encourage or discourage reflection.

Schön's findings in this area, however, are incomplete as regards individual managerial reflection. His macro focus placed attention on organizational-level systems and structures that affect reflection (like the allocation of resources across a corporation). While such forces are important, so too are more meso-level ones that are a part of a manager's immediate work environment. These forces, including things like the norms, people, and available information that directly impinge upon managers when they are grappling with a specific experience, should also significantly affect reflection. But to date these external forces (i.e., forces external to the manager's internal cognitive processing) have received minimal attention in the management literature on reflection. Although the existence of external forces has been acknowledged, previous discussions have focused on reflection as an internal cognitive process.

Finally, Schön did not draw generalizable conclusions about the macro-level forces he discussed, preferring rather to emphasize the uniqueness of each organizational learning experience. If the management literature gives incomplete attention to the internal process of managerial reflection, it gives even less consideration to the effect of organizational work environments on reflection.

The Major Deficiency in the Existing Management Literature

It should now be clear that there is insufficient research on the nature of reflection in on-the-job managerial learning. Kolb (1984) and especially Schön (1983) provide some useful rudimentary ideas on managerial reflection, but their work only scratches the surface of this rich phenomenon. In addition, virtually all of the more recent interest in reflection (e.g., Robinson and Wick, 1992; Sherman, 1994) has been largely atheoretical and prescriptive. Recent writing has been about how managers should reflect, not about how they actually do reflect. While there is nothing wrong with prescriptions, the dearth of descriptive information on reflection is disturbing. A solid theoretical understanding of managerial reflection is a prerequisite to sound practice, yet this is just the type of information that is currently incomplete in the literature. The theory-building research reported here is intended to fill that gap by exploring the ways managers actually reflect when they are involved in a challenging experience in an organization. This is intended to produce theoretical insights into the nature of that reflection as well as the conditions in the organizational environment that impact managers' reflection.

Attention will now be turned to the conceptual framework that will be used to guide the theory-building research described in subsequent chapters. The focus of this work is the role of reflection in learning, not from just any experience, but from developmental experiences. These challenging job experiences, as discussed earlier, have been demonstrated by prior research to provide the best opportunity for learning. By further exploring these experiences, this research will build on prior research and will have implications for practice, since this is the type of experience companies are currently using to promote their managers' learning and development.

Figure 1-1 provides a model of the preliminary conceptual framework of the role of active reflection in managerial learning. Active reflection begins with a genuinely challenging, developmental experience. Forces external to the manager provide the context within which the experience unfolds. These *contextual conditions* consist of factors in the manager's immediate work environment. Although individual differences in learning from experience do exist (including individual differences in reflective abilities), the framework assumes that forces exist in organizations that are powerful enough to transcend the range of individual differences and produce consistent effects across different managers.

The notion of contextual conditions is at the heart of the research proposed here. That managerial learning occurs in and is thus affected by a particular organizational context has been verified empirically, so it is reasonable to assume that the organizational context within which developmental experiences occur should also significantly affect managers' reflection. Indeed, such experiences can be understood only in context, since it is the organizational context that produces the experience.

The notion of contextual conditions is also consistent with the view that as open systems, organizations create contexts in which a multitude of factors simultaneously shape rather than determine behavior (Hackman, 1985). According to this view, conceptions of simple, linear causality (i.e., that *x* causes *y*) are inadequate for understanding the dynamics of complex systems. The idea of mutual causality (loops rather than lines) provides a richer and more accurate picture of organizational systems (Morgan, 1986).

Figure 1-1
Conceptual Framework of the Role of Active Reflection

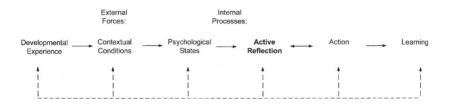

Moreover, in contrast to contingency theories, which posit that knowledge of a few moderating variables enables the prediction of precise outcomes, a "multiple possibilities perspective" maintains that perfect predictability has very limited validity in the social sciences (Tyler, 1983). Because an observed effect may be linked to one or more of several possible causes and because any particular cause can produce several possible effects, adopting a stance that is open to multiple possibilities is a more effective way to study the social world. The focus thus becomes thinking of all possible influences on behavior and studying them as an organized system.

In terms of how managers learn from experience, this means giving attention to how organizations do or do not produce conditions that enable managers to reflect on their experiences at work. The discovery of enabling conditions would delineate those conditions that increase the likelihood that a manager in the midst of a developmental experience would engage in meaningful reflection. Examples of possible conditions include time and space for reflection and a cooperative atmosphere where ideas are openly shared and debated. The actual conditions will emerge from analyzing the data collected during the research. No attempt will be made to prove the existence of preconceived conditions (like those just mentioned). Rather, effort will be directed toward discovering whatever conditions actually exist as indicated by the data.

As important as contextual conditions are, their influence is not directly on reflection. Rather, as illustrated in Figure 1-1, these external forces impinge upon the manager, resulting in particular psychological states internal to the manager that in turn stimulate active reflection. The term *psychological states* refers to the manner in which conditions in the organizational context are experienced by the manager. Whereas contextual conditions involve forces external to the manager, psychological states consist of processes within the manager. Both are central to understanding the process of active reflection. Examples of psychological states include awareness (i.e., heightened sensitivity to one's surroundings) and acceptance (i.e., a nonevaluative response to the outcomes of reflection).

The importance accorded to psychological states is based on the premise that the psychological experience of work drives people's attitudes and behaviors (Hackman and Oldham, 1980). The mediating influence of persons' psychological experiences by their work contexts has received empirical support. Psychological states are a central factor in Hackman and Oldham's theory of job enrichment as well as in Kahn's (1990) model of personal engagement and disengagement at work.

Psychological states and the ensuing reflection are processes that occur internal to the manager. They produce a behavioral response, or action, by the manager (see Figure 1-1). As Kolb (1984) has demonstrated, learning from experience involves a cycle of active engagement with experience and more detached examination of the meaning of the experience. The arrow between reflection and action is bidirectional since their relationship is better described as cyclical rather than linear. Each causes the other, and a person moves back and forth between action and reflection over the course of an experience, an interaction that ultimately produces learning. Action is just as important to producing experiential learning as is reflection, but the focus here is on the presently understudied reflective element of the learning cycle. The dotted lines in Figure 1-1 indicate that the results of learning modify the other elements of the process of learning from experience.

We assume here that reflection is necessary for learning to occur, but we also acknowledge that reflection alone is not sufficient to produce learning from experience. Other factors such as being faced with a truly developmental challenge and then engaging that experience behaviorally are also critical. Among other factors, the unavailability of rewards for learning may also result in deficient experiential learning. The intent here is not to dismiss these other factors but rather to focus on the understudied phenomenon of reflection.

SUMMARY

Reflection is best conceptualized as a contextually embedded and dynamic process, not as an isolated event. Much more needs to be learned about how managers actually engage in reflection during developmental experiences. Managerial reflection is also best viewed as a means to an end, not as an end in itself. Reflection produces some form of understanding or appreciation of learning experiences. To be truly comprehended, the process of reflection cannot be divorced from the experience that engenders it or the learning it helps produce. Reflection involves making sense or meaning of experience, examining something new in relation to one's current understanding and then making changes in one's understanding as indicated. These changes are the fundamental stuff of learning, and they require reflection.

Reflection is as relevant to managers as it is to the scholars, monks, and vacationers described at the beginning of this chapter. Even so, data demonstrate that managers are more inclined toward action than reflection. Kolb's (1984) work on learning styles found that managers prefer more active styles. Mintzberg (1973) and Kanter (1986) attribute this to the fragmented, varied, and unrelenting pace of managerial work. According to Robinson and Wick's (1992) action research, the bottom-line orientation of business organizations discourages reflection.

Even though reflection is beginning to be incorporated into some corporate management development programs, and despite recently being connected to strategic planning (Hammer and Stanton, 1997), reflection continues to have minimal impact on management practice. This is probably because of the perception that managers are action-oriented and not reflective. This also helps explain the minimal attention given to reflection in the management literature. Just the opposite has been the case in another field where reflection is also relevant—education, to which attention will now be turned.

Chapter 2

Reflection in Education

Reflection is well documented in the education literature as an important part of learning (Boud, Keogh, and Walker, 1985; Hullfish and Smith, 1961; Knapp, 1992; Osterman, 1990; Thomas and Harri-Augstein, 1977). Though a computer search of the management literature using the keywords *reflection* and *manager* yields very little, a search of the education literature for the role of reflection in learning will produce many citations. Reflection is not only a central part of education theory but is a regularly used method in a variety of educational settings.

This chapter reviews the history of the use of reflection in education, definitions, phases of reflection, the methods used, the use of questions in reflection, and requirements for effective reflection. The section on methods used reviews the literature on the three methods used most commonly to facilitate experiential learning—individual, peer group, and tutor—from both a theoretical and an experiential framework. Finally, the literature reviewed is summarized and analyzed to develop implications for the experimental study of reflection reported here.

INTRODUCTION TO REFLECTION FROM AN EDUCATIONAL PERSPECTIVE

Historical Background

Using reflection to learn has ancient roots. According to Knapp (1992), Socrates was one of the first to actively use this process, as he tried to discover the nature of goodness by asking questions of others. Socrates constantly challenged the statements and beliefs of his students, including Plato, whose work developed as a consequence of Socrates's training in how to reflect. Other early proponents of reflection as a way of learning include Sophocles, who declared that one learns by observing what one does time and time again, and John Locke, who believed that knowing is purely a function of thoughtful reaction to experience (Shuner, 1990).

In discussing the medieval process of education, Sayers (1979) reports that the medieval system concentrated first on "forging and learning to handle the tools of learning" (p. 92) and later upon the teaching of subjects. Educators of that time divided the curriculum into two parts: the trivium and quadrivium. The trivium, consisting of grammar, dialectic, and rhetoric, provided the discipline necessary to learn the quadrivium—arithmetic, music, geometry, and astronomy. Sayers argues strongly for a return to the emphasis not just on reflective practices but on the formal teaching of reflective practices in educational systems.

In this century, the strongest early advocate of the use of reflection in education was John Dewey. In *How We Think* (1910), Dewey states, "Education consists of the formation of wide-awake, careful, thorough habits of thinking" (p. 78). This thinking is a special type he defines as "reflective thinking—the kind of thinking that consists in turning a subject over in the mind and giving it serious and consecutive consideration" (p. 3). Dewey's writing in the early part of this century influenced educators and gave rise to the trend called "reflective teaching" in the education literature and to the use of reflective practices in student teaching, one of the most popular current uses of reflection in making sense of learning experiences.

Another common application of reflection in nonclassroom learning situations is its formal use in the many outdoor learning experiences that gained popularity in the last decade. As with student teaching, outdoor learning events (i.e., survival simulations, physical challenges such as ropes courses and white-water rafting) are full of teachable moments that seem to cry out for analysis and reflection (Flor, 1990; Stehno, 1986).

Definition of Reflection

The word *reflection* comes from the Latin root *reflectere*, meaning "to bend back." Horwood (1989) believes the concept of bending back is important in understanding the nature of reflection:

There is something importantly backwards about reflection. The thinking involved must scan memory of the past, seeking connections, discrepancies, meanings. The notion of bending or folding is also useful because events in memory acquire new meanings over time, especially as they may be molded and reframed by the reflective processes (Horwood, 1989, p. 5).

Knapp (1992) provides the following synonyms for reflection: debriefing, processing, critiquing, bridging, reviewing, thinking about thinking, critical thinking, facilitating, analyzing, publishing, generalizing, teaching for transfer, evaluating, interviewing, inquiry, and consideration. He states that in reflection the learner is becoming aware of, exploring, and transforming parts of an experience to produce a new understanding or appreciation. The learner does this, according to Knapp, by drawing conclusions, communicating, evaluating, or describing, often within a supportive group or environment.

Hullfish and Smith (1961) define reflective thinking as the ability to "entertain and explore meanings, to draw inferences, to respond conceptually, to name objects and events, to talk and write one's way out of difficulty" (p. 104). They believe that reflection differs from "looser" kinds of thinking primarily because it is directed or controlled by a purpose. Mezirow (1991; Mezirow and Associates, 1990) also differentiates reflection from other types of thinking.

Mezirow (1991) has written extensively on the role of reflection in the way adults learn from experience. The crux of learning to Mezirow is critical reflection; that is, critical assessment of the way one gives meaning to experiences. This requires surfacing and questioning that which is taken for granted. Such reflection can produce "transformational" learning, which involves the formation of new, more accurate mindsets that allow for a more open, discriminatory, and integrative understanding of one's experiences. Although most learning is not at this deep level, Mezirow believes that ultimately this is the only learning that really matters.

Mezirow contrasts thoughtful action with reflection, and he distinguishes between different types of reflection. These differences are best described through an example he provides:

Becoming aware of, say, negative feelings toward an acquaintance named John is *introspection*, simply being aware of ourselves feeling, perceiving, thinking, or acting. Deciding that "John is bad" is a *thoughtful action*, making a judgment based upon evidence or prior learning. This involves *content reflection*—reflection on *what* we perceive, think, feel, or act upon. *Process reflection* is an examination of *how* we perform these functions of perceiving, thinking, feeling, or acting and an assessment of our efficacy in performing them. We might, for example, ask ourselves whether we could have misinterpreted some incident that we used as evidence in concluding that "John is bad." The act of *premise reflection* leads us to question whether *good* or *bad* is an adequate concept for understanding or judging John. Premise reflection involves our becoming aware of *why* we perceive, feel, or act as we do and of the reasons for and consequences of our possible habits of hasty judgment, conceptual inadequacy, or error in the process of judging John (Mezirow, 1991, pp. 107–108).

Although it is necessary to question one's premises less frequently than to examine the content or process of one's reflection, only premise (or critical) reflection makes possible genuine learning through the powerful transformation of personal perspectives. According to Mezirow, reflection can occur only after an experience and, in the case of premise reflection, requires a hiatus from action.

Mezirow's ideas have been criticized as presenting an unrealistically rational view of adult learners and as decontextualizing learning by minimizing the effect of social and historical conditions on adult learning (Clark and Wilson, 1991). The empirical base for his view of reflection is of questionable relevance in understanding managerial reflection; it was a study of women's reentry programs in community colleges in the 1960s and early 1970s, with a focus on learning in formal educational environments (Mezirow, 1978).

One educator who has applied techniques of reflection to a business setting is Marsick (1990). Drawing on Mezirow's ideas about premise reflection, Marsick and O'Neil developed a method for helping business professionals become more critically reflective (O'Neil and Marsick, 1994). Critical reflectivity entails surfacing, examining, and questioning the beliefs and assumptions that influence one's decisions and actions. Marsick (1988) also describes another aspect of reflection, termed simply "reflectivity," which is aimed at increasing personal awareness. In comparison to critical reflectivity, reflectivity focuses on self-understanding. According to Marsick, reflectivity is important not only for learning about oneself, but also for task-related learning since that learning is often embedded in social norms that have an impact on one's personal identity.

Boyd and Fales (1983) report an exploratory study from which they conclude that reflection is the key to learning from experience. As a result of interviews with adult educators, graduate students in education, and practicing counselors, all of whom were interested in experiential learning, Boyd and Fales define reflection as the process of internally examining and exploring an issue of concern, triggered by an experience, which creates or clarifies meaning in terms of the self and which changes one's conceptual perspective.

The following were discovered to contribute to reflection: foregoing the need for immediate closure; setting aside the problem and being receptive to whatever "pops up"; reading something apparently unrelated to the issue; talking with someone else; involving oneself in a different type of activity, such as shifting from mental to physical activity; and asking oneself difficult questions. Boyd and Fales admit to selecting a highly unrepresentative sample, one that was made up of very intelligent and self-aware individuals who strongly valued self-directed and experiential learning. This limits the generalizability of their findings; nevertheless, their work provides empirical support for the centrality of reflection to learning from experience.

Two other definitions of reflection appear in the education literature. They are "the ability to step back and ponder one's own experience, to abstract from it some meaning or knowledge relevant to their experiences" (Hutchings and Wutzdorff, 1988, p. 15) and the "active, persistent, and careful consideration of any belief or supposed form of knowledge in the light of the grounds that support it and the further conclusions to which it tends" (Dewey, 1910, p. 9).

By combining elements of these definitions, the following operational definition of reflection emerges: the process of stepping back from an experience to carefully and persistently ponder its meaning to the self through the development of inferences. Using this definition, reflection is the mechanism that results in the product of learning. This way of defining reflection is qualitatively different from the management literature's focus on naturally occurring active reflection. Active reflection is akin to Schön's (1983) reflection-in-action. In contrast, the education literature focuses on what we call proactive reflection, which is like what Schön called reflection-on-action. Kottkamp (1990), an educator, points out the value of reflection-on-action, citing the importance of paying full attention to the analysis of what happened in an experience without the necessity for immediate action and with the added opportunity to receive assistance from others. If active reflection occurs spontaneously, proactive reflection involves thinking about an experience that is deliberate and temporally and spatially removed from the experience. Proactive reflection is the focus of the remainder of this chapter.

The Phases of Proactive Reflection

Some authors have divided proactive reflection into phases. Hullfish and Smith (1961) identify four phases of reflective activity: (1) recognition of a problem; (2) clarification of the problem; (3) hypothesis formulation, testing, and modification; and (4) action. Dewey (1910) defines the process very simply as a two-step sequence of observation and inference that begins with "a state of doubt, hesitancy, perplexity, or mental difficulty" and moves to "an act of searching, hunting, or inquiring to find material that will resolve the doubt, and settle or dispose of the perplexity" (p. 12).

Boyd and Fales (1983) identify six steps based upon their research: (1) a sense of inner discomfort; (2) identification or clarification of the concern; (3) openness to new information from internal and external sources; (4) resolution, expressed as "integration," "coming together," "acceptance of self-reality," and "creative synthesis"; (5) establishing continuity of self with past, present, and future; and (6) deciding whether to act on the outcome of the reflective process. Although they describe specific steps, they found that reflection is not a one-way, linear process, but is more comparable to "an alternating current flowing back and forth between intense focusing on a particular form of inner experience and outer experience" (Boyd and Fales, 1983, p. 105).

Although each description has its own unique way of separating the stages of reflection, there appear to be four common steps: articulation of a problem, analysis of that problem, formulation of a tentative theory to explain the problem, and action (or deciding whether to act).

METHODS OF PROACTIVE REFLECTION

Theoretical Framework for Three Methods

Since the self is the source of learning in reflection, the methods used to reflect vary greatly. In their research with sixty-nine adult educators, Boyd and Fales (1983) found that each individual reflected differently: they had different strategies, different "trigger" experiences, and different levels of awareness of their reflective processes. Fritts (1989), studying public school principals, developed a list of sixty-four activities that foster reflective thinking. Kottkamp (1990) identified five categories of variation in methods of reflection: (*a*) temporal— past or present experience; (*b*) medium—writing, reading, observing, listening, talking, electronic reproduction; (*c*) numbers involved—alone or with others; (*d*) locus of initiation—self-initiated, suggested, structured, or facilitated by external agents; and (*e*) reality—actual or contrived experience.

Additional researchers have developed methods that fall into one of three categories: those that approach reflection as an individual activity, those that approach reflection through a discussion of events with others who are not in a position of authority, and those that use the advice, guidance, and interpretation of someone with more expertise or experience. The remainder of this section on methods reviews first the theoretical support for using these three distinctions and then the experience of education practitioners in using these methods.

The three distinctions in methods of reflection are supported by the work of three of the most well-known theorists of this century: Jean Piaget, Kurt Lewin, and John Dewey. Each theorist developed a conceptual framework that addresses how individuals use reflection to learn and that also supports the use of one of the three methods. The following summary of their work is taken from a review of the foundations of experiential learning conducted by Kolb (1984, pp. 5–19).

The work of Piaget supports the development of a reflective process centered on the individual. Piaget, a cognitive psychologist in the rationalist tradition, explored the nature of intelligence and how it develops. His initial research on the age-related differences in children's reasoning processes led him to conclude that learning is a cyclical interaction between the individual and the environment that requires an integration of concepts and experience. The integration occurs in two ways: (*a*) as the individual modifies concepts based upon experience, and (*b*) as the individual fits experiences into existing concepts. Piaget calls this "intelligent adaptation" and classifies it as a cognitive, not social, process.

Lewin conducted research in group settings that gave rise to the laboratory training movement. His work supports the development of a reflective process involving peer group discussion. Using a phenomenological perspective, Lewin studied the dialectic tension and conflict between immediate concrete experience and analytic detachment. Underlying all his work was a belief in a spirit of inquiry, expanded consciousness and choice, and authenticity in relationships. He collected data and observations about "here and now" experience to produce feedback used to modify behavior. Nonevaluative feedback from others is a key element; Lewin believed that much individual and organizational ineffectiveness can be traced to a lack of feedback processes.

Dewey, a pragmatist, believed that learning transforms the impulses, feelings, and desires of concrete experience into higher order purposeful action. This, according to Dewey, is a complex intellectual operation that involves (*a*) observing surrounding conditions, (*b*) linking those observations to similar past situations, and (*c*) using judgment to link what is observed and what is recalled to see what is significant. Dewey believed that one accomplishes the second phase of the process—linking observations to similar past situations—with information, advice, and warning of those who have had a wider experience. This use of expert advice in his model that supports the third distinction in type of reflective method: guidance by a tutor.

Empirical Research on Methods

Individual

Most of the individual types of reflective activity surveyed in the literature involve some kind of recording of one's experiences. According to Hedlund (1989), writing in journals is a form of "talking to oneself" and as such is an important component of learning and of seeking balance, direction, and meaning in life. From her work with individuals participating in outdoor learning activities, Permaul (1982) found that writing about experiences, when properly guided, is one of the most effective tools for monitoring and supporting learning. One technique she has used with success is a log assignment, in which participants first select an incident, describe it, and analyze it in writing. She also advocates using ongoing journals to record questions, perceptions, feelings, and fantasies about an experience.

Recognizing the value of journal writing in educational curricula, Fulwiler (1987) edited a volume call *The Journal Book*, soliciting contributions from forty-two educators who use journal writing in the classroom. Barnett and Brill (1989) found writing to be a powerful medium for learning and a powerful means of facilitating reflection, since it causes one to pause, cycle back, and rethink the ideas one is in the process of formulating and inscribing. In writing exercises created by Barnett and Brill, participants record (*a*) a brief summary description, (*b*) important questions, (*c*) new concepts, (*d*) reactions, and (*e*) a description of what was learned and how it might alter future responses.

Wutzdorff and Hutchings (1988) identify four elements that should be included in written logs to extract meaning from specific incidents: questions raised, personal insights, challenges, and environmental factors. Finally, Flor (1990) reports the use of these procedures in a reflection workshop using writing as the primary tool: (*a*) introduce participants, (*b*) provide a quiet period for personal reflection and relaxation, (*c*) ask participants to recount a transforming experience in any written form (narrative, poetry, fiction, etc.), (*d*) share the writing with others and elicit responses, (*e*) articulate goals for future action, (*f*) envision a world in which the goal has been realized, and (*g*) create a group account in writing.

Peer-based

Although discussing experiences with others is a natural human social process, it has not received much attention as a formal learning tool outside its use in small group discussions in educational environments. Belenky, Clinchy, Goldberger, and Tarule (1986) report that "through mutual stretching and sharing, the group achieves a vision richer than any individual could achieve alone" (p. 119). Revans (1982) found that through the social process of communicating with others in small groups, there is less chance of error in learning.

Peer discussion groups are used for personal learning in many interpersonal development workshops offered through institutions such as the National Training Laboratory based in Bethel, Maine, and the Gestalt Institute in Cleveland, Ohio. The use of peer discussion groups is rooted in the group relations conferences that originated in Tavistock, England, and in Lewin's (1947) work through the Research Center for Group Dynamics.

In recent research being conducted at the Organization Learning Center at the Massachusetts Institute of Technology, use of peer discussion groups is being investigated in what is called The Dialogue Project (Isaacs, 1995). Based upon the Latin roots of the word *dialogue* (*dia* = "through" and *logos* = "meaning"), Isaacs defines dialogue as "the flow of meaning," flowing in this case through a group of people. Isaacs reports that dialogue provides the opportunity for people to step back from problems to reflect on what lies beneath them, at more subtle levels of thought. This research is aimed at creating "settings in which people may create a pool of common meaning from which they may draw and in which they may participate" (Isaacs, 1992, p. 8). In these dialogue groups, there is no leader (only a facilitator who guides the group at the beginning) and no agenda. Isaacs describes the process as follows:

Dialogue is a space of deep listening, where there is nothing to prove, where well-worn ways of thinking and being can be let go of. In a dialogue, there is nothing to be solved and nothing to be defended. Respect for oneself, for one another, and for the commonly-created pool of meaning is at the heart of the process (Isaacs, 1992, p. 1).

Tutor-guided

A third way individuals may reflect on experience is through the use of someone with content or process expertise—a guide, facilitator, or tutor. Direct assistance from someone with more experience than the learner is the essence of the tutor method of reflection. Through a one-on-one, coaching-type relationship, the tutor and the learner work together to surface insights from the learner's experience.

Based on their work implementing development programs that use action learning principles, Hoberman and Mailick (1992) have developed a technique called "preceptorial meetings." These involve individuals who serve as catalytic agents, sounding boards, and consultants to learners. Called "preceptors," they help participants induce learning from experience by encouraging and pointing the way for continued learning, coaching participants to try new approaches, and helping with problems. Special training programs are held to prepare preceptors for their task.

Schön's work on reflection-in-action is also relevant here. Indeed, the greatest practical application of Schön's ideas has been in the training of teachers in traditional educational settings (Sparks-Langer and Colton, 1991). Following his book introducing reflection-in-action (1983), Schön (1987) published *Educating the Reflective Practitioner*, wherein he presents an alternative model of professional education based on reflection. A central piece of this model is the one-on-one relationship between a master teacher and a learner. Schön describes a method that involves active coaching by an experienced professional—giving students opportunities to face real problems, test solutions, make mistakes, seek help, refine approaches, and reflect-in-action along with a seasoned professional—and recommends how professional schools can use such coaching to produce professionals with useful reflection skills. This tutorial approach has helped student teachers learn how to move beyond acquiring facts, rules, and procedures to developing the ability to construct and test new categories of understanding, strategies of action, and ways of framing problems.

Permaul (1982) discusses the importance of mentors as guides for reflection on experiential learning and identifies four roles for mentors: raising questions, challenging observations, sharing experiences, and providing positive reinforcement. Finally, Knights (1985) argues for a relationship with a person who will listen to a learner verbalize what she is experiencing in a particular situation. The role of the listener is to place all of her awareness and attention at the disposal of the learner and to listen with interest and appreciation without interrupting. From the perspective of the person engaged in a learning experience, "talking through one's ideas with the thoughtful attention of another person is a powerful way of clarifying confusion, identifying appropriate questions, and reaching significant insights" (Knights, 1985, p. 90).

THE USE OF QUESTIONS IN REFLECTION

Regardless of the method chosen, posing and answering questions appears to be an important part of any formal reflection process. Knapp (1992), who developed a guide for teachers to use in reflecting upon their experiences, states, "The most widely used strategy for conducting a reflection session consists of the teacher posing carefully selected and sequenced questions to which students respond" (p. 71). Canning (1991) asserts that through access to the right questions, reflection uncovers the answers needed for meeting life's challenges. Studying student reactions to the use of reflection in a student teaching program, Canning found that students learn to ask questions of themselves as a way of promoting an internal dialogue. The questions were promoted by a conflict between what students professed to value and what they were doing in actual practice. Dewey (1910) claims that questions are used to extract meaning from situations but warns that they should be used carefully so as to continue a discussion, not end it.

According to Brookfield (1987), questions used to promote reflection should be specific (i.e., should relate to particular events, people, or actions; should work from the particular to the general; and should be conversational, expressing something of the personality of the individual, with no academic jargon). Paul and Binker (1990) offer six categories of questions with examples of each: (1) questions of clarification (What do you mean by ___ ?); (2) questions that probe assumptions (Why are you asking ___ ?); (3) questions about viewpoints (Why do you think that is true?); (4) questions about perspectives (Why have you chosen this rather than that perspective?); (5) questions that probe implications and consequences (What effect would that have?); and (6) questions about the question (How can we find out ___ ?).

Several researchers use questions in a sequential way during a reflection session. Justice and Marienau (1988, p. 56) suggest the following order:

What is the problem?

How is the problem similar to or different from other management problems I have solved successfully?

What concepts and principles will guide my approach to this problem?

What criteria will I have met when the problem is resolved successfully?

Glenn and Nelson (1989, pp. 55–56) suggest proceeding from *what* to *why* to *how* questions as follows:

What happened?

What did you see?

What are you feeling?

What was the most important thing?

Why was that significant to you?

Why do you think it happened?

How can you use this information in the future?

How can you do it differently next time for different results?

REQUIREMENTS FOR EFFECTIVE PROACTIVE REFLECTION

Certain requirements must be met for the formal use of reflective practices to be effective. These include attitudes of the individual reflecting on the experience, attitudes of peers or tutors who assist the learner, and general procedures by which the activity will take place.

Attitudes of learners greatly influence the quality of the reflective experience. Dewey (1910) believes that individuals who will benefit most from reflection possess three attributes: open-mindedness, or being hospitable to new themes, facts, ideas, or questions; whole-heartedness, since when one is absorbed, questions occur spontaneously and suggestions "pour over him"; and responsibility, or the need to consider the consequences of a projected step (p. 31). In addition, Dewey states that three situations will stimulate reflection: practical needs, curiosity, and intellectual problems.

Another major influence on the quality of the reflective experience is the attitude of any helpers involved (as in peer group and tutor-based processes). According to Justice and Marienau (1988), helpers in the process of reflection must perform three central tasks: they must listen, support, and challenge. Brookfield (1987) identified five behaviors important to helping others think critically—a necessary condition, in his view, for reflection. First, helpers must affirm the critical thinker's self-worth through questions that do not threaten the person's integrity and through body language or verbal responses that communicate acceptance. Second, they must listen attentively. Third, they should show support for the individual's efforts. Fourth, they must help the thinker by reflecting ideas, acting as a mirror for ideas and actions. Fifth, they should provide an atmosphere that motivates.

Brookfield believes that reflection is a learning conversation, and people involved in good conversations behave in special ways. Conversations always involve either talking or listening. In good conversations, talking involves responding to previous comments, replying to questions posed, building on earlier arguments, illustrating general ideas with particular examples, and initiating new areas for discussion. Listening involves processing others' ideas and interpreting them in the context of one's own experience. In addition, Brookfield believes that good conversations cannot be anticipated. "When we begin a conversation, we embark on a journey without knowing our final destination" (Brookfield, 1987, p. 239). Therefore, participants must be willing to allow the conversation to go where it will. Finally, good conversations entail diversity and disagreement. If there are no counterpoints and individuals always agree with each other, they are probably not really listening to each other.

Isaacs (1992) identifies the following behaviors and qualities as important to successful dialogue: generative listening (paying close attention and putting the self aside), suspending assumptions (refraining from imposing one's views on others), a spirit of inquiry (letting go of the need to defend one's views, or equating them with the person), respect for self and others; and ability to observe the observer (increase one's awareness of one's reactions).

Following certain general procedures is also critical to developing successful formal reflection sessions. Knapp (1992) lists twenty-one tips for teachers in leading reflection in a classroom. The most relevant to managers in corporations include allowing an adequate length of time to reflect, stressing the importance of confidentiality, being attentive to the physical arrangement of the group, taking notes, and moving from the concrete to the abstract.

Separating the formal reflective process from the normal place of activity appears to be important for effective proactive reflection. Boyd and Fales (1983) suggest that "reflective learning is the process of creating a resting place" (p. 106). Likewise, Hutchings and Wutzdorff (1988) state that "situations that encourage reflection are often characterized by some degree of distance, which may mean removing a student from a given situation or experience, either through spatial or temporal separation" (pp. 15–16).

ANALYSIS AND IMPLICATIONS

The education literature says very little about the active type of reflection, aside from its application to training teachers. Instead, the education literature focuses on what is here referred to as proactive reflection: stepping back from an experience to carefully and persistently ponder its meaning to the self through the development of inferences. Whether the researchers are Boyd and Fales (1983), Hutchings and Wutzdorff (1988), Mezirow (1991), or Marsick (1990), reflection is framed differently than in the management literature. An emphasis on a formal, structured approach to reflection that removes learners from their experience is consistent with the way learning is approached in the field of education.

Figure 2-1 provides a model of the preliminary conceptual framework of the role of proactive reflection in managerial learning. The basis for this form of reflection is a challenging, developmental experience, something that by definition must be responded to behaviorally by the manager, who takes action to engage the experience and attempts to affect it in desired ways. Such action will produce some type of result, but it will not necessarily lead to learning. For learning to occur, external forces outside of the manager must be introduced. The three reflection methods introduced earlier—individual, peer group, and tutor—summarize what the education literature indicates are forces that promote reflection. Much attention has been given in the literature to these three methods, hereafter referred to as interventions. *Interventions* is a useful term in the context of how managers learn from experience, since it connotes the need to intervene in such situations if managers are to learn all they can.

All such interventions are designed to stimulate the internal process of proactive reflection in managers. The education literature has also given considerable attention here, examining such things as the proper attitude for reflection

Figure 2-1
Conceptual Framework of the Role of Proactive Reflection

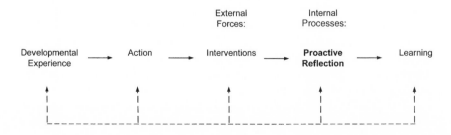

(Dewey, 1910) and the use of questions in reflection (Justice and Marienau, 1988; Paul and Binker, 1990). The education literature assumes that external interventions are necessary to stimulate internal reflection, both of which are necessary to produce learning from experience. The potential then exists for that learning to feed back to all elements of the experiential learning process (as illustrated by the dotted lines in Figure 2-1).

In addition to these broad issues, the preceding literature review raised several specific questions, the answers to which determined the design of the research study described in chapter 10. That chapter describes an experiment involving managers who participated in a proactive reflection process to test three specific reflection techniques. The questions raised by the literature review are: (*a*) What steps will managers be asked to follow as they reflect, regardless of the intervention used? (*b*) What specific questions will be used to stimulate reflection? (*c*) What general procedures should be followed to ensure an effective reflection experience? and (*d*) How will the interventions be structured? Each question is answered through the following analysis of the literature reviewed in this chapter.

General Steps in Proactive Reflection

Boyd and Fales (1983) and Hullfish and Smith (1961) identified sequential steps in the reflective process. Through an analysis and synthesis of their results, the following general steps will be used to guide managers through the process of reflection in the study: (*a*) identification of a specific challenging, developmental experience; (*b*) articulation of a problem that is present in that experience; (*c*) analysis of that problem; (*d*) formulation of a tentative theory to explain the problem; and (*e*) development of a plan of action to resolve the problem.

In addition, Kottkamp's (1990) research influenced the study in the following way: Using each of Kottkamp's five dimensions, the subjects were asked to reflect upon a current experience (temporal category) that was based on actual experience (reality); to reflect upon the experience by writing, listening, and talking (medium); and to respond to direction from a facilitator (initiation).

Questions for Proactive Reflection

As reported earlier, posing and answering questions were found to be important parts of most reflective processes. The following list of questions, derived from a combination of questions used by Glenn and Nelson (1989), Hullfish and Smith (1961), Justice and Marienau (1988), and Ryan (1988), was used to conduct the third step in the general process described previously: analysis of the problem. The questions follow the progression from *what* to *why* to *how* questions suggested by Glenn and Nelson, since that progression also follows the sequence of clarification, theory generation, and action planning inherent in the general process.

SPECIFIC PROACTIVE REFLECTION QUESTIONS

1. What happened? (What did you see, what were you feeling, what was the most important thing?)
2. What is the fundamental likeness of this problem to others?
3. What is the fundamental difference?
4. Why was that significant to you?
5. Why do you think it happened?
6. How can you do it differently next time for different results?
7. How can you use this information in the future? (What concepts and principles will guide your future approach?)

General Procedures

The following general procedures for creating a setting for effective reflection were developed by combining several elements from the work of Bartunek and Louis (1988), Brookfield (1987), and Knapp (1992). They were used in two ways in the study: to guide the researcher in designing an appropriate intervention, and to create a set of guidelines to be distributed among and reviewed with all participants.

Provide an adequate length of time to reflect.

Stress the importance of confidentiality.

Ensure comfort in the physical surroundings.

Encourage managers to take notes throughout the process.

Move from the concrete to the abstract.

Allow managers to determine which events to reflect upon and to assess their own level of the importance of these events.

Respect the personal nature of reflection by allowing individuals to draw their own boundaries around what to share.

Suspend assumptions.

Practice generative listening (with others and/or oneself).

Adopt a spirit of inquiry, letting go of the need to defend one's views.

Practice observing the observer by paying attention to thoughts and feelings as they occur throughout the session.

Resist the tendency to judge or evaluate responses until the last stages of the process.

Allow thoughts and insights to proceed where they will (within the general guidelines imposed by the process).

The Three Proactive Reflection Interventions

The steps, questions, and procedures described were followed in each intervention or treatment group. The basic tool in each intervention was asking questions of learners that were designed to probe the significance of what happened to them, why it happened to them, and what they can do about it. All three interventions were facilitated by someone other than the learner, with the central difference among them being whether the reflection occurred individually, in a group setting with peers, or through one-on-one discussion.

The following differences occurred across the three interventions, based on the unique characteristics of each as discovered in the literature on methods. For learners who would reflect individually, the log assignments developed by Permaul (1982) and the writing exercises of Barnett and Brill (1989) were used to capture the responses to the reflection questions in writing. In the peer discussion group, the dialogue process of Isaacs (1992) guided small-group discussions of the reflection questions. Finally, in the tutor group, Permaul's (1982) description of mentors of experiential learners were used to describe the type of relationship needed to effectively guide reflection. Hoberman and Mailick's (1992) guidelines for preceptors were used to formulate the specific task of tutors in these relationships.

SUMMARY

The education literature is far more advanced than the management literature in its treament of reflection, which is understandable given the different orientations of these two fields. But even in education, important questions remain unanswered. What are the relative effects of the three different reflection interventions on managers? Are they equally effective in surfacing learning from experience? Do the different interventions produce different types of learning? No research exists that directly assesses and compares the effects of these three reflection interventions on learning. Furthermore, no research has applied these three interventions to managers undergoing a learning challenge in a business organization.

The field of education provides an exceptional springboard for applying knowledge about proactive reflection to managers. Doing this will provide important insights into the way this mode of reflection is directly applicable to managerial learning.

Chapter 3

Approaches to Investigating Reflection: Inductive and Deductive Research

The previous two chapters discussed the current state of understanding of reflection in both the management and education literatures. Each of those literatures points to areas greatly in need of additional research. The bulk of this book is devoted to describing the results of two studies addressing gaps in the literature on reflection. The purpose of this chapter is to introduce the two approaches to studying reflection taken by the investigations discussed in the next two sections of the book. This chapter will also explore how two researchers who started with the same topic could study it in two such different ways.

Most of this chapter is written in the first person voice since it offers testimonials of why we approached our research the way we did and because it illustrates the way the personal characteristics of researchers influence their work. We will begin by describing the similarities between our two studies, followed by the way the approaches we took to studying reflection began to diverge. Next, we will discuss separately the backgrounds of our research, including what influenced our choice of research approach. We conclude the chapter by exploring the different choices of approach to inquiry faced by researchers and the way a researcher's identity influences those choices.

SIMILARITIES BETWEEN THE TWO STUDIES

Since both of us studied the role of reflection in helping managers learn from job experiences, it is not surprising that there are similarities between our studies. Before discussing those, it is important to note that our collaboration started after we were both well into our independent studies, and we had minimal contact during the research. Most of our discussions, including collaboration on this book, came after our studies were completed and documented. When we first met, we were quite pleased to find another researcher interested in managerial reflection.

We quickly discovered that we both started with the same issue: many businesses today recognize the value of developmental experiences for growing managerial talent, yet little support is given to managers to help them learn from these experiences. This was one of the findings of the Center for Creative Leadership's path-breaking research on learning from experience (McCall et al., 1988). We both used that research, especially its typology of five developmental experiences, as the foundation for studying how managers learn from experience. We both also recognized that despite previous research indicating the importance of reflection to experiential learning, little prior work had looked directly at the role reflection played in managers' learning.

A final similarity between the two studies is that both were designed to integrate and contribute to both scholarship and practice. The initial impetus behind both studies was the practical problem described. In the true spirit of action research (Argyris, et al., 1985; Lewin, 1951), we highly valued research aimed at helping people by addressing their problems. But we also were committed to the conventional scientific model of research, which emphasizes building on prior research by addressing holes in the existing scholarly understanding of issues. Thus our research needed not just to address a practical problem but to do it in a way that built upon prior knowledge and used sound scientific methods.

The two studies, then, shared a similar starting point and similar values concerning the overall purpose of research.

DIVERGING APPROACHES TO INQUIRY

Despite the similarities between our starting points and basic values, we pursued very different lines of research using different methods. One of us conducted an inductive, theory-building study using qualitative methods, while the other carried out a deductive, experimental study using quantitative methods. How could this happen? Should not such similar origins for the two studies necessitate that they also be similar in design?

The explanation for the different approaches we took that is consistent with traditional positivist science is that they resulted from the different literatures that were our starting points. Kent drew primarily from the management literature, whereas Marilyn relied primarily on the education literature. As discussed in chapters 1 and 2, these literatures frame reflection differently, the former emphasizing its active nature and the latter focusing on its proactive character. There are significant differences in the fields of management and education concerning the understanding of the nature of reflection as a phenomenon. Given these differences, contrasting approaches to studying it are not surprising.

Not only is reflection framed differently in the two fields, but the extent to which it is currently understood is different as well. Management researchers are just beginning to appreciate what reflection is, whereas education researchers have been examining it for about a century. This too should lead to different approaches to studying reflection. Many of the differences in our approaches, then, can be explained by the fact that although we were interested in the same topic, we operated in different academic disciplines.

This accounts for many but not all of the reasons behind the different research approaches we employed. A complete picture of the differences emerges only after separately examining our situations.

KENT'S QUEST TO KNOW

It was my professional desire to complete research that would contribute to both the theory and practice of managerial learning and my personal desire to better understand the role of reflection in managerial learning. The research was intended to generate theory grounded in data that explains the nature of managers' active reflection while learning during developmental job experiences. Prior to the research reported here, such theory did not exist. Schön's (1983) work comes the closest; however, my research differed from his in notable ways.

In collecting data, Schön concentrated on episodes when a senior practitioner tried to help a junior one learn a job skill. Thus, what Schön discovered is most accurately described as reflection-in-action in the context of a coaching relationship. My research focused on active reflection during managers' naturally occurring developmental experiences. Another important difference is that Schön's work was structured around professions (e.g., architecture, psychotherapy), but my work was grounded in the world of business organizations. How managers learn from experience must be understood in the context in which it unfolds. Other than the four management cases Schön provided (only one of which looked at an individual manager), the contextual influences on active reflection during developmental experiences had not received any attention by scholars.

I hoped that in addition to developing a much-needed theoretical model of active reflection, my research would significantly contribute to practice. I reasoned that prescriptions about how to facilitate managers' active reflection would be stronger if they were based on a better understanding of how that reflection currently occurs in organizations. Organizations need to do more than just put managers in developmental situations; they also need to support the learning that potentially accrues from those situations. Providing an environment that fosters active reflection is certainly one type of support that organizations can give.

If this is what I hoped the research would contribute, the next issue was designing a study that would accomplish those objectives. In considering how to approach my investigation of active reflection, I considered the basic nature of active reflection as a social–psychological phenomenon and the extent of existing knowledge about it.

Active reflection while learning from experience is a complex and inexact, if not messy, activity. "Development is not magic. It is not a science. It does not lend itself to neat formulas, precise measures of this and that," claim McCall et al.

(1988, p. 183). Active reflection is also by definition context-bound. The reflection that happens during an experience directly results from the experience itself and the specific setting that has produced the experience. Unlike taking a class or reading a book, the reflection that occurs cannot be divorced from the setting that stimulates it; indeed, it is precisely a function of what is happening in that setting.

Complex, inexact, context-bound social phenomena of this sort are best studied using what alternatively has been called "inquiry from the inside" (Evered and Louis, 1981), "direct research" (Mintzberg, 1979), and "naturalistic inquiry" (Marsick, 1990). In contrast to the detached and controlled positivist approach, which has characterized research of management development historically (Campbell, Dunnette, Lawler, and Weick, 1970; House, 1967), these approaches share the belief that organizational research should take a more involved, flexible, open-ended, and contextually aware stance. Additionally, because qualitative methods are ideally suited to realizing such a stance, I employed them in my research.

In addition to being useful for studying complex, inexact phenomena in context, qualitative methods are the most effective way to explore the social world from the perspective of the actors in that world. This phenomenological approach (Sanders, 1982) was the primary one taken here; namely, I focused on the process of active reflection as it was experienced personally by managers. Given the nature of the phenomenon in question, naturalistic inquiry through qualitative methods was the logical approach.

My choice of approach was also based on the current state of knowledge of active reflection in the management literature. Deductive theory-testing through quantitative methods is typically called for when a substantial amount of research has accumulated on a given subject (Eichelberger, 1989). On the other hand, new research areas and those that have received minimal empirical attention are best addressed through inductive, theory-building research (Glaser and Strauss, 1967). Inductive research builds specific observations, usually of less well understood phenomena, into general theory, which can then be tested later. It involves inferring, from a set of instances in which a phenomenon occurs, that it occurs in like fashion in all similar instances. The researcher starts without a priori analytical categories, seeking to let those emerge from the data that are observed.

As demonstrated in chapter 1, managers' active reflection during developmental experiences has received minimal direct empirical and theoretical attention by scholars; thus the use of an inductive, theory-building approach is called for. Glaser and Strauss's (1967) grounded theory technique (which is described in chapter 4) is especially applicable to studying a phenomenon like active reflection, so I chose it for my inductive research.

I used qualitative methods for data collection and analysis for the reasons described earlier and since they are inherent in the grounded theory technique. Of course, qualitative methods are not without their critics (e.g., Passmore,

1990). Nevertheless, their use by those who study management (Gummesson, 1991), career development in organizations (Brown and Brooks, 1990), and reflection in learning from experience (Boyd and Fales, 1983) continues to grow. Qualitative methods are certainly relevant to studying an emerging phenomenon like the active reflection of managers undergoing developmental experiences.

Qualitative methods typically recognize that researchers are not detached, purely objective observers during the research process, and that researchers may even intentionally use themselves as research instruments (Reinharz, 1979). Personal characteristics of the researcher are made an explicit part of the research. It is to these characteristics that I now turn, since they played a significant role in my research.

I have a deep personal interest in managerial learning that stems from my intense commitment to the importance of growth and development throughout a person's life. More specifically, this interest originates from both my own managerial experience in business and my former responsibilities as a management trainer. It has long been clear to me that managers learn more outside the classroom than they do inside it.

As I transitioned from a business career to an academic one, this interest was further nurtured by my affiliation with Boston University's Executive Development Roundtable, a group of executive development professionals and scholars who share an interest in managerial learning. They also provided significant funding for my research. The roundtable's director, Dr. D. Tim Hall, who is also an internationally recognized expert in management and career development, has served as a personal mentor, providing further support for my interest in this area.

My choice of how to approach this research topic is also rooted in my past. As a former manager and corporate trainer, I am less inspired by elegant and rigorous research approaches than I am by those that are relevant to life in actual organizations. Much of organizational life is inherently messy and difficult to predict due to its complexity, interconnectedness, and fluidity. Research approaches that ignore this or attempt to eliminate it distort organizational reality. I believed that the best approach to supporting natural managerial learning would be a natural approach, which also seemed to be the approach that would be most acceptable to managers and their companies.

All of this is consistent with a naturalistic and qualitative approach to management research, but why the emphasis on inductive theory-building? This stems from my training in the field of organizational behavior and from a deep, life-long quest to know. When I was a manager I was never satisfied to make something work; I also always wanted to know why it worked. My need to understand how social–psychological processes work has always been as strong as the desire to make those processes work more effectively. This, coupled with a proclivity to develop abstractions based on the particulars of a situation, lends itself naturally to an inductive approach to research.

I also believe that things should be thoroughly described before they are tested. This is obviously consistent with a preference for theory-building rather than theory-testing research. Although this belief is readily accepted in my field, in principle, it is not always practiced. It seems as though the methods of a mature science are often used—because of their sophistication, rigor, and ability to quantify—even though management as a science (especially when it deals with social and psychological issues) is still quite young. The rush to be accepted as a legitimate science in scholarly circles as well as the pressure to produce prescriptions useful to practicing managers has often led researchers to bypass inductive research in favor of deductive approaches. Both approaches are needed, and, in many areas, more basic research using descriptive techniques would be very helpful in advancing theoretical knowledge and ultimately in promoting practice as well.

Finally, my choice of research approach was driven by my valuing research that treats human beings as participants in the research process rather than as subjects to be studied. Especially when it comes to applied topics with very practical implications, this seems like not only the appropriate approach but also the most useful one. These, then, are the various factors of which I am aware that influenced my decision to approach the study of managerial reflection using inductive theory-building.

MARILYN'S QUEST TO APPLY

My choice of a deductive approach to studying proactive reflection in managerial learning was initially met with skepticism from both the corporation that supported the research and the academic institution from which it was based. Since previous research studies conducted in the company used techniques such as surveys, participant observation, and in-depth interviewing, managers participating in the study and company representatives were more comfortable with these techniques. The rigors imposed by experimental design and the use of formal statistical processes to analyze and report the results were not widely understood. In addition, my university contacts cautioned me about the difficulties involved in conducting experimental research in this setting. They were especially concerned about the need to control for extraneous variables and to eliminate researcher bias.

With these cautions in mind, I decided to pursue a deductive approach for three reasons: my desired research outcomes would best be served by this methodology; an empirical approach is consistent with my academic and professional background; and this methodology fits with my personal style, skills, and values. Each of these reasons is explained later in this section.

As the literature reviews in earlier chapters pointed out, reflection is an important part of learning. The literature also shows that challenging work assignments provide powerful opportunities for learning. A unique contribution of both sets of research described in this book is the linking of these two important bodies of knowledge. My specific process for creating this link was: (*a*) identifying or creating specific proactive reflection interventions that managers could use to enhance learning from developmental experiences and (*b*) testing them to see which of these proactive reflection interventions are most effective as tools to enhance learning. A preliminary review focused primarily on the education literature revealed that many proactive reflection interventions already exist and could be classified into three broad categories (as described in chapter 2). Therefore, the focus of my contribution became testing these interventions to see which are most effective when used with managers in challenging work situations. I decided that an experiment using a treatment group for each proactive reflection category and a control group would be the best way to test these interventions.

While Kent's study used an inductive process (creating generalizations derived from specific observations that were then used to build theory), my research followed a deductive process. This involves testing existing knowledge via specific observation to draw conclusions in previously untested arenas. Using a deductive approach, the researcher takes established ideas, presents them as specific predictions (or hypotheses), collects data relevant to them, and then tests the veracity of the predictions.

The experimental method is ideally suited to a deductive approach, because it provides an established format for hypothesis testing in a controlled setting. Control of extraneous variables, including the influence of the researcher, allows the effect of the variables under study to be measured and analyzed. The a priori establishment of analytical categories and careful measurement of independent and dependent variables leads naturally to the use of quantitative data analysis. The deductive approach also uncovers knowledge that can be generalized to many situations.

The second reason I chose a deductive, experimental approach is based upon my work in the management development department of a large corporation. Most of the managers I worked with were practical, results-oriented people. My professional experience as a provider of developmental opportunities for this group taught me that they learn best when focusing on subject matter that is immediately relevant to their work challenges and when they are given specific, reliable tools to facilitate their learning.

As a consequence of my management development experience, I knew that a focus on challenging work experiences would appeal to managers; however, an emphasis on proactive reflection would be less appealing. As Mintzberg notes, "Study after study has shown that managers work at an unrelenting pace, that their activities are characterized by brevity, variety, and discontinuity, and that they are strongly oriented to action and dislike reflective activities" (Mintzberg, 1973, p. 422). It would be necessary to provide practical tools that yield predictable results to help managers see the value of proactive reflection. An experimental design that evaluated three specific interventions and provided statistical proof of their effectiveness would counteract the perceived "softness" of proactive reflection, as described by Marsick:

Workplaces are not typically associated with reflection or critical self-reflection, ideas that are often considered "soft" and somewhat irrelevant to the hard-nosed, bottom-line results-oriented world of business. In the workplace, reflection of any type has been considered a luxury, something that takes place only in the ivory towers of academe, and by its very nature somewhat unrelated to "real life" (Marsick, 1990, p. 23).

Finally, a deductive and quantitative approach appealed to my own set of skills and values and my professional goals. I like rules and order, procedures and clarity. My most important contributions in the business world have involved taking complex information and simplifying it for new users. In short, I am driven by a quest to apply knowledge to assist others. This drive to apply knowledge has required me to publish handbooks, guidelines, and tools to help managers bridge the gap between general data and their own specific circumstances. My inclination to take general, established information and translate it into use in specific situations is also consistent with a deductive approach to research.

My ultimate interest in understanding how reflection can be used to help managers learn from their developmental experiences comes from 15 years as a program manager and internal consultant in the leadership development department of a Fortune 500 corporation. Professionals in management development are in a unique and powerful position to create the time and structure needed for proactive reflection. In designing my research, I hoped that it would help corporate management development groups take advantage of their position by providing (*a*) an empirically sound argument for promoting proactive reflection as a tool for learning from developmental experiences; (*b*) models of proactive reflection interventions that can be used to create workshops in reflection; and (*c*) guidelines that will help consultants, supervisors of managers, and others be more effective coaches as managers attempt to learn from their developmental experiences.

My research did in fact lead to the creation of techniques and guidelines for each of the three interventions tested in the experiment (Daudelin, 1996a). It was my hope when I designed the research that in addition to providing these specific tools, it would provide the basis for a new direction for management development in corporations, a direction that emphasizes the role management development can take in promoting proactive reflection that helps managers use the valuable learning inherent in their developmental experiences.

EXPLORING THE DIFFERENT CHOICES OF APPROACH TO INQUIRY

Which approach—induction or deduction—is most defensible for studying reflection in managerial learning? Based on the circumstances surrounding each study, the answer is an unequivocal *both*. The differences in the two literatures that served as the foundation of each study partially explain the differences in our approaches. The limited understanding of reflection in management as well as the way reflection is framed as a natural, active process points to the need for inductive research. In contrast, the advanced state of understanding of reflection in education and the way it frames reflection as a structured, proactive intervention suggests the need for deductive research.

Indeed, both approaches to research are equally necessary to advancing knowledge. Inductive research observes reality and builds general theory based on those observations. Hypotheses can then be derived from general theory and tested through additional specific observations. This deductive research can then fuel further observation and theory-building. The two approaches complement one another in developing and then verifying empirical views of reality; understanding a phenomenon like reflection requires both.

However, as the personal stories we shared in the previous two sections suggest, there was more to our choice of research approach than how it was previously understood in our respective fields. Our respective literature reviews led us toward inductive and deductive studies, but they did not necessitate these choices. Both literatures at least suggested the alternative framing of reflection (i.e., active versus proactive), yet we each chose to view reflection in one way. Why? Here is where our personal styles, values, interests, and identities as researchers came into play. We studied reflection the way we did because of who we are.

According to the traditional, positivist view of science, the researcher's personal characteristics are irrelevant to the research being conducted. If these characteristics come into play at all, it is in possibly contaminating the research. Science is objective and value-free. But as Kuhn (1970) has persuasively argued, science is a human endeavor driven by paradigms that reflect value judgments. The world and how we come to know it has a subjective as well as objective dimension to it. The traditional positivist is incorrect in believing that values do not affect the results of scientific procedures. Reinharz (1979) takes this view further and claims that research method and personal identity are connected for the social scientist.

Our identities, which include our respective drives to know and to apply, certainly influenced our choice of approach to studying reflection in managerial learning. A summary of the major influences on the choice of our approach is presented in Figure 3-1. Our research shared in common an initial interest in managerial learning, developmental experiences, and the role of reflection in experiential learning. But as we approached the literatures of our respective fields, the focus of our studies started to diverge, ultimately ending in very different inductive and deductive designs.

We have placed "personal factors of researchers" toward the bottom of the figure, reflecting our idealized hope that we let our respective literatures speak for themselves before letting our personal inclinations influence how we approached our research. However, it is just as likely that personal factors influenced how we

Figure 3-1
Influences on the Choice of Research Approach

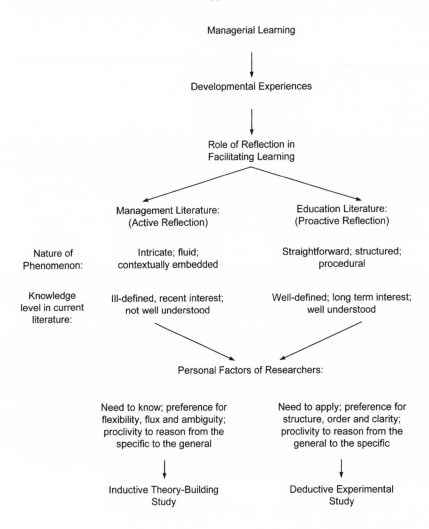

approached our literatures in the first place, in which case that portion of the fig-ure really belongs at the top. Indeed, if our initial interest in managerial learning was based on our experience as management development professionals, then personal factors came into play long before we decided on a research approach. In reality, personal factors and scientific procedures are intertwined throughout the research process.

While this discussion may be disturbing to traditional, positivist scientists in that we "admit" our lack of pure objectivity in conducting our research, it may be equally disturbing to those constructivists/postmodernists who believe we have not gone far enough in celebrating our subjectivity. To them, reality is relative and socially constructed (Guba and Lincoln, 1994). We, however, are reluctant to "throw the baby out with the bath water" in critiquing positivism and the scientific method. As modest realists, we hold to the view that although purely objective science is humanly impossible, neither is reality entirely, and probably even predominantly, subjective. Taking a critical and modest stance in examining both the objective and subjective aspects of reality seems most prudent to us.

We certainly believe that a purely positivist approach to research is naive at best and deceptive at worst, which is why we devoted an entire chapter to exploring our disparate research approaches and personal inclinations. We believe doing so assists others in evaluating the potential effect of our biases on our work. But we also believe that our self-awareness has enlivened our research. We value research conducted with self-awareness on the part of the researcher. We also value both inductive and deductive research, which is why both approaches appear in this book. Admittedly, neither of our individual studies combined induction and deduction. However, when taken together they provide an example of a holistic approach to research.

Our initial surprise that we would study reflection in such different ways has evolved into a deeper appreciation of the value of different research approaches as well as greater awareness of who we are personally and how that affects our work. Our individual horizons broadened to encompass a different type of reflection, a different field's view of it, a different approach to studying it, and a different means to enhancing managers' learning through it. In so doing we have grown professionally and personally and, after all, is that not what learning from experience is all about?

SUMMARY

This chapter described how scientific procedures and our personal inclinations as researchers interacted to produce the research we report in this book. We hope this chapter has given the reader insight into the background behind two major research studies as well as two researchers. We also hope the chapter has raised the reader's awareness of the importance of both professional and personal issues in the selection of research approaches and methods.

The chapter began by describing the similarities between the two studies reported here, followed by discussion of how, despite almost identical foundations, the approaches taken in the two investigations diverged. Then we shared the stories behind the genesis of our individual studies. We concluded by exploring at a more general level what influences the different choices of approach to scholarly inquiry.

This chapter concludes the first, introductory section of the book. Kent's inductive exploration of active reflection is described in the next section. Marilyn's deductive examination of proactive reflection follows in the third section. In the final section we integrate the findings of our separate studies and discuss their implications for theory, research, and practice.

PART II

An Inductive Exploration of Active Reflection at Food Corp. and Health Co.

Chapter 4

A Theory-Building Study of Active Reflection

This chapter presents the research methodology used to study active reflection. As the literature review in chapter 1 demonstrated, the field of management has framed reflection as a natural cognitive process involved in responding to a developmental experience. This focus derives from the current, rather underdeveloped state of the management literature on reflection and from the discipline's basic desire to increase understanding of how people behave in organizations.

Because reflection has not been a central construct in the management literature, there are several fundamental gaps in the knowledge of reflection. Much more needs to be learned about both the external forces that influence reflection and its nature as an internal process (refer to Figure 1-1). Specifically, information is needed on the contextual conditions in managers' immediate work environments that influence their inclination to engage in active reflection. Information is also needed on the internal process of active reflection, including the state of managers' minds ("psychological states" as defined in chapter 1) when they are actively reflecting. Addressing these gaps in current knowledge is the purpose of the theory-building study described here.

SPECIFIC RESEARCH QUESTIONS

This research is intended to explore the nature of managers' active reflection while they are engaged in developmental job experiences, particularly the contextual conditions within business organizations and the psychological states within managers that enable them to reflect. The primary purpose of this research is to produce a grounded theory to explain how these phenomena operate. Given that this is exploratory, theory-building research, the research questions are intentionally open-ended. They are as follows:

What is the process of active reflection for managers undergoing developmental experiences? This includes exploring issues such as the way managers do or do not reflect during developmental experiences; the fundamental nature of active reflection; variations in the reflective process; and the consequences of active reflection.

What range of contextual conditions influence active reflection in business organizations? Relevant issues here include exploring the immediate work environment surrounding managers' experiences with an eye toward identifying working conditions that foster or inhibit active reflection during experiences.

What psychological states give rise to reflection in managers? What psychological states foster (and inhibit) active reflection? In what ways do contextual conditions in organizations and psychological states interact to influence active reflection?

Answering these questions will increase our understanding of the internal process of active reflection as well as the external forces within organizations that influence it.

METHODOLOGY

The basic method used here to answer the research questions is grounded theory building (Glaser and Strauss, 1967) using qualitative data. Given the exploratory nature of the research as well as the naturally occurring and contextually embedded nature of the phenomenon under study, a qualitative, theory-building approach is called for. A more detailed explanation of the rationale for using this methodology appears in chapter 3.

The intended product of the research is a model of the process of active reflection and the external and internal influences that enable managers to reflect during developmental experiences at work. As inductive research, the study is not intended to prove anything but rather to develop a framework that can be tested in future research.

INTRODUCTION TO THE TWO RESEARCH SITES

Comparative analysis forms the basis of the grounded theory approach to theory building (Glaser and Strauss, 1967; Strauss and Corbin, 1990). Comparative analysis begins by selecting groups to study through theoretical sampling. The basic criterion for selecting groups is their theoretical relevance, which refers to their likelihood of providing data suggestive of meaningful categories. Thus, to enable comparisons and to stimulate the generation of theoretical concepts, active reflection was examined here in two contrasting companies (whose names have been disguised). This also allows for concepts that emerge from the first site to be tested (in a theory-building sense) and refined in the second organization.

Food Corp.

The first company is a large Fortune 500 food producer. The company, with about 15,000 employees, manufactures more than 125 different products and markets them through more than twenty brand names. It is a highly successful player in the relatively stable yet very competitive U.S. food industry. Conservative in its culture and management philosophy, Food Corp. pursues a strategy of active but prudent growth.

Succession planning and management development for the entire corporation are coordinated by a group within the corporate human resources function. The company uses what it calls cross-training to facilitate on-the-job managerial development. Cross-training experiences involve moving managers from one business function to another (e.g., from marketing to production) and between major divisions of the company (which differed primarily according to the type of product they produced). Cross-training assignments are generally reserved for managers who are considered by the company to have "high growth potential."

Health Co.

The second firm is a health care insurer and Medicare Part B administrator. At the time of the study, the company ranked among the top twenty U.S. health insurers/health services providers in terms of revenues. The firm, which has approximately 7,000 employees, is run for the benefit of its policyholders (called "subscribers") as a nonprofit business. Health Co. serves nearly six million subscribers in such programs as traditional medical–surgical insurance, dental programs, and a vision program.

Health Co. also solely or jointly owns several health maintenance organizations as subsidiaries. The company has recently emerged as a leader in managed health care. Finally, Health Co. is one of the U.S. government's major Medicare administrators, which involves processing the claims of several million Medicare beneficiaries. The company has had a history of financial strength in what until recently has been a stable industry. In the 1990s, the health care and health insurance industry moved into a period of major turbulence and uncertainty. The research for this study was undertaken during the first term of the Clinton administration, when the President's health care reform initiative was being actively debated.

While striving to position itself favorably in the future health care arena, the company had a reputation as being conservative, risk-averse, and operationally focused (for efficient processing of a very heavy volume of insurance claims). With respect to its human resource development practices, although Health Co. had an extensive system of formal training and education, there was no formal succession planning process. Instead, managerial-level positions were filled as they came open. Neither was any systematic effort made to use job assignments for developmental purposes.

The specific procedures used in this study at each company are described next.

FOOD CORP.

Sample

Twelve management-level employees from Food Corp. participated in the study at the first research site. This purposive sample was obtained as follows. The person in corporate human resources responsible for coordinating cross-training assignments was asked to identify about a dozen managers who were currently or recently (within the past 6 months) involved in a major developmental experience on the job. The intent was to obtain information on reflection as it naturally occurs for managers by studying active reflection while an experience was happening (or shortly thereafter).

The human resources representative was given the following criteria for identifying potential research participants. Only managers in a major developmental experience—an experience intended to produce learning and development in the manager—were to be considered. "Major developmental experience" was defined as a challenging experience that was understood by all parties (i.e., the manager, the manager's boss, and the organization) as providing the opportunity for learning and growth. "Challenge" meant a new experience that pushed the manager significantly beyond the limits of her current capabilities. In short, a major developmental experience was one in which the manager had to acquire new knowledge and skills to function effectively in the job.

The human resources representative was given the typology of developmental experiences developed by McCall et al. (1988) to help identify potential research participants. That typology describes five experiences that are particularly conducive to learning and development: project/task force (temporary assignment to address a specific issue); line-to-staff switches (moving from line operations to a staff role); start-ups (building something from nothing); fix-its/turnarounds (stabilizing a failing operation); and leaps in scope of responsibility (significant increase in the number of people, dollars, or functions to manage). It was emphasized to the human resources representative that the focus of the research was learning not just from any experience but from a developmental experience.

Developmental experiences were emphasized for three reasons: (1) the intent of the research was to learn more about an aspect of managerial learning, so it was necessary to select managers who were in situations where learning was likely to happen; (2) by focusing on the types of experiences already demonstrated by prior research (McCall et al., 1988) to contribute to learning, this research would build on existing knowledge; and (3) by concentrating on experiences that companies were already using to promote development, the research would have practical relevance.

The human resources representative thus began his search for participants by using the pool of managers currently and recently involved in cross-training assignments. Corporate-wide this pool consisted of approximately one hundred managers. Forty were immediately eliminated because they worked in remote geographic locations. Of the remaining sixty, only those meeting the criteria described earlier were considered. Fifteen managers were contacted about becoming involved in the research, twelve of whom agreed to participate.

The developmental experiences of the twelve research participants are summarized in Exhibit 4-1. The names of the participants and particulars of their experiences have been disguised. Each experience is classified in the right-hand column into one of the five developmental experiences identified by McCall et al. (1988). The only type of experience not represented in the sample from Food Corp. was the "fix-it." The most common experiences were leaps in scope of responsibility and start-ups, each occurring four times. One participant's experience involved elements of two types of experience.

Exhibit 4-1
Descriptions of Participants' Experiences at Food Corp.

Participant	Developmental experience	Center for Creative Leadership type
1. Pete	6-year assignment as operations director of manufacturing plant in Mexico.	Leap
2. Gill	Designing a new executive development program having no prior training experience.	Project
3. Mark	Promotion to director of governmental affairs.	Leap
4. Patrick	1-year cross-functional assignment as public relations director.	Switch
5. James	1-year cross-functional assignment as general manager, visitors' center.	Switch
6. Rick	Cross-training assignment from marketing director for Division A to corporate training.	Switch
7. Cliff	Leader of cross-functional task team exploring application of new distribution technology.	Project; Start-up
8. Jerry	Establishing company day care that would be run as a self-sustaining business.	Start-up
9. Ted	Cross-training assignment as national field sales manager for venture group.	Start-up
10. Bob	Project leader responsible for developing and test-marketing a potential new product.	Start-up
11. Christine	Promotion to director of newly created regulatory affairs function.	Leap
12. Phyllis	Promotion to human resources manager at major plant as member of plant's new management team.	Leap

Demographically, the sample was composed of ten males and two females, ranging as a group in age from 36 to 55 ($\underline{M}$ = 45). All the participants were white. The shortest tenure with the company was 3 years, while the longest was 27 years ($\underline{M}$ = 15). The participants represented a wide variety of job functions (e.g., corporate staff, human resources, operations, marketing, and research and development). All were at the level of middle manager or director.

Data Collection

The usefulness of qualitative research for building theory has been cogently argued by Eisenhardt (1989) and Marsick (1990). The approach to qualitative theory-building taken here is "grounded theory" as introduced by Glaser and Strauss (1967) and refined by Strauss and Corbin (1990). This approach is designed to provide in-depth explanations of complex social phenomena that are not yet well understood, and is ideally suited to studying active reflection of managers in developmental experiences. The research reported here collected "thick descriptions" (Geertz, 1983) of managers' experiences and reflection as well as the working conditions in which they occurred. The intent was to mine the terrain of reflection in managerial learning rather than to survey it.

The primary method of data collection was open-ended interviewing (Bouchard, 1976). Each participant was interviewed for at least 90 minutes on each of two separate occasions. All interviews were tape-recorded, and participants were assured that their responses would be treated confidentially. A structured set of questions was employed. However, in the spirit of qualitative research, the attempt was made to minimize the imposition of predetermined categories when gathering data (Patton, 1980). Therefore, a flexible framework was provided within which participants could express their own understandings in their own terms.

In the first interview, after basic background information on the participant was obtained, interview questions solicited detailed descriptions of a challenging, on-the-job learning experience, how the manager thought about the experience while it was happening, and what occurred in the manager's immediate work environment during the experience. Participants' initial responses were clarified and elaborated through follow-up probes. Earlier versions of the interview had been piloted on four other persons before the interview format used in the study was finalized.

Getting participants to talk about important issues involving learning was the primary means of obtaining information about reflection and its influences. Only after this information had been obtained were participants directly asked how they reflected and what in their work environment helped or hindered that reflection. Participants knew that they would be interviewed about their learning during a developmental experience; however, they did not know that the primary focus of the research was reflection, because this could have inappropriately influenced their responses.

The second interview, completed approximately 3 months after the first, had two purposes. The first was to obtain data on participants' learning style by asking participants to complete the Learning Style Inventory (Kolb, 1986). Participants were given a copy of their completed inventory along with scoring instructions. I did not score the inventory with them because I did not want to be influenced by knowledge of their learning style. Learning Style Inventories were scored at the conclusion of the data analysis phase for Food Corp.

The other purpose of the second 90-minute interview was to engage participants in a "conceptual encounter" (de Rivera, 1981). This interview was designed to engage the manager in a discussion of how effectively the model I was developing described the manager's active reflection. As de Rivera explains it, "The abstract conceptualization that has been created by the investigator encounters the concrete experience as comprehended by the partner (i.e., research participant). Is there an enlightening 'fit' between ideas and experienced reality or is something wrong?" (de Rivera, 1981, p. 4).

Thus, the second interview allowed for provisional testing of conceptual ideas generated from the first round of interviews and for refinement of the emerging theoretical model. It also allowed for deeper probing of the participants' experiences and provided them with deeper insight into their own experience and active reflection. The theoretical model discussed with participants evolved during this round of interviews based on feedback provided by participants in the conceptual encounters. This process is discussed further in the section on data analysis later in this chapter. The conceptual encounter interview was piloted on two people who were not participants in the study before it was used with the twelve research participants.

Data were also collected through informal observation during organizational entry, interviewing, and conceptual encounter. Special attention was given to the ways in which participants answered the interview questions (e.g., thoughtfully–impulsively, concretely–abstractly) since this could provide meaningful information about how they reflect. These data were recorded in journal entries made following each interview.

The final method of data collection was self-analysis. Theory-building research is enhanced when researchers use themselves as a research instrument (Mirvis and Louis, 1985; Reinharz, 1979). My own experience conducting the research represented relevant data since I was in the role of learner myself (i.e., learning about active reflection in an organizational setting). My ability or inability to reflect on what I was learning in the company was another source of data on contextual conditions that influence reflection. Self-analysis also meant being aware of the potential impact of my personal history and demographic characteristics on the research process (Kram, 1985).

Field notes were made to record the results of informal observations and self-analysis. The use of multiple data collection methods both stimulated the generation of theoretical insights and checked the credibility of the conclusions drawn (Marshall and Rossman, 1989). Unlike ethnographic research, only data that were germane to the emerging theoretical model were collected.

Collecting data during this research itself represented an intervention into the systems being investigated. It was likely that approaching organizations and managers about the nature of reflection during developmental experiences would heighten their awareness of reflection. An important issue is the distinction between reflection that occurred during a manager's experience and reflection that occurred as a result of the research interview. Which was I capturing in the interview?

I took several steps to keep the focus on the reflection happening during the actual developmental experience. First, only managers who were currently or very recently involved in such an experience were interviewed. Second, the term *reflection* was not used with participants until the very end of the interview. Instead, emphasis was placed on their experience and how they thought about it as it occurred.

Participants were specifically asked to put themselves back into the experience and describe what happened then, instead of describing how they were thinking about the experience now. Moreover, while they were discussing their experience, I worked hard to help them stay in the situation by redirecting them to describe what they were doing, feeling, and thinking during the experience.

Despite these efforts, it is still likely that the interview had some effect as an intervention, a limitation of this research that I fully acknowledge. Given the nature of the phenomenon studied here, any approach to data collection would suffer from this limitation. Accordingly, I will note in the discussion of the results instances where it seemed possible that what was being shared was being influenced by the interview intervention.

HEALTH CO.

Sample

Twelve management-level employees participated in the study at Health Co. A purposive sample was selected following the same procedure as described previously for Food Corp., with the director of training and development identifying potential participants. Since Health Co. did not use formal succession planning or assignment management programs, the training director used his judgment to identify managers he believed met the criteria for a developmental experience (as described previously).

The training director began with a pool of about fifty managers he considered to be currently or recently involved in a challenging learning situation. Given the recent demands of national health care reform on Health Co., he expressed confidence in being able to identify managers in learning situations, even if they had not been placed there intentionally for developmental purposes. In attempting to identify managers who met the criteria for a developmental experience and who were diverse in terms of job responsibilities, gender, and age, he narrowed his list to twelve. The twelve managers he initially contacted all agreed to participate in the study. It is coincidental that both research sites ended up with samples of twelve managers.

The developmental experiences of the twelve participants from Health Co. are summarized in Exhibit 4-2. Once again, the names of the participants and the particulars of their experience have been disguised. The only type of developmental experience, according to McCall et al.'s (1988) typology, not represented in the sample from Health Co. was the leap in scope of responsibility. Given Health Co.'s risk-averse culture and lack of formal assignment management, this is not surprising. It was the norm in the company to give promotions that involved gradual, incremental increases in responsibility.

Fix-it was the most common type of developmental experience in the Health Co. sample, occurring four times. Coleen's and Loretta's experiences are not classified according to McCall et al.'s (1988) typology because they do not fit any of the five types of experience in the typology. This became evident by the

Exhibit 4-2
Descriptions of Participants' Experiences at Health Co.

Participant	Developmental experience	Center for Creative Leadership type
1. Tim	Merging dental HMO into dental business unit to form new for-profit dental subsidiary.	Start-up
2. Steve	Reorganization of dental marketing function.	Fix-it
3. Doug	Reorganization, including integrating two different computer systems from two different parts of the organization.	Project
4. Matt	Assisting in reorganization of major division.	Fix-it
5. Brad	Moving from private medical practice to Health Co., and automating his new area.	Switch
6. Coleen	Promotion to corporate secretary.	"Leap"
7. Paul	Moving from hospital administration to Health Co.	Switch
8. Sarah	Promotion to manage operations at subsidiary.	Switch
9. Loretta	Promotion to vice-president of a subsidiary.	"Leap"
10. Todd	Assisting in developing and marketing a major new product.	Start-up
11. Meg	Promotion to president of subsidiary and reorganization of same.	Fix-it
12. Harry	Promotion to lead and revitalize a major division that was struggling.	Fix-it

conclusion of the first interview with these two managers. It was originally thought that they had experienced a leap in scope of responsibility. And although each had recently received promotions to positions of considerable responsibility, neither promotion was really a stretch for the person since each had already been performing many of the duties of the new position in her previous position (Colleen as assistant corporate secretary and Loretta as a director).

Indeed, Colleen's and Loretta's promotions were typical of Health Co.'s risk-averse approach to promotions, which meant that managers received promotions only when they were already capable of performing effectively in the new position. This contrasts sharply with Food Corp., where the most common type of experience was a leap in scope of responsibility and a start-up.

The eight male and four female research participants at Health Co. ranged in age from 35 to 52 (M = 46). All the participants were white. In terms of tenure with the company, the shortest was 3 months and the longest was 22.5 years (M = 9.3). All of the managers with less than 3 years tenure had extensive previous experience in the health care industry. The participants represented a wide variety of job functions (e.g., corporate, dental operations, Medicare, traditional indemnity insurance, managed care subsidiary). All were at the level of director or above.

The job titles at Health Co. are at a higher level than those at Food Corp. Because it is a smaller organization and it has a strong operational focus, the titles at Health Co. are inflated relative to Food Corp. In terms of the level of actual job responsibilities, however, the participants from both companies were equivalent.

Data Collection

The same process of data collection was employed at Health Co. as was used at Food Corp., with one important exception. The first round of interviews at Health Co. was not a replication of the first round at Food Corp. Data similar to that gathered at Food Corp. were collected in order to shed light on the veracity of the theoretical concepts developed at Food Corp. In addition, however, a major focus of the interviews at Health Co. was to probe more deeply into areas identified from Food Corp. as important but that were still underdeveloped conceptually. The notion of provisionally testing and building upon emerging theoretical concepts at additional research sites is a central principle of grounded theory (Glaser and Strauss, 1967).

Therefore, the first interview at Health Co. had a different focus than at Food Corp. First, the following were obtained: basic background information on the participant; a description of a challenging, on-the-job learning experience; and a detailed description of situation within that experience where the manager found himself doing a lot of thinking. Then attention turned to two other areas. These areas—a difficult period when the manager's thinking was confused or stuck and the type and intensity of emotions felt while thinking—required significant additional attention. These areas were probed extensively during Health Co. interviews. Earlier versions of the Health Co. interview were piloted on two persons.

The second interview at Health Co. was completed about 3 months after the first. It followed the format of the second round of interviews at Food Corp. closely, including having participants complete the Learning Style Inventory (Kolb, 1976) and engage in a conceptual encounter. Of course, the theoretical concepts shared in the conceptual encounter with participants at Health Co. were at a later stage of refinement since they were based on the findings from Food Corp. as well as from the first round of interviews at Health Co. The theoretical model discussed with participants evolved during this round of interviews based on feedback provided by participants in the conceptual encounters.

Informal observation and self-analysis rounded out the data collection at Health Co., as they had at Food Corp. In total the data collection phase of the study took approximately 18 months.

DATA ANALYSIS

All interview data were transcribed word for word. This resulted in over 2,000 pages of interview transcripts formatted according to The Ethnograph (Seidel, Kjolseth, and Seymour, 1988) software program. This written material, along with the observation and self-analysis notes, was then coded and analyzed using standard qualitative analysis and grounded theory techniques (Miles and Huberman, 1984; Strauss and Corbin, 1990). Grounded theory consists of the inductive discovery of theory from the systematic collection and analysis of empirical data. This involved two different but complementary activities. The first was to mechanically follow prescribed data analysis techniques and the second was to extract meaning creatively from raw data. How I went about these activities is described next.

As should be the case when building grounded theory, data collection and data analysis occurred together. Thus, data analysis began long before data collection was complete. The iterative relationship between data collection and analysis in this study is illustrated in Figure 4-1. A summary of the data analysis activities performed in conjunction with each round of data collection is presented in Exhibit 4-3.

The first phase of data analysis occurred after the first round of interviews at Food Corp. When I read the interview transcripts, a variety of categories emerged from the data itself that were then used to code the interviews. All comments that seemed to pertain in any way to reflective thinking, psychological states, or contextual conditions that encouraged or impeded reflection were coded. Although I was guided in this inductive process by the understanding I already had of active reflection (which is provided in the literature review in chapter 1), I sought to let the data speak for itself when defining codes.

Exhibit 4-3

Summary of Data Analysis Activities Corresponding to Rounds of Data Collection

---

Food Corp.
Data analysis
after first-round   Inductive analysis of data to discover characteristics
interviews   of reflection and types of organizational conditions.
                         Preparation for conceptual encounters (CE) by applying emerging,
                            preliminary models of reflection and conditions to each
                            participant's experience.

Analysis during
second-round (CE)   Adjustment of models after each CE based on participants'
interviews   feedback regarding the models' fit to their experience.

Analysis after
Food Corp.   Inductive analysis of CE data.
interviews   Development of revised models of reflection, conditions, and
                            psychological states based on all Food Corp. data.
                         Identification of areas in need of further investigation at second site.

Health Co.
Data analysis
after first-round   Examination of data in light of existing models.
interviews   Inductive analysis of data to discover characteristics of areas in
                            need of further investigation (i.e., difficult periods of thinking,
                            emotions).
                         Revision of models.
                         Preparation for CEs by applying latest models to each
                            participant's experience.

Analysis during
second-round (CE)   Adjustment of models after fourth and eighth CEs.
interviews

Analysis after
Health Co.   Inductive analysis of CE data.
interviews   Revision of models based on all Health Co. data.
                         Reexamination of Food Corp. data in light of latest models.
                         Final revision of models based on complete data.

This initial process of developing codes resulted in a list of over eighty codes describing various characteristics of active reflection and the forces affecting it. A review of this list of codes revealed that many overlapped with others and that some were used only once or twice across all twelve interviews. It thus became possible by collapsing and eliminating codes to cut their number in half. Although this process is described here as an orderly one, in reality it was messy and confusing.

Figure 4-1
Iterative Process of Data Collection and Data Analysis

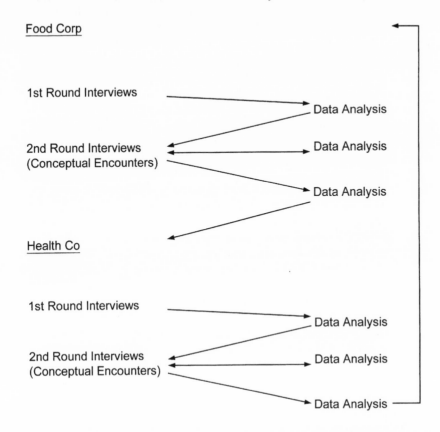

Food Corp

1st Round Interviews

Data Analysis

2nd Round Interviews
(Conceptual Encounters)

Data Analysis

Data Analysis

Health Co

1st Round Interviews

Data Analysis

2nd Round Interviews
(Conceptual Encounters)

Data Analysis

Data Analysis

Based on the revised list of codes, it was possible to construct a very prelimi-nary model of the process of active reflection, including its key elements and their relationships. This was done by examining each participant's responses in relation to the three primary research questions in this study. The codes were also used to produce a very preliminary model of the operation of psychological states and contextual conditions in relation to active reflection. Next, each inter-view was reread in light of these preliminary models. During this reading, the interviews were recoded with the narrower list of codes.

Transcribing interviews according to the formatting parameters of The Ethnograph qualitative data analysis program (Seidel et al., 1988) allowed for hard copies of interviews to be printed with each line of text numbered sequentially. These numbered transcripts greatly facilitated manual coding. The results of the recoding with the narrower list of codes were then entered into The Ethnograph program, enabling me to search for individual codes across interviews. For exam-ple, all interview comments coded "feedback" could now be produced.

While this feature was useful, the following two techniques were the most helpful in actually moving from the raw data to the abstract models that depicted them. First was rereading transcripts each time a new concept emerged or a change was made in the models. Each participant's interview was thoroughly read at least five times over the course of data analysis. Second was the conceptual encounters. Much of the model development occurred in dialogue with research participants during the second round of interviews. More will be said about this later.

At this point in the data analysis, specific aspects of each participant's responses that illustrated parts of the models were also identified and recorded. This information—the preliminary models and supporting examples from participants' responses—formed the basis of the second-round conceptual encounter interviews. Specifically, this information was then fed back to participants in their second interview in order to engage participants in a discussion of the extent to which they felt the model accurately represented their experience.

Data analysis also occurred during the conceptual encounter interviews at Food Corp., in the interviews during the discussion with managers. The process of examining the models in relation to their developmental experience and associated reflection shed light on the strengths and deficiencies of the models. For example, the participant in the first conceptual encounter commented that "emotions" affected his reflection, yet this concept was missing from the models.

After each conceptual encounter, the models were adjusted based on the feedback provided by the participant. Thus analysis also happened between each conceptual encounter. The models produced by this study represent the collaborative efforts of the research participants and me. I adjusted the models only if the changes were also consistent with the experiences of participants whose conceptual encounter had already been completed.

The next phase of data analysis was after the Food Corp. conceptual encounters. Based on the models that emerged out of these twelve interviews, the list of codes was refined down to twenty-six more complex and comprehensive codes, which were then used to recode both rounds of Food Corp. interviews. Revised models of reflection and contextual conditions, including the psychological states they affect, were constructed after this recoding. These models were then applied to all twelve participants to verify the models' fit to participants' responses and to identify exemplars as well as variations. Exemplars are examples that are particularly effective at illustrating aspects of the models, while variations refer to notable exceptions to the models.

The preceding analysis set the stage for Health Co. data collection by providing models of reflection and contextual conditions that could be provisionally tested and revised at Health Co. It also illuminated deficiencies in the models. Two areas were especially in need of more attention: the role of emotions in the process of active reflection, and difficult periods when reflection was unclear or confused. While the data at Food Corp. suggested that these were important issues, they were inadequately addressed in the models that emerged from the Food Corp. analysis. These deficiencies, then, influenced the questions asked in the first round of interviews at Health Co. Therefore, the data collection and analysis at Health Co. expanded upon the findings from Food Corp., rather than merely replicating those findings.

After the first round of interviews at Health Co., another phase of data analysis ensued. This phase was very similar to the first phase of data analysis at Food Corp. except that interviews were coded using existing codes (i.e., those developed from Food Corp. data) and particular emphasis was given to the two areas in need of further attention listed earlier. A handful of new codes emerged to address those issues, and another version of revised models emerged from this analysis. I then prepared for the Health Co. conceptual encounter interviews by applying these latest models to each participant's responses in the same way I had done for the Food Corp. conceptual encounters.

Data analysis occurred during and between conceptual encounter interviews at Health Co. as it had at Food Corp., with one important difference. Adjustments were made to the models twice (after the fourth and eighth interviews) instead of after each interview. Fewer adjustments were required because my conceptualization of active reflection and the forces affecting it had grown much sharper over time. Whereas Food Corp. participants had many comments about deficiencies in the models, by the time I got to the Health Co. conceptual encounters, participants' comments were overwhelmingly confirmatory of the models. Glaser and Strauss (1967) refer to this as reaching "saturation." That is, a point is reached at which further data collection is deemed unnecessary because little new information is being produced in the interviews. I definitely had this sense in the latter stages of the Health Co. conceptual encounter interviews.

Another phase of data analysis occurred after the Health Co. conceptual encounter interviews. This phase paralleled the analysis that took place at the conclusion of both rounds of interviews at Food Corp. The purpose here was to reexamine all the Health Co. data in light of the models that emerged from the conceptual encounter interviews. This resulted in yet another revision to the models of active reflection, contextual conditions, and psychological states. These revisions centered around fully incorporating emotions and difficult periods of reflection into the models.

There was one final phase of data analysis, which involved returning to the Food Corp. data to examine it in light of the most recent models. The intent was to ensure that the changes made to the models as a result of data collection and analysis at Health Co. were still consistent with managers' responses at Food Corp. This needed to be the case if the eventual models were to represent a generalizable descriptive theory. A final set of slight revisions to the models was required based on this analysis. Overall, the models went through eight major revisions during data collection and analysis. The movement between data collection and analysis across sites tested the findings (in a provisional, theory-building sense) and ensured that theory was produced that was truly grounded in data. The resulting models represent a generalizable and grounded theory of active reflection and the forces that affect it.

Both self-analysis and discussions with experienced researchers who supervised my work contributed to the analysis of the data. I tried, with their help, to remain self-aware throughout data collection and analysis and to consider the implications of what I was experiencing. I kept a written record of thoughts and feelings that I deemed to be significant, and I referred to those notes frequently during data analysis.

For example, I made a note after the first Health Co. interview that I felt unstimulated. I attributed the feeling to perhaps beginning to reach saturation in my understanding of active reflection or to general fatigue. I felt the same way after the second Health Co. interview. Before heading home after that interview, I paused in my car to think. I was parked in the visitor's section of Health Co.'s parking lot, from which there is a good view of the company's two buildings. As I starred at the two drab, brown brick buildings, each the mirror image of the other, I literally saw that Health Co. was an unstimulating organization (at least relative to Food Corp.) The architecture was uninspiring, the basic work the company performed—processing mountains of insurance claims—was boring (this was something several research participants would refer to), and the general atmosphere was noticeably less stimulating than at Food Corp.

I realized that I was not tired nor was I anywhere near saturation; instead what I was feeling was tangible evidence of the differences in climate between Food Corp. and Health Co. Such differences have important implications for managerial reflection and learning. This example also illustrates how an awareness of my own emotional reactions played a part in the analysis of the data.

SUMMARY

The method used in this investigation of active reflection was grounded theory development. Qualitative data were collected through extensive open-ended interviews with twenty-four managers from two companies. Managers' responses were analyzed to shed light on these questions: What is the process of active reflection for managers undergoing developmental experiences? What factors influence their ability to engage in active reflection? Specifically, what external, contextual conditions in managers' work environments affect their reflection and what internal, psychological states resulting from these environmental conditions give rise to active reflection?

Managers' responses to interview questions as well as my informal observations and self-involvement in the research process were analyzed using The Ethnograph (Seidel et al., 1988) program and standard qualitative data analysis techniques. Finally, limitations of the study were raised and means for addressing them were considered.

Chapter 5

Overview of Active Reflection

The four management cases discussed by Schön (1983) demonstrate that when faced with unusual or perplexing challenges, managers naturally shift into a mode of mindful cognition that Schön calls reflection-in-action. Schön provides an excellent but rudimentary description of this type of reflection for managers. This type of reflection is here called "active" to distinguish it from "proactive" reflection, as reflection is framed in the field of education, and to differentiate it from Schön's "reflection-in-action." It will become apparent from what follows that active reflection bears much in common with reflection-in-action as Schön conceptualizes it but that it also involves significant dimensions not reported by Schön; hence the use of a different name for the reflection managers naturally engage in during challenging experiences.

The next six chapters discuss the results of the analysis of the data collected at Food Corp. and Health Co. This chapter introduces the internal, cognitive process of active reflection during developmental job experiences. It is intended to offer an overview answer to the first research question posed by this investigation: What is the process of active reflection for managers undergoing a developmental experience? In other words, what is actually happening when managers naturally reflect?

This chapter will introduce the theoretical model of active reflection produced as a result of this research. The next two chapters will flesh out the details of the model. Following that are two chapters describing research results relevant to the external, contextual forces and internal, psychological states that influence the manifestation of active reflection.

In this and subsequent chapters, selected quotes from research participants will be provided to illustrate and substantiate the concepts presented. Notable variations from the more typical responses will also be shared. Extended examples that appear (e.g., Jerry in this chapter and Sarah in chapter 8) were chosen because of their representativeness. Other participants were reported on at length because they represent an exception or provide an informative countercase (e.g., Coleen in this chapter). Some of the results presented here were first reported in abbreviated form elsewhere (Seibert, 1999).

It will be shown that the essence of active reflection during a developmental experience is an internal dialogue involving moments of inquiry and interpretation in an effort to produce increased insight. Active reflection occurs amidst uncertainty and includes both task-oriented thinking and thinking that is more personal. Active reflection is thinking that occurs during the process of learning and growing. In contrast to the thinking that happens when one is trying to find a solution to a routine problem, active reflection actually changes managers as they expand their base of knowledge and skill.

OVERVIEW OF A MODEL OF ACTIVE REFLECTION

It is important to note two things about the theoretical model presented here. First, the model underwent several revisions during data collection and analysis at Food Corp. and Health Co. The actual procedure involved in developing the model is described in chapter 4. Second, the model makes sense only when it is considered in context—that is, the context of a manager who is involved in a challenging developmental experience. The basic response to the experience is to engage in a cycle of action and reflection, of behaviorally responding to the experience and cognitively processing what is happening in the experience (recall Figure 1-1). This movement back and forth between acting and reflecting ultimately produces learning. Although the material described here focuses on the reflective part of this cycle, it is essential to remember that managers were also responding behaviorally to the challenges they faced.

The Model

A descriptive model of the process of managers' active reflection is presented in Figure 5-1. Unless indicated otherwise, I created the terms used for the concepts presented in the model (as well as in the models that follow in subsequent chapters). Of course, the terms were shared with research participants in the conceptual encounter interviews, where there was general agreement as to their accuracy in describing various aspects of reflection.

Managers' natural reflective thinking involves the specific thoughts managers have about different aspects of a challenging experience over the course of the experience. The core aspect of a developmental experience is that it challenges the manager. Facing a significant challenge on the job is experienced cognitively as deep interest in how the challenge can be successfully met. Managers' need to know is motivated not by a desire for knowledge for knowledge's sake but by a practical desire to become capable of performing new responsibilities (desig-

Figure 5-1
Model of the Process of Active Reflection

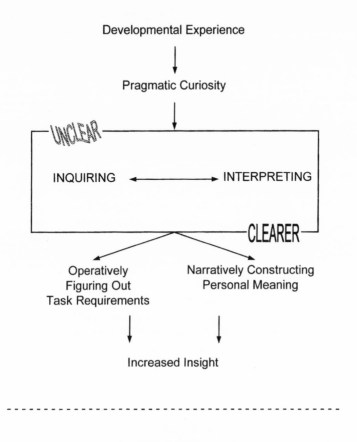

Developmental Experience

Pragmatic Curiosity

UNCLEAR

INQUIRING ←————————→ INTERPRETING

CLEARER

Operatively
Figuring Out
Task Requirements

Narratively Constructing
Personal Meaning

Increased Insight

Three Additional Dimensions:

Timing:	Approach:	Activity:
On-Line & Off-Line	Analytical & Intuitive	Cognition & Affect

nated in the model as pragmatic curiosity). The curiosity is "pragmatic" since managers operate in the bottom-line, results-oriented domain of management. The pragmatic quality of the curiosity may be unique to workplace learning, owing to its utilitarian nature. Since the situation is unfamiliar, initial thoughts are of the questioning or inquiring variety: What's going on here? What do I need to know? How do I proceed?

All this happens amidst great uncertainty and lack of clarity. Unlike attending a training seminar with concrete learning objectives or even learning something straightforward on the job (like how to prepare a capital budget), challenging developmental experiences are fraught with ambiguity and obscurity. As choices in organizations are made under conditions of ambiguity (March and Olsen, 1979), so too happens active reflection during developmental experiences in business. Developing a new product, which was required of one manager at each company, illustrates this. Not only did the managers have to learn about new product development, but they had to do so in a situation where it was unclear just what the best new product would be.

Once questions are formulated by inquiring, attempts are made to develop answers or interpretations to those questions. Answers come in the form of "interpretations" because the issues at hand are too complex for simple, black-and-white answers and because managers have limited information-processing abilities (March and Simon, 1958). Initial interpretations are formed based on existing knowledge and first impressions of the situation. Although these may provide an initial basis for action, they usually prove inadequate, resulting in further inquiry, which necessitates further interpreting. Over time, the interpretations become more and more refined, and they translate the complexities of the experience into more understandable terms. The initial uncertainty of the situation begins to give way to an emerging sense of clarity.

Thus managers' active reflection moves back and forth between moments of inquiry and moments of interpretation over the course of the experience. This internal dialogue of inquiring and interpreting represents the essence of active reflective thinking. It can be oriented in one of two ways: operatively or narratively. Operative reflection involves thinking oriented to the business task at hand. This is reflection whose purpose is to enable managers to take effective action (or "operate") in the situations they face. Operative reflection contributes to what Hall (1986a) calls task learning.

Narrative reflection, in contrast, is more personal, determining what the experience means for the manager personally. Through it a manager creates the meaning of the experience to himself, almost as if by constructing a personal story (hence the use of the term *narrative*). Active reflection that is oriented toward the self provides the opportunity for personal learning (Hall, 1986a).

The result of active reflection is usually increased insight into the experience or an aspect of it; specifically, what the experience actually involves, what it means, and what should be done about it. The manager does not necessarily have complete insight, but she has more insight than she began with. Finally, strong emotional reactions to an experience can interfere with developing insight or can lead to outcomes other than insight.

The concepts listed along the bottom of Figure 5-1—on-line and off-line, analytical and intuitive, and affect and cognition—represent important additional dimensions of the active reflection of managers, which are discussed in chapter 7.

The external and internal factors affecting active reflection are presented in chapters 8 and 9.

An Illustrative Case

Jerry (not his real name) was a research participant from Food Corp. He will be used to illustrate the basic process of reflection, since his experience was representative of most research participants. Examples from other research participants will be provided in subsequent chapters. A brief overview of Jerry's experience and active reflection will help ground the model before providing more detailed explanations and illustrations in the following chapters.

The challenging developmental experience

Jerry, a 48-year-old male, had spent his career in human resource management. His challenge involved establishing day-care services for the company's employees, an experience that can be classified as a start-up assignment according to the developmental typology of McCall et al. (1988). Simply having to contract with a day-care provider would not represent a very challenging experience; Jerry's experience involved much more. He became responsible for establishing day-care as a self-sustaining business separate from Food Corp., which required the construction of a $1 million day-care facility across the street from the company's oldest plant. Jerry saw this as essentially starting a small business. He summarized the experience, which stretched him to grow in areas beyond human resources, this way:

That's been a major effort that required putting a business case together and analyzing the marketplace and computing the targeted rates of return. We wanted to make it a thriving business. It's been a wonderful experience. It allowed me to serve as a general manager of that whole project because it required coordination with engineers and architects, attorneys, business people, marketing research, outside contractors, the township, educational accreditation institutes, and financial institutions. What an experience that was!

Pragmatic curiosity

The day-care opportunity sparked Jerry's interest, and he quickly became very curious about day-care. "I didn't know anything about day-care, not a thing," he shared. "I love a project (like this one) where I know little or nothing about it. It's like an almost infinite opportunity to learn." Jerry's curiosity was on a very practical level, stemming from his desire to figure out how to make day-care work at Food Corp., not from having any personal interest in day-care. Hence his curiosity can be called "pragmatic."

Inquiring and interpreting

Since Jerry knew practically nothing about day-care or starting a small business when he began this project, his initial response was to wonder what was required to run an effective day-care business. Jerry began reflecting spontaneously by forming a host of questions to which he needed answers. These ranged from questions as broad as the fundamental purpose of day-care for Food Corp. to those as specific as the local laws that apply to day-care. He then developed an interpretation of what was the essence of each of these issues. Throughout this he had to learn basic skills necessary to move the project along (like market research to assess the demand for day-care and break-even analysis to figure out how big a center was needed to be economically feasible). Learning these skills and making decisions to advance the project required repeated inquiry and interpretation.

Jerry moved back and forth between inquiring and interpreting throughout his experience. These two moments of active reflection fed back and forth into each other. As a result of early inquiry, Jerry developed initial interpretations of how to establish day-care. He also began to realize how much he did not know about day-care. Based on these initial insights he engaged in more reflection (as well as, of course, action), which deepened his insight but also necessitated further reflection (and action). His active reflection is best understood thus not as one moment of inquiry followed by one moment of interpretation, but instead as a series of alternating moments of inquiry and interpretation, each of which drew from and then contributed to the refinement of the other.

Obscurity – clarity

Most of the reflecting Jerry did, especially early in the assignment, occurred amidst uncertainty and obscurity. Since day-care was so new to him, the issues he dealt with early on were usually unclear to him. For example, the crucial role of careful financial planning became clear only after he had been working on the project for some time. He described how "filtering" and "distilling" helped him move from being unclear about how to build a successful day-care to a clearer understanding of what was required. This notion is illustrated by the diagonal dimension in Figure 5-1.

Operative and narrative reflection

Jerry reflected both operatively and narratively. On an operative level, he had to figure out how to perform many work tasks to complete the project (e.g., computing targeted rates of return, assessing educational accreditation requirements). These issues occupied a considerable amount of his thinking. But Jerry also thought about the implications of the experience for himself and his career. Through this narrative reflection he constructed a story that captured the personal meaning of the experience to him. Day-care became a highly visible issue at the company, especially when construction of the new center began across from the main plant. Jerry realized that the success or lack thereof of his efforts would have a direct bearing on his future at the company. He also realized that he enjoyed having bottom-line responsibility for an entire project.

Increased insight

As a result of inquiring and interpreting in both operative and narrative ways, by the completion of this assignment, Jerry's insight into day-care, small business development, and himself had all deepened significantly. He had finally begun to grasp the overall nature and meaning of his experience. Jerry felt that he had made great strides in, for example, the financial area. As he said in reference to financial issues, "It was very helpful to really understand a subject." On the personal level, Jerry began to see himself in a new and broader way. "Now I can see why people become general managers because it's fun," he reported. "One thing I learned is that I have more capacity than I realized." No longer would he limit his career aspirations to just human resource management. Based on the day-care project, he could now see himself as a potential general manager. The initial curiosity he felt had been satisfied on both the technical and personal levels.

Three additional dimensions

Three other aspects of managers' active reflection are noted in Figure 5-1. Jerry reflected both on-line and off-line; that is, he reflected both when he was in the midst of taking action directly related to the day-care assignment and when he was temporarily removed from such action. Additionally, he approached reflection in both analytical and intuitive ways, moving between periods when his reflection was more logical or on more of a gut level. Finally, Jerry's active reflection was influenced not only by what he was thinking (cognition) but also by how he was feeling (affect). Emotions were both a cause and a consequence of reflection. Detailed descriptions of these three dimensions of active reflection are presented in chapter 7.

A caveat

It is useful to emphasize the distinctive nature of reflection as it is conceptualized in the model in Figure 5-1. The reflection described in this research is that involved in responding to a developmental challenge requiring learning. Existing knowledge and skill were inadequate for effective performance, so the manager had to learn new things to respond adequately to the situation. Since an automatic response that draws on current skills was not possible, active reflection occurred naturally.

The inquiring and interpreting that the manager engaged in resembled the cognitive activity involved in problem solving (March and Simon, 1958), but there were important differences. The problem-solver (an experienced detective solving a murder, for example) reflects on the problem at hand using existing skills. If the crime is solved successfully, the detective feels good about herself (i.e., her self-image is positively reinforced). A learner, in contrast, reflects not only on the issue at hand but also on new skills that must be acquired to address the issue. If new skills are acquired in the process of confronting the issue, the learner feels changed and developed because he can now do something he could not do before the experience.

Based on the research reported here, it can be postulated that active reflection during learning experiences is qualitatively different from reflection during problem solving or other similar activities. However, the actual verification of this proposition awaits further research. It appears as though, in learning situations, inquiry and interpretation bring about fundamental change in a person (in contrast to simply solving a problem). Inquiry and interpretation are at least as much about "becoming" as they are about "doing."

Jerry illustrates this very nicely. His experience required that he address many problems, but the only way he could do this was by developing beyond the manager he was when he began the assignment. Active reflection—inquiry and interpretation—played a central role in enabling him to do this.

A Countercase

Reflection as a dialogue involving moments of inquiry and interpretation meant that managers actively engaged themselves in developmental experiences on a cognitive level, seeking to bring clarity to situations that were unclear. They did this to learn how to effectively perform new and unfamiliar tasks. This was the basic process of active reflection for managers.

Four research participants did not fit the model of active reflection presented in Figure 5-1, primarily because they were not in genuinely challenging experiences. One of those managers, Coleen, will be briefly described here. Her situation nicely illustrates that while active reflection may be a natural response of the manager who faces a developmental challenge, it is not a natural response for managers in less challenging situations.

Coleen, an attorney, was originally chosen to participate in this study because she had recently received a promotion to corporate secretary, a senior-level position at Health Co. involving regular interaction with executive management and the board of directors. It was believed that her promotion represented a "leap in scope of responsibility" (McCall et al., 1988).

When asked to describe an incident in her promotion that stretched her and required her to do serious thinking, however, she drew a blank. The specific response listed in her interview transcript reads, "Oh (pause, long pause, no response)." After a follow-up probe she cleared her throat, paused again, and then began to talk about a personality conflict in the office that did not directly involve her. Upon further discussion it became clear that her promotion had not led to noticeable inquiring or interpreting on her part. The work simply did not engage her cognitively in a serious way.

When asked more about the promotion itself, she revealed that she had been assistant corporate secretary for a year before the promotion to corporate secretary. Far from being a "leap in scope of responsibility," her move up to corporate secretary had intentionally been a gradual and incremental one. As she said,

I just moved into the corporate secretary position in February, but my responsibilities really didn't change all that much. You see, basically as the assistant corporate secretary I was doing most of the responsibilities. I watched William (the previous corporate secretary) and then they groomed me for this position and then I took over.

"Grooming" people gradually for new responsibilities seems much less conducive to promoting active reflection than does thrusting them into new situations that really stretch them. This is consistent with research demonstrating that experiences providing major challenges are the most advantageous to development (McCall et al., 1988). The grooming approach to promotion was not uncommon at Health Co. The way Coleen's promotion had been handled was probably less a reflection on Coleen's abilities than a reflection of Health Co.'s cautious approach to doing business.

As an insurance company, Health Co. understandably operated in a way to minimize risks. While this approach may have minimized the business mistakes the company made, it also diluted opportunities for personal growth and development. Coleen's situation also illustrates the important influence of the broader conditions in managers' work environments on their reflective learning.

Evidence from the interviews with the research participants strongly suggests that engagement in active reflection is associated with an experience at work that stretches managers to the limits of their current capabilities. Without that stretch, there is minimal active reflection. With it, managers cannot help but engage in inquiring and interpreting as they seek to organize and understand their experiences.

THE INPUTS TO AND OUTPUTS OF ACTIVE REFLECTION

At its core, active reflection is about inquiring and interpreting that are oriented both operatively and narratively. The details of those aspects of active reflection will be fleshed out in the next chapter. However, a few more words need to be said about the input to inquiry and interpretation as well as the ultimate output of those processes. As indicated in the previous section, having a genuinely challenging developmental experience is a necessary stimulus to active reflection. The importance of the developmental challenge a manager faces is described further in the next section.

The Catalyst for Active Reflection

Whether a manager's experience was truly a challenging developmental one was crucial to her active reflection. Recall that the primary criterion used in selecting the research sample was the manager's involvement in a stretching experience of the type identified by the Center for Creative Leadership (McCall et al., 1988). Although I intended to interview twenty-four managers in this type of situation, it turned out that two managers from each company, although in a new job, were not in a truly stretching experience. This was the case for Gill and James from Food Corp. and for Coleen and Loretta from Health Co. Loretta and Coleen had recently received promotions that upon further inspection, really involved little more than a change in title. Gill moved from one human resource function to another while assuming responsibility for a major project. But due to circumstances beyond his control, the project never got off the ground, leaving Gill with less than challenging responsibilities.

James's situation is intriguing. His experience involved swapping jobs with Patrick for one year, which can be classified as a "switch" assignment (McCall et al., 1988). Since both jobs had significant responsibilities at a high level, it seems as though the switch should be a stretching experience. Indeed, that is how it was perceived by Patrick, who viewed the switch as a significant opportunity for learning and development. He called it "interesting, challenging, and exciting." "The one thing I didn't want to do was to do it just to go through the motions," he added.

James, however, approached the assignment differently and felt he had become a "caretaker" (of Patrick's job) for a year. He did not think he would learn anything significant from the experience and he wrote it off as a wasted year. Thus, an important element of whether an experience is challenging developmentally is the manager's own perception of the experience.

As research participants, James, Patrick, Coleen, and Loretta have two things in common. First, their experiences did not provide substantial challenge (or were not perceived as providing challenge). Second, the model of reflection introduced here does not fit the way they experienced their assignment. These participants were the only ones out of the entire sample who had trouble responding to interview questions about their thinking. They found it difficult to describe their thought processes during their experiences and they admitted that the experiences did not require them to do much reflecting. Without the catalyst of a genuinely challenging learning experience, there was minimal active reflection, a finding consistent with cognitive research on the types of situations that produce active cognition (Sims and Lorenzi, 1992).

The discussion that follows draws primarily on the other twenty research participants. Occasional reference will be made to James, Patrick, Coleen, and Loretta when they provide instructive contrasting data. The finding that these participants' experiences do not conform to the models presented here actually lends credence to the validity of the models. The models should not apply to managers who are not in challenging situations, and indeed they do not. I decided not to add to the original samples to make up for these four cases for two reasons: (1) these cases provided useful contrasting data in and of themselves, (2) the ten remaining participants at each site produced a sense of saturation indicating that additional interviews would provide only diminishing returns.

The other twenty participants had genuinely challenging experiences, as perceived both by me and by themselves. For these managers, the key catalyst for active reflection was their involvement in truly challenging experiences. Interestingly, managers reflected regardless of their learning styles, as determined by their score on the Learning Style Inventory (Kolb, 1976). The style for each manager is plotted in Figure 5-2, which shows that managers' scores are

Figure 5-2
Learning Styles of Health Co. and Food Corp. (*in italic*) Research Participants

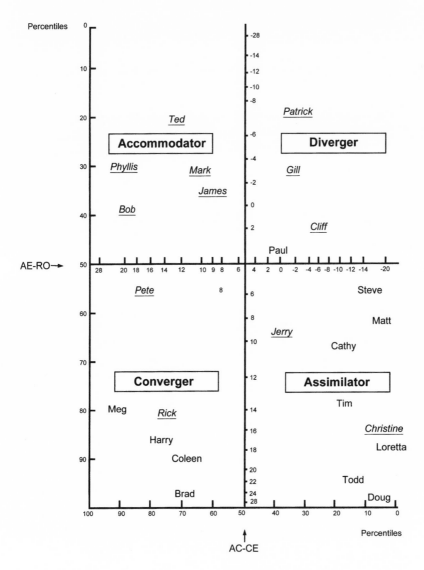

spread fairly evenly across all four quadrants. Also of note is the fact that the four research participants who did not exhibit active reflection—James, Patrick, Coleen, and Loretta—are also located in all four quadrants. Thus, their lack of reflection is more readily attributed to not having a challenging experience than to having a less reflective learning style, in which case one would expect that they would all appear in the same quadrant.

Although the sample size is small, the data on learning styles suggest that something other than learning style determines whether managers engage in active reflection. I assert that the major determinants of active reflection are a challenging developmental experience that occurs in the context of a particular work environment. The importance of the experience itself is argued here. The case for the importance of conditions in the work environment will be made in chapters 8 and 9.

What about the experience itself served as a catalyst for active reflection? Words like *excitement* and *complexity* were common descriptors of the developmental experiences of the research participants. Jerry described the day-care project this way: "It got more challenging and more complex and that's what really turned me on." When managers were faced with a challenging situation, their natural reflection was activated by encounters with novelty or discrepancy. For most[1] managers, the novelty of the situation got their thinking started.

Whether it was Ted's exposure to a brand new product line, Harry's introduction to providing health insurance through the government (i.e., Medicare) after having spent his career in private insurance, or Jerry's responsibility for day-care, managers were confronted with something with which they had no experience. Their natural response was an eagerness to figure out what they were facing so they could take effective action. In short, the novelty of the situation produced pragmatic curiosity (refer to Figure 5-1). According to Jerry, "I love a project where I know little or nothing about it. It's like an almost infinite opportunity to learn."

The trigger for active reflection for one-third of the research participants was discrepancy rather than novelty. An example is Tim, whose experience involved assuming responsibility for managed care dental insurance. His previous experience had been with traditional fee-for-service dental insurance, and he did not recognize at first how different the two types of insurance were. He assumed that most of what he knew about traditional insurance could be applied to managed care. When this proved not to be the case, the difference between his initial perception and his emerging awareness provoked reflection. He became pragmatically curious about managed care, but his curiosity was stimulated by an awareness of discrepancy rather than novelty. The distinction between novelty and discrepancy is similar to Louis's distinction between what she calls a rude awakening and a dawning awareness (Louis and Sutton, 1991).

The initial catalyst for active reflection is a challenging developmental experience and the pragmatic curiosity it produces. The ultimate output of having engaged in active reflection—increased insight—is described next.

The Outcome of Active Reflection

The potential ultimate outcome of active reflection, of engaging in a dialogue of inquiry and interpretation, is increased insight into the situation (see Figure 5-1), meaning that managers grasp or understand the nature or meaning of their experiences. A small minority of the research participants did not experience this consequence of reflection either because their assignment was not complete or it was complete but they had not yet come to terms with it. Mark, whose situation is described in detail in the next chapter, is one such participant.

In contrast, Jerry had clearly come to the point where he understood himself as capable of not just staff but line responsibilities as well. This insight came through narrative reflection. He had also developed insight into the way to develop a day-care business (by assessing demand, projecting costs and revenues, establishing facility requirements, and so on). An important area where he acquired significant insight was financial analysis, which previously had been a mystery to him. This came through operative reflection. As he stated,

I had to learn the intra-play of the financial model that we had. I didn't know anything about targeted rates of return. And I didn't understand cash-flow as I do now, believe me. For me it was very helpful to really understand a subject, you know, getting and sweating the details. None of this superficial stuff, but really get in there and understand how it works.

Insight ensued both from positive experiences, like Jerry's day-care experience, and from negative experiences, like Bob's, where the new product he worked to develop (a beverage) never came to fruition. Despite the lack of success of the new beverage, Bob finished the experience with a much deeper insight into how to develop a new product than he had when the project began.

Insight emerged out of the evolving, specific interpretations a manager developed during an experience. Insight is thus broader and more general than specific interpretations, and it is less changeable. Even though insight could be modified, it tended to be less mutable because it was the result of several iterations of inquiring and interpreting. Finally, although interpretations are better thought of as journeys than destinations, insight is more narrowly a destination or ultimate outcome of active reflection. Recall that pragmatic curiosity, based on the novelty or discrepancy inherent in a challenging experience, is the initial trigger for reflection. Developing insight means managers satisfied that curiosity.

SUMMARY

This chapter introduces a model of how active reflection operates during developmental experiences in business organizations. According to the model, active reflection is best described as an internal dialogue involving moments of inquiry and interpretation, both of which are intended to increase insight into a situation. A case illustrating the model as well as a contrasting countercase was also presented. Finally, the inputs to and outputs of active reflection were discussed to place the process of active reflection in its broader context. This chapter was intentionally introductory and general. Specific details of the process of active reflection are presented in the next two chapters.

NOTE

1. Specific numerical counts across research participants of the frequency with which novelty activated reflection (as well as counts of variations on other concepts) are not provided for two reasons. First, with such a small sample, size counts carry little meaning. Second, counts are often unavailable because not exactly the same set of questions was asked of each manager. This study used the grounded theory technique of letting the content of specific interviews evolve over the course of the research as concepts emerged and developed. Detailed explanation of the interview methodology is provided in chapter 4. The concepts presented here are in all cases representative of the experiences of at least a majority of research participants, unless otherwise stated.

Chapter 6

How Active Reflection Operates

The model presented in Figure 5-1 illustrates several dimensions of active reflection, three of which will be discussed in detail here: process, outlook, and orientation. Taken together, these dimensions capture the essence of how active reflection operates. At its core, active reflection is a process of inquiry and interpretation. Its outlook begins with obscurity from the manager's perspective, which over time shifts to increasing clarity. Finally, the reflection is directed or oriented either toward the task at hand (i.e., operatively) or toward the manager himself (i.e., narratively). Data in the form of extensive quotes from research participants will be provided to illuminate these three important dimensions of active reflection.

THE CORE PROCESS OF ACTIVE REFLECTION: INQUIRY AND INTERPRETATION

What exactly do managers do when they engage in active reflection? Viewed as a cognitive process (recall Figure 1-1), active reflection is best described as an internal dialogue. While managers do not actually "talk to themselves" when they reflect, it is as though they carry on conversations in their minds. They formulate questions, interpret incoming information, and develop insights. They strive to understand all the new, ambiguous, and confusing stimuli they are encountering. The initial response to being curious about all these stimuli is to wonder what they all mean.

Inquiry

Research participants did not explicitly talk about internal dialogue, but the term *dialogue* captures nicely what it meant for them to reflect naturally. One manager, Phyllis, did refer to her reflection as a "conversation." In describing active reflection she commented, "I play it (a situation) back in my mind. I probably do that not so much visually as conversationally. What I said and what someone else said, and try to think of the verbal and nonverbal reactions I got."

Inquiring and interpreting represent two distinct moments of reflection. A moment is a brief but important interval of time, and the conventional view is that reflection inherently takes a lot of time. That was not the case for the active reflection of managers. Active reflection was brief, often lasting several seconds or at most a few minutes, but those moments were important ones. Indeed, they were crucial to helping the manager work through the experience. Additionally, the two moments interacted iteratively. Each required the other if the manager was to move from a state of ignorance and incompetence to one of increasing insight and skillfulness.

Inquiry is the first moment of reflection, which involves formulating questions in the quest for information and comprehension. Since the situations managers faced were unfamiliar, initial thoughts were of this variety: What's going on here? What do I need to know? How do I proceed? This type of thinking preoccupied Jerry early in the day-care project. As he shared,

I didn't know anything about day-care, not a thing. I've found that when I'm in that type of situation, I try to break it down. What do I know? What are sources of information that I can get answers to my question? What are the facts, what are the relationships between all the facts, and how do I feel about it? It's not knowing the answers, but it's knowing the right questions. I firmly believe that having the right set of questions is more important than anything else.

The relationship of action to active reflection

It is necessary to digress momentarily to explain the role of action in the model of active reflection as described in Figure 5-1. Not only did two distinct moments of reflection—inquiring and interpreting—interact iteratively, but so too did each moment interact with action (i.e., taking behavioral action in the situation). Inquiry as it is described here is a mental activity; questions arise and are formulated in managers' minds. But once the questions are formed, they are usually verbalized, which means they move from pure cognition to behavior. Put simply, managers ask someone their questions. This is how reflection and action interact iteratively in the process of learning from developmental experiences (see Figure 1-1). Strictly speaking, inquiring as it is presented in the model in Figure 5-1 refers only to mental activity. Obviously, however, mental inquiry leads to behavioral inquiry. That is, questions formed inside managers' minds are spoken audibly so that answers to the questions can be obtained.

Taking action occurs in conjunction with all the mental activities presented in Figure 5-1. According to the findings of this study, action took the form of exploring the environment (i.e., acting on the thoughts produced while inquiring), sharing emerging interpretations with other people, and task performance (i.e., actually trying to perform whatever it was a manager was learning). Selected examples of action and their relation to moments of reflection are provided in the discussion that follows. However, little elaboration of action is given because the focus of this research is the reflective rather than the behavioral nature of learning from experience.

Returning to the first moment of reflection, questions formed in inquiry could be categorized as one of five basic types. Listed in order of increasing complexity and depth, they are questions of fact, of function, of approach, and of purpose; a fifth type, questions of self, involve examining the personal implications of the experience. These questions will be discussed later in this chapter in the section on narrative reflection. The five types of questions are summarized in Figure 6-1.

Questions of fact

These questions, the simplest and shallowest, were designed to solicit specific information. Jerry wondered with whom the company currently contracted for day-care as well as how many children were presently enrolled. Although such questions required cognitive effort on Jerry's part, that effort is not considered active reflection here since the answers to the questions do not require forming an interpretation. Since the answers are self-explanatory, reflection is not

Figure 6-1
Five Common Types of Questions Formed in Inquiry

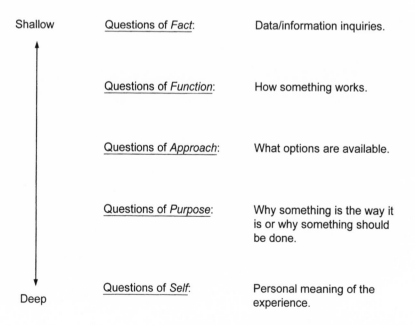

involved. The next four levels of questions all involved reflection because answering them required the deliberate development of interpretations.

Questions of function

Questions of function were questions of how something works, operates, or "functions." For Jerry, these included a question as broad as how day-care was structured under the current provider, to one as narrow as how a break-even analysis is performed (which was something he needed to learn to establish a financially viable day-care operation). The answers to these questions, although not really open-ended, did permit a degree of interpretation in understanding them.

These questions also got at the heart of learning. The situations the managers found themselves in required that they take effective action to attain certain performance goals. In order to do this they had to learn new things (such as how to manage a sales staff made up of brokers versus employees or how managed dental care operates in comparison to traditional fee-for-service insurance). Much of this learning involved simply figuring out how things currently worked so the manager could take informed action.

Questions of approach

These questions involved a deeper level of active reflection than questions of function. Here managers inquired into the various ways a particular situation could be handled. The basic question was: What is the best approach to take? Jerry considered several "options" (his term): continue to contract with Food Corp.'s current day-care provider, have Food Corp. get into the day-care business and offer the service itself, rent day-care facilities, or construct new ones. This represented a deeper level of inquiry because it required not only comprehension of issues but also an evaluation of the merits of various alternatives.

Questions of purpose

The deepest level of inquiry involved formulating questions of purpose, which were questions about the underlying reason for doing something. These questions typically included the word *why*. Jerry referred to these as "basic questions."

The first thing I did, which is always sort of in my mind, was to get a big picture. What did we have here? What's the situation we have here? So the big picture was very important to me in taking on that assignment. Well, what is our company policy and belief about day-care? Should we have it and why?

Questions of purpose were the deepest form of inquiry because their answers were the least readily apparent and because ultimately they were of a philosophical nature. Determining whether Food Corp. should offer day-care and, if so, why, required serious and arduous reflection. It also necessitated recognizing one's values. A major part of the reason Jerry concluded that Food Corp. should indeed offer day-care and should do so wholeheartedly was because the company had a long history of seriously promoting the welfare of children.

Questions of purpose were associated with challenging experiences that were new not only to the manager but to the company as well. At Food Corp., Ted and Bob worked with products and Cliff worked with an automated distribution technology, all of which were brand-new to the company. Their task was thus not to learn something that was new to them but familiar to others at Food Corp. Instead it was to learn something that both they and the company knew nothing about. Bob put it this way:

That whole theme of "unique and new to the world" plays through this whole thing [of developing a new beverage]. That's why we're struggling with this. Otherwise it would be more straightforward. You follow the leader, if you will. In this you can't because we are the leader!

Established modes of thinking and acting were unavailable in these situations, leading managers to question why the company wanted to undertake this innovation and whether it really made sense to do so.

Finding out what other people already knew through questions of function required reflection at a more superficial level. Essentially it involved simply becoming informed. In comparison, fundamental questions of purpose required reflection at a much deeper level because managers were attempting to decipher something that no one at the company knew about. This involved a process of discovery, not just becoming informed.

Inquiry at this level involved the most serious active reflection because it required getting at the underlying reason for things and exploring previously unexplored areas. It involved learning that is similar to what Senge (1990) calls generative learning. In contrast to adaptive learning, which is about coping, generative learning is about creating. Creating involves expanding one's capability to effect one's environment, not just reacting to the environment. The findings of this study indicate that generative learning requires reflecting deeply on questions of purpose.

Questions of purpose were common for Ted, Bob, Cliff, and Jerry at Food Corp. At Health Co., questions of purpose were readily evident among three participants who were exploring new areas for the insurance company. Questions of purpose occurred occasionally among the other research participants but were most clearly associated with "generative" experiences. The other levels of questions were common among all participants. The breadth of managers' involvement in inquiry ranged from Bob, who developed a list of 200 questions when he began his assignment, to Todd, who inquired sparingly. Todd described himself as a former Marine whose responsibility was to implement orders, not to ask questions. Todd's comment also suggests that individual differences are not irrelevant here; however, they are not the focus of this research.

Questions of fact, function, approach, and purpose were here discussed in order of increasing depth. In managers' actual experience, these questions emerged in no particular order. Once again Jerry provides a useful illustration. He initially dealt with questions of purpose because it was unclear to him whether Food Corp. should even provide day-care. These were followed by questions of function by which Jerry simply tried to comprehend what day-care was all about and how the current contractor performed it.

These questions led to different questions, such as the financial viability of the company's current day-care provider. The issue here was not simply whether the provider was viable, but also how to conduct the financial analyses necessary to make such a determination (recall that Jerry's previous experience had been entirely in human resources). Jerry needed answers, but he also needed to learn the financial techniques necessary for arriving at those answers. Questions about the actual demand for day-care followed, succeeded by questions concerning the possible ways to meet the identified demand (an example of questions of approach). So it went. At each step, new questions at varying levels emerged.

If the formulation of questions was a key element of the cognitive process of reflection, developing answers required that action be taken. This Jerry did, by visiting area day-care centers and meeting with parents, employees, and relevant experts (financial, legal, governmental, etc.). Through observation and dialogue he sought information relevant to his inquiries.

Intentional inquiry was central to managers' active reflection during developmental experiences. Managers naturally inquired into the meaning of their experiences. They also reflected in another important way: interpretation.

Interpretation

Inquiry represented managers' initial response to the unfamiliar. After questions were formed and action was taken to collect relevant information, data became available. These data were then processed mentally, organized, and deciphered in an effort to make sense of them. Through this moment of reflection, information began to be translated into knowledge, and the manager thus began to unravel key issues and determine what learning was required to address them. According to Bob, this consisted of "figuring out what all this [new information] means."

The term *interpretation* is used to describe this moment of reflection because the issues managers were inquiring about were too complex and indeterminate to result in unambiguous answers. There is a clear-cut answer to the question, for example, of how to complete an expense report. But there was no unequivocal answer to the question of how to market a new health insurance product. Such questions required managers to develop their own explanation or interpretation of the situation. In this way, developing interpretations parallels the process of *satisficing* in decision making (March and Simon, 1958).

Interpretations were generally provisional and subject to revision. They also had an element of subjectivity, in that a situation could be reasonably understood in more than one way. Certainly some interpretations captured reality more accurately and validly than others, but rarely was there one "correct" interpretation. The learning the managers in this study were involved in thus contrasts sharply with conventional, structured approaches to management development where explicit learning objectives are defined and used to assess learning outcomes. That approach works well for relatively simple skills taught in a controlled environment (like a classroom); in such settings it is more likely that there are "right" answers. On-the-job developmental experiences, in contrast, are by definition ill-defined and fluid. What is learned as well as how it is learned results from an interpretive process as much as from a strictly rational one.

For Jerry, interpreting meant taking the raw (financial, marketing, architectural, etc.) information he was collecting and manipulating it in order to draw conclusions. This involved a form of internal dialogue.

It's my own intellectual approach of gathering information, categorizing it, putting it in places. Here's what I need for marketing. Here's what I need on finance. Here's the legal issues. So to categorize and organize the information in a sensible way was very helpful. Then the ability to shift from one subject to the next and focus on it, really understand it. The ability to step out of that and then go back and forth between different functions. Like the business case and the cost of the building. You know, the shifting and tying that all together. Pretty soon it starts to create a picture.

As a specific example, once he had learned and applied several financial techniques, Jerry concluded that the day-care needed an occupancy rate of 140 children. He interpreted this to be the optimal number of children for the day-care to be profitable, although he later discovered that this interpretation was incomplete. The point, however, is that Jerry developed an initial interpretation through reflecting by "categorizing, organizing, and going back and forth between" the information he had. Later he would refine that interpretation.

Part of Ted's experience involved increasing his sales responsibility from one region to the entire nation. He described his emerging interpretations of the requirements of various regions as getting an "MO" (modus operandi) of the market. Being able to learn various regional market conditions was critical to Ted's success in his assignment.

Managers formed interpretations about many things during their experiences. One participant from Health Co. referred to these interpretations as "mental schematics." Jerry used similar terminology in describing this type of reflection:

I have sort of models and theories in my head, things that other people have thought out and I've filed them away. Sometimes I use those and they make brilliant sense of things. And sometimes they don't help at all. There are a lot of different, and I'll use the term *model* or *theories*, different ways of breaking complex things down into components so you can do something with it. And if you don't like the answer you get from the components, then it's, well, let's come up with a different model.

So, in addition to developing his interpretations based on existing mental models, Jerry developed new interpretations in trying to make sense of day-care. If an interpretation led to action that attained the desired result, the interpretation produced insight. That is, the interpretation validly translated the complexities of the experience into understandable terms. In contrast, an interpretation that did not contribute to desired results elicited new questions, which necessitated further inquiry and interpretation.

Because managers were dealing with complicated issues, several rounds of inquiry and interpretation were usually required before clearer understanding emerged. Jerry said, "I put some preliminary understanding together and see if I can make sense out of it." Another participant, who was in the midst of his experience when interviewed, shared, "I'm getting a little closer to (what I need to know)." He was not there yet but he felt as though he was making progress.

Reflecting by inquiring and interpreting helped managers move from an initial sense of uncertainty and confusion toward one of greater clarity. Recognizing that the moments of inquiry and interpretation just described occurred amidst uncertainty and a lack of clarity is critical to understanding the process of active reflection. This dimension of active reflection is described next.

THE OBSCURITY–CLARITY DIMENSION OF ACTIVE REFLECTION

The description of active reflection provided so far, while accurate, is incomplete. Managers' active reflection was not nearly as antiseptic as the previous description implies. To the contrary, such words as the following were used by participants to describe their mental state during their experience: *muddy water*, *puzzled*, *unclear*, and *confused*. As the full complexity of organizational decision making is appreciated only when the ambiguity within which it occurs is recognized (March and Olson, 1979), so too the role of ambiguity in natural managerial reflection cannot be underestimated.

Steve described his experience as being in a cloud or a haze. Since his use of the word *haze* captured nicely what it was like reflecting when things were obscure, it is used here to describe this important aspect of reflection. It was as though Steve could not get a clear view of the "terrain" of his experience. Often the haze was thick and things were very indistinct. Occasionally the haze would lift (even if only momentarily), and he would see something clearly.

For the research participants in this study, the sense of being in a haze was the strongest early in their experience. Gradually, things became clearer (as their interpretations of what they were facing became more refined). The idea of movement from less clarity to more clarity is illustrated in the model in

Figure 5-1 by the diagonal dimension (labeled *unclear–clearer*). It is significant that one endpoint of this dimension is labeled *clearer*, not *clear*. While issues generally became more apparent to managers over time, it was rare that these issues became perfectly distinct; thus a bit of haze still remained. Moreover, it was possible to feel perplexed at any point in an experience. Indeed, three participants—two at Food Corp. and one at Health Co.—who had been in their experience for at least a year by the time of the second interview still faced issues that were quite unclear to them.

Operating in a haze required managers to tolerate ambiguity. Ambiguity existed about identifying the key issues of a situation and what they meant. It also existed regarding what exactly needed to be learned and how it should be learned. This required managers to learn as they worked and to be comfortable taking action even when they were not certain of the best course of action. If active reflection is thought of as an internal dialogue, then operating in a haze means managers were sometimes at a loss for words.

Functioning in the midst of obscurity and reflecting in order to achieve some clarity was common among all research participants. Tim, a senior manager at Health Co., demonstrates this well. His developmental experience involved merging a dental HMO with a traditional dental insurance business unit to eventually form a new for-profit dental subsidiary. He entered this assignment having no prior experience with HMO/managed dental care.

The three major functions of the HMO that had to be integrated into the traditional insurance area (which was referred to as the DBU, for Dental Business Unit) were claims processing, customer service, and professional relations. Initially Tim thought that this integration would be straightforward, that these functions should be similar in the HMO and the DBU. But what Tim first thought was a clear-cut issue turned out not to be so straightforward. His lack of knowledge of HMOs had caused him to oversimplify a complicated issue. Once he became aware of this, the result was a sense of confusion. As he put it,

The confusing part of it was, at times I sort of said: What did I get myself into here? I mean the thing is a total can of worms. I mean, what do we have here? Is this ever going to work? So that was the confusion. What I thought was going to be a simple organizational structure issue turned out to be, the more we dug into it, very complex. There were other issues and other problems below the surface that needed to get resolved.

In the professional relations area, for example, dentists who were part of an HMO had to be treated differently than those who were part of a traditional insurance plan. Tim recognized this basic principle early, but it took him time and significant reflection to work through the financial complexities involved in developing a network of HMO dentists. The basic issue was how Health Co. could get dentists to join their HMO network when doing so meant dentists accepted a reduced fee for services provided. First it had to become clear for Tim that this was an important issue, and then he had to resolve it.

This issue was typical of the type encountered by managers in developmental experiences. First, the issue presented itself as a business problem that the manager had to resolve. Second, to resolve it, the manager had to learn something new. For Tim this meant learning how pricing professional services in HMOs differed from pricing in traditional fee-for-service insurance plans. Third, the issue itself was not initially clear to the manager and, even once the issue became clearer, the manager found it confusing and difficult to comprehend. Fourth, this comprehension emerged gradually over time as the manager engaged the issue both behaviorally and reflectively.

Tim described the process of working from being unclear to a greater sense of clarity:

It is really a repetitive process. Things often tend to be not what they initially appear to be. So when you look at it you form a question and get an answer. You think you understand the answer but you may not. There just aren't black and white answers. Further probing is required to understand just what is. Sometimes you tend to oversimplify or underestimate what is the problem. You ask a few questions and then you think a little bit more about it as you're assimilating the information. And then you ask more questions. Because it's a new experience you don't have a laundry list of all the questions. As you're developing more questions, you're learning and you're getting a feel for what the real situation is. You constantly refine and move up a ladder as you're asking questions.

This describes how inquiring and interpreting happen in the muddy waters of managerial reality. It also implies that interpretations become increasingly more refined over time. Paul also expressed the evolutionary nature of interpretations as he moved from a vague understanding of the Health Care Finance Administration (HCFA) of the federal government to a clearer view:

It's basically been a growing awareness or a growing understanding. A progressive increase in understanding of what our relationship [with HCFA] needs to be. I think I'm still on the road to complete understanding. There's a lot of political elements to the relationship that I still need to understand more clearly.

There were two basic causes of haze for managers. The first was oversimplifying issues, as illustrated by Tim. In these cases the confusion came not initially but only after managers recognized that things were not as simple as they first appeared. Meg provides another example of oversimplification. Her experience involved promotion to president of a subsidiary of Health Co. that was losing money. Much of the challenge she faced involved returning the subsidiary to profitability. Her first interview happened when she had been in her new position only 2 months. She spoke at length about the need to reorganize the subsidiary but gave no indication that there were any major issues that she found hazy or confusing. When asked about this directly she responded that the experience was "going pretty smoothly" because "I'm a quick study."

During her second interview, which was 2 months later, Meg felt differently. During those 2 months she had discovered that the financial situation at the subsidiary—in particular, the way it priced its services—was more difficult to understand than she first realized. Her initial interpretation of the situation was that prices were set too low. Eventually she revised her interpretation to deal with the component prices of services rather than with one overall price. Once she had clarified this issue she felt that she was in a much better position to begin to return the subsidiary to profitability. But this subtler insight had not been apparent to her earlier.

I had an overall view that oversimplified it to, well, I've just got to get my PMPM [per member per month fee] up enough to cover my costs. But then I came to realize that the better way to go would be to componentize it and take those pieces where I could off-set other pieces.

The second cause for haze was the sheer complexity of the situation. Most managers felt overwhelmed by how new and complicated their experiences were. Whether Peter had just arrived at Food Corp.'s Mexican plant or Brad had just joined Health Co. after a career as a pediatrician, the reaction was much the same as Mark's after his leap in scope of responsibility: "I had a great deal of uncertainty and confusion in my mind about how to do this. I was not operating from something I had any experience at this level doing." Part of the reason Bob developed a list of 200 questions at the beginning of his assignment was to help him cope with what he felt was information overload. A definite sense of being in a haze resulted from being overwhelmed with so much new information.

With only one exception, the managers in this study never got completely stuck in their thinking; they never felt they were in so much haze that they were at an impasse, unable to proceed. They may have been confused or slowed down or off-track, but they continued to try to move forward. This seemed to be because they operated under substantial performance demands or tight deadlines. To completely stop, even for a short period of time, would be fatal and was not an option.

Sarah, for example, struggled through haze in her assignment, and, like the other managers, she worked for superiors who expected tangible results within a limited time frame. Specifically, she faced a deadline for a report summarizing her findings from investigating cost allocation problems. This requirement to act decisively forced her to continue to advance despite being unclear about the meaning of the cost data she was uncovering. Bob likewise felt that time pressures actually facilitated his active reflection. He had limited time to develop his new product and get it to market. He felt this forced him to reflect hard and fast because he had to keep moving forward, even when he wasn't comfortable that he fully understood all the issues needing his attention.

The one exception was Brad. His active reflection stalled, and for one entire month early in his experience he basically did nothing about an important issue.

Brad's experience involved moving from a private medical practice to becoming the medical affairs director for Health Co. Shortly after assuming his new responsibilities, he determined that the manual systems currently used in the medical affairs area needed to be automated. Doing this required selling the idea to a boss who had no interest in computers. As someone who was not used to needing permission to do things, Brad was at a loss as to how to proceed or even whether to proceed. He experienced this as "internal conflict" that momentarily prevented him from doing anything. Having always felt capable as a physician, this was a new and unpleasant feeling for him.

I had no conception of hierarchy within a company at this point. You're talking about somebody who was his own boss and practiced medicine. So I was faced with walking in as the new kid on the block and perceiving something that I thought needed to be changed and not knowing how to do it without stepping on toes. And doing it to the wrath of my boss, who had no interest in this stuff. So that was a tremendous conflict for me. It took me so much time to work through on a personal level, doing this back and forth, back and forth. Should I do it? Shouldn't I do it? And what will happen if I do it?

Brad differed from the other research participants in two important ways that help explain why a lack of clarity led Brad to get stuck while other participants never reached that point. Brad was the only participant who did not have prior professional experience in a corporate context. His professional training and socialization were as a doctor, not as a manager. Thus it took him time to even recognize the need to be persuasive to get what he wanted. In this sense Brad came across more like someone who was brand-new to corporate life rather than someone at the director level. Periods of feeling paralyzed are not uncommon among persons new to the ranks of corporate management (Hill, 1992).

Additionally, unlike other participants, Brad did not receive clear performance goals and deadlines from his boss. Brad could take a month before deciding what to do because, if he got any message at all from his boss, it was that the status quo was acceptable and that automation was unnecessary. Unlike the other managers, Brad felt pressure to *not* act. It is understandable that his reflection got stalled in such a situation.

Feeling stuck was thus an exceptional outcome to the experience of reflecting in the midst of haze. The most common outcome was an incremental refinement of interpretations leading to a slowly developing understanding. Paul's "growing awareness" and "progressive increase in understanding" of the HCFA, as shared earlier, exemplifies this outcome. The haze slowly dissipated.

Occasionally a manager would receive a sudden burst of insight. One participant expressed this as "the light goes on." Another described it as "the sun shines through the clouds." A final outcome of haze was that it never completely left before the manager had to take action. Matt described this in explaining his attempt to learn how to reorganize one of the two major divisions of Health Co.:

I'm not sure that the haze goes away all the time. There were some times where I got to the point where I had to make a decision and it was still there. I tried to see as best I could through that haze but I realized that it just wasn't that cut and dried. I got to the point where black and white didn't exist and it never became clear, so I went with my best instincts.

A final word about active reflection when things are obscure: it can be both the cause and consequence of strong emotions. Brad felt significant "internal conflict" over being unclear to the point of getting stuck. For other research participants (particularly Harry, Steve, and Mark), feeling deep, negative emotions contributed to haziness over an issue. Active reflection as iterations of inquiring and interpreting is not solely about clarity; it also involves haze and confusion. Likewise, active reflection is not solely about cognition; it also involves significant emotional responses. The specific role of emotions in managers' active reflection is covered in the next chapter.

ORIENTATIONS OF REFLECTION

The core of active reflection is an internal dialogue that occurs in moments of inquiry and interpretation. This dialogue took one of two directions for the participants in this study: it was oriented toward the business issues and tasks at hand, or it was oriented toward the manager himself. These two orientations are here referred to as operative and narrative, respectively (as indicated in Figure 5-1). Although the interview guides that I used had questions dealing with potential personal learning, the questions were heavily slanted toward task-related issues. It is thus a significant finding that all research participants demonstrated a significant amount of narrative reflection.

Operative Reflection

In operative reflection, the issues under reflection are job tasks and requirements, business issues, technical problems, and the technical learning required to handle them. The task-oriented nature of active reflection should be clear from the many examples already presented in this chapter. Whether Jerry reflected on the necessary occupancy rates for the day-care center to break even or Bob inquired into the possible ways to package his new product or Tim interpreted how customers of an HMO needed to be serviced differently than customers of fee-for-service insurance, all these thoughts were oriented to the business task at hand. The purpose of operative reflection was to better enable managers to take effective action in their situation: it helped them "operate" in the situation.

When reflecting in an operative way, managers were immersed in the details of their experiences. They needed to reflect in order to learn things and solve problems to perform acceptably. Recall Cliff, whose experience involved implementing a cutting-edge distribution system at Food Corp. This new technology, called Quick Response, enabled Food Corp. to be connected electronically with its major customers. So, for example, sales of Food Corp. products rung up at Wal-Mart would automatically be transmitted to Food Corp., enabling Food Corp. to keep Wal-Mart continuously supplied with its products.

According to Cliff, "We're trying to understand their [Wal-Mart's] ordering system and what their business is like. A lot of it I have to just sort of figure out." This required that Cliff learn the various computer requirements of Quick Response systems. It also required that he learn about Food Corp.'s major customers and how they did business, which was something he knew nothing about. This required considerable interactions with customers as well as considerable inquiring and interpreting on an operative level.

Operative reflection is similar to Hall's (1986a) notion of task learning. It also parallels what Kram (1988) has referred to as the career functions of developmental relationships. When managers engaged in operative reflection, they used the first four levels of questions listed in Figure 6-1 (i.e., questions of fact, function, approach, and purpose).

Narrative Reflection

The term *narrative* is used to describe inquiry and interpretation that are oriented toward the self because managers expressed this reflection as though they were constructing a personal story. They thought deeply about their experiences, not only in terms of how to address the business tasks at hand but also in terms of how the experiences fit into their careers and lives. Narrative reflection is consistent with interpretive views of adult development (Neugarten, 1984), which frame development as the individual's subjective construction of a life course or story. If operative reflection entails trying to discover the objective reality of events in an experience, then narrative reflection involves working to construct the personal meaning of the experience to oneself.

In analyzing the interview data, I initially read the interview transcripts line by line and issue by issue. Operative reflection was obvious when participants' experiences were viewed in this reductionistic way. After coding the interviews at this level, I was left believing I was still missing an important aspect of managers' experiences. During subsequent quick and more holistic readings of the transcripts, the gestalt of participants' experiences became evident in the form of personal stories. It was clear that most managers reflected about what the experience meant to themselves during the experience itself.

Managers' considerations of the personal implications of experiences may have been stimulated artificially by the interview process. Knowing that I would be asking them about their learning may have prompted participants to think more deliberately about what the experiences meant to them personally. Thus, the interview, though not designed to, may actually have assisted managers in constructing personal stories of their experiences. Even if it did, I got the definite sense that the process of constructing the story had already begun during the experience itself.

Jerry clearly engaged in considerable operative reflection aimed at helping him learn how to establish a viable day-care operation. But he also reflected in a narrative way, which enabled Jerry to see himself in an entirely new way. For example:

That whole process of learning the dynamics of that [day-care] business was a challenge for me. One thing I learned is that I have more capacity than I realized. I had set my career goals, I mean I thought maybe I could learn more about HR and grow up through it as I have. One day I was having breakfast with a consultant we use and I said, "Hey, I would like to get some career advice." So I was talking about my interests and he said, "Did you ever think about running a company?" I said, "Yeah, for about one nano-second." Because quite frankly, I didn't have all the experience in marketing and finance. And I don't know that I want to do what those guys do and live and breathe general management, and have the accountability for a whole business because it's a tremendous responsibility. So he said, "Well I think you ought to seriously think about it." It just all of a sudden made me realize that perhaps I had put some self-imposed barriers around my own capacity. And so it just kind of laid there and I didn't think too much about it. Well then all of a sudden some new opportunities started to occur here. [He then mentioned the day-care project.] It awakened me to the fact that I may have limited my own perceptions about my capacity. So that was a very personal experience, a learning point for me. That not only can I do it, but it's one heck of a lot of fun. Major learning point. If somebody asked me tomorrow to go try to run a sector of this business, I'd do it without a blink of an eye.

Prior to the day-care experience Jerry had always seen himself as just an "HR guy." But after it he envisioned himself in a way he never had before, as a potential line manager with bottom-line responsibilities. This fundamental change in his professional identity illustrates the power of reflecting narratively on a developmental experience, especially when it involves deep inquiry around questions of purpose. The focus of inquiry in narrative reflection thus was questions of purpose and questions of self. Questions of purpose involved considering the reason for the experience, not for the company but for oneself. Questions of self, as illustrated by Jerry and other participants described later, centered around a self-examination of abilities, motivations, and identities.

Reflecting in a narrative way was demonstrated in a variety of forms by managers. Rick, whose assignment moved him from a divisional marketing function to corporate human resources, used the phrase "change is as good as rest" to describe how his line-to-staff switch came at a time in his life when he really needed to try something different in order to keep stimulated at work. He said,

After 20 years in packaged goods marketing, a chance to try something different has been extremely stimulating. Doing something different, breaking a mind set, and becoming refreshed through that, is certainly valuable.

The stories did not always have a happy ending, however. Bob was enthusiastic during our interview about his experience and the new beverage he was developing. Just days before his second interview (which was about 2 months after his first interview), Bob decided that, based on disappointing market research data, he would not recommend proceeding with the production and sale of the beverage. He was noticeably discouraged in the second interview. He was just beginning to reflect on what the experience meant to him personally and professionally. At the time of this interview he was unclear about these issues as he struggled to cope with what could be perceived as a business failure.

Mark's personal story was one of struggle and self-doubt and also illustrates an interaction between operative and narrative reflection. Mark's experience involved being promoted to director of governmental affairs at Food Corp. The promotion involved both a modification in functional duties and the assumption of supervisory responsibilities for a professional staff, which was new for Mark. In the first interview Mark briefly mentioned the challenge of becoming a manager of professionals, but the focus of his comments were on a particularly demanding project—revitalizing the company's political action committee (PAC). What he described was almost entirely operative reflection concerning the PAC.

The second interview with Mark was a mirror image of the first. He talked at length about the difficulties of being a strong manager. Despite repeated attempts on my part to review the PAC project, he kept returning to his struggles as a manager. This interview was decidedly narrative in orientation as Mark personalized his experiences as a new manager and began to express significant self-doubt over his ability to manage. While the first interview centered on the PAC and the tasks required to improve it, the second interview focused on Mark and his abilities or lack thereof as a manager.

The primary reason for this intense narrative reflection by Mark was the recent loss of one of his four subordinates, whom Mark's boss had taken away from reporting to Mark. Mark's interpretation was that this was because his boss did not perceive Mark as having strong managerial skills. The former subordinate now reported to Mark's boss, who himself had recently had some of his own responsibilities taken away. Taking away Mark's subordinate may have been as much a reaction of Mark's boss to the boss's own loss of responsibilities as it was an indictment of Mark's managerial skills, but Mark did not see it that way. He was not sure what it all meant, but he was starting to doubt himself.

This whole change from being an individual contributor to a manager has been so difficult. If I get dispirited or concerned, then I get down on myself. And then I don't learn at all. You talk about how to learn, I mean, the learning experience right now is a very tough one for me to absorb. Because I don't know what it means yet. And I don't know yet whether I've reached the limits of my competence. I mean that's the real question here. The area where right now I'm questioning myself is this whole question of, am I capable?

Mark was feeling a lot of stress. He was clearly experiencing a lack of clarity, but for him it was on a personal or narrative level. Until he reached some clarity through reflecting about himself, he was not able to meaningfully reflect about the business tasks he faced. In order to reflect operatively he needed to make progress narratively. This was demonstrated by the fact that Mark continued to return to personal issues in the second interview even when prompted to discuss task issues. Mark's situation also illustrates that narrative reflection was not primarily a function of the research interview. He may have used the interview as an opportunity to vent, but the issues he shared were clearly ones he had been wrestling with on his own for some time.

Narrative reflection parallels Kram's (1988) psychosocial functions of developmental relationships. It is also involved in producing personal learning (Hall, 1986), one outcome of which is identity change. For Mark, the key issue in interpreting his experience and trying to integrate it into his career story involved determining whether being a manager was his true professional identity. Identity issues were also central to Jerry's narrative reflection.

SUMMARY

When viewed as an internal cognitive process, active reflection is about developing clarity about operative and narrative issues in a developmental experience by inquiring and interpreting. Inquiry is the initial moment of active reflection. This involves formulating questions of fact, function, approach, purpose, and self in order to probe the experience. Inquiry leads to the next moment, interpretation, which entails developing a tentative understanding of the situation by examining incoming information. All this is done amidst a haze or lack of clarity, which is caused by oversimplifying issues or by the sheer complexity of the experience. Inquiry and interpretation are used to work toward an increasing sense of clarity. Finally, alternating moments of inquiry and interpretation are oriented toward the business tasks facing the manager (operative reflection) or toward the manager herself (narrative reflection). In reflecting narratively, managers examine what they are learning about their abilities and their identity through the experience.

This chapter described the primary characteristics of active reflection. Three additional dimensions of active reflection, which proved further refinements to the reflection construct, are described in the next chapter.

Chapter 7

The Role of Timing, Intuition, and Emotion

The previous chapter presented the basic process of managers' active reflection during developmental job experiences. Inquiring and interpreting to clarify confusing situations represent the core of active reflection; however, there is much more to reflection. The purpose of this chapter is to discuss three additional dimensions of the way managers reflect naturally (see the bottom of Figure 5-1). Timing, intuition, and emotion all play significant roles in the expression of active reflection. Once again, representative comments of research participants will be provided. This chapter will demonstrate that active managerial reflection is more complex than simply engaging in an undisturbed and rational process of forming questions and interpretations.

THE TIMING DIMENSION OF ACTIVE REFLECTION

This dimension refers to the point at which active reflection occurs in relation to taking action during a manager's developmental experience. Before explaining this dimension, it is necessary to reiterate the distinction between action and reflection in learning from experience. Reflection is a mental experience. Thus, inquiring and interpreting in order to develop insight into an experience represent cognitive activities. They can be contrasted with action or behavior—actually doing something, not just thinking about what could be done. Although active reflection is distinct from taking action to respond to a developmental challenge, it does interact with action in the overall process of learning from experience. Managers respond to challenging experiences by a combination of reflecting and acting (recall Figure 1-1). The iterative nature of the relationship between action and reflection is described by Health Co.'s Tim:

> You *gather* more information that conflicts with your original information. So you have to go back and *probe*. Sometimes you *take action* based on the initial information and it doesn't work so you have to back off. I'm sure there are learning experiences which are, you gather some information, you make a decision, and you sit back and say, "Yep, that was the right decision; I learned something." But most don't work that way. I think it's more complicated and it's more of an ongoing type of thing. In complicated situations it's more of a back and forth between *gathering* information and thinking about it [emphasis added].

The words in italic are examples of action Tim took, in either following up on an inquiry or trying out an interpretation.

Recall that the action that managers in learning situations took fell into one of three types: exploring, sharing, and trying to perform. Exploring involved investigating the situation at hand by asking the questions or making the observations formed while inquiring. For Tim this meant gathering more information about how HMOs differed from fee-for-service insurance plans. Sharing meant expressing one's emerging interpretations to other people involved in the project. Tim did this in meetings and one-on-one discussions with employees responsible for various aspects of both types of dental insurance. Finally, trying to perform entailed actually attempting to do whatever it was a manager was learning. This involved taking action based on interpretations. Tim did this, for example, by directing that the claims processing areas of both types of insurance be combined after deciding they were not that different. The struggles he faced trying to make the integration work enlightened him to the inadequacy of his initial interpretation by revealing the significant differences between HMO and fee-for-service insurance. But this became apparent to him only because he tried to do something; that is, because he took action.

Additional attention will not be given to the action component of experiential learning here because the focus of this research is the cognitive rather than the behavioral aspect of learning from experience. Even so, it was important to briefly review the action component for two reasons. First, active reflection makes sense only when understood in relation to action and second, an important dimension of active reflection—on-line and off-line—involves the *timing* of reflection in relation to when action is taken. This research found that managers reflect both while they are in the midst of acting (on-line) and separate from acting (off-line).

On-Line Reflection

On-line reflection is thinking that occurs while managers are directly engaged in whatever they are trying to learn. Doug used the term *real-time* to describe this. It involves inquiring into and interpreting elements of an experience while in the midst of acting in that experience. Here managers arrive at interpretations that serve as immediate guides to action. The following are three short examples. First, Christine described how she thought about the way she was handling a difficult meeting while it was happening: "I was reflecting while the meeting was going on." Second, Pete talked about learning how to interact interpersonally with Mexican business people: "It only takes a thousandth of a second to think some of these thoughts, and you think, wait a minute, that's completely different than somebody in the States would react." Third, Phyllis explained how she tried to learn the culture of a new plant: "So much of what I do is have to respond to the situation that I'm presented with. So I do tend to think before responding, but that's all during the actual situation."

Reflecting on-line while managers were directly involved in responding to specific demands of their experiences was common for all research participants. Jerry described how he responded to an obstacle that arose during the course of the day-care project:

We were kind of singin' and dancin' in the street, feeling really good about the whole project, and one of the finance guys was crunching our numbers late one night, and he said, "You know what? We really goofed. Our occupancy rates of 140 slots, we're assuming that they're going to be filled at all times. I don't think that's right." So our model was off. So we recomputed the numbers (based on less than 100% occupancy) and we fell below the necessary targeted rates of return for the business. The whole thing was virtually ready to collapse. And we went back in and scrutinized all the assumptions we made in the model. And we started to rethink what the available interest rates would be, and what we could do to modify the building to drop the cost down to preserve the project, which we did. We lopped off about 1,000 to 1,500 square feet of that building.

Jerry's initial interpretation of occupancy rates and associated targeted rates of return was faulty. He assumed that all 140 slots at the day-care center would be filled at all times, an assumption he later realized was false. Alerted to the incorrect assumption, he responded in the situation (i.e., on-line) by reflecting to correct the situation. This reflection involved both inquiry (i.e., asking what assumptions were made in the model and whether they were valid) and interpretation (i.e., examining the relationship between occupancy rates, interest rates, and the like).

Another example is provided by Ted, who felt the only way he could learn his new assignment as national sales director was to get out into the field where he was forced to reflect on-line. "I'm the type of person that has to go out and shake their hand and ask the questions and walk through the store—actually see the building," he shared. In doing so, he reflected while he was acting by, for example, formulating questions and interpretations during conversations with customers from whom he was gathering information.

Active reflection, therefore, contrasts sharply with views of reflection as something that can only happen when one is removed from daily activities.

Rather, these examples clearly show that by its very nature, on-line reflection is connected to the context in which it occurs.

Active reflection is similar to Schön's (1983) reflection-in-action, a kind of on-the-spot experimenting that by definition occurs in the moment when it can still make a difference in the situation at hand. Both Schön and I found reflecting while acting to be common among managers facing challenging experiences. However, whereas Schön found that reflection separate from action (he called it "on-action") was rare, the majority of managers I interviewed engaged in a noticeable amount of it. They often thought about an activity even when they were not actively engaged in the activity. This type of active reflection is here called "off-line."

Off-Line Reflection

Here managers inquired into and interpreted an experience as it occurred, but not while they were in the midst of taking action directly related to the experience. Off-line reflection, thus, is thinking that occurs separate from action directed at task performance. Two research participants, Cliff at Food Corp. and Doug at Health Co., used the term *off-line* when describing reflecting in this way. They are credited with the use here of the off-line/on-line terminology.

Jerry referred to off-line reflection as "re-reflecting." Early in the morning, commuting, and even going to the "john" were particularly productive times for him to engage in this reflection. Here is how he describes it:

I'll re-reflect. When I have spare time, I'll go back over and review what I think, what my judgments and conclusions are. You can't be doing that during the fray of the battle. Sometimes I just retrace my steps. When I get up in the morning my mind races. I have lots of thoughts about new ideas before I ever leave the house. And then I have a 45-minute commute and I use that time.

This reflection occurred during the day-care experience, but it happened while he was in activities unrelated to the day-care project.

Managers reflected naturally off-line, but this does not mean they spent time sitting around just thinking. Although off-line reflection happened separately from action directed at task performance, off-line reflection usually occurred when the manager was involved in an unrelated activity. This type of reflection, thus, involved multitasking; while engaged in one task, the person was consciously reflecting on another task. According to Jerry, "The work environment demands multiple tasks. I can be doing a lot of different things and be thinking about something else." This form of active reflection was widespread and frequently occurred during a variety of activities unrelated to managers' developmental experiences: traveling, commuting, exercising, showering, chauffeuring children, waking up at night, mowing the lawn, doing housework, and engaging in a hobby (wood carving). These were potentially times of very productive reflection.

Since they could be performed relatively mindlessly, activities like those just listed provided an opportunity for managers to engage in fruitful reflection about aspects of their experience. Ted provides some specific examples:

I think the [venture start-up] job, because of being able to experience new things and having that time period where you had to drive to the next meeting or you're by yourself in the hotel, not with the family at home, or you're on the airplane or you're in [the office] on Sunday, gave me time to think.

A reduction in the opportunity for off-line reflection bothered Ted and interfered with his thinking. One of the few things he missed about traveling when his start-up assignment was finished was the opportunity for reflecting while in airplanes. In addition, as autumn turned to winter, he complained that "tremendous quality time thinking on my lawn mower" was no longer available.

Off-line reflection occurred at work (walking to get a cup of coffee, for example), getting to or from work, or away from work at home. For many managers, home provided a better setting for off-line reflection than work because there were fewer distractions. It is worth noting that active reflection transcended traditional work boundaries; additionally, multitasking was involved in both off-line and on-line reflection. The difference involved whether the activity managers were engaged in was unrelated or related to the work tasks they were learning to perform.

Off-line and on-line reflection differed in more than just their relationship to action. They also differed in the functions they performed. On-line reflection helped managers respond immediately to the demands of a situation, whereas off-line reflection served other purposes. First, it enabled managers to gain perspective on specific events by putting some time and space between the event and when they reflected on it. In describing how she reacted to some negative feedback about her management style, Christine said, "I felt pretty beat up and it was hard to sort of separate those feelings. Now I'm distant enough from it that I'm able to take in the information and process it."

Second, off-line reflection also provided an opportunity to simply "clear your mind" (in Cliff's words), since being removed from an experience freed a person from having to make an immediate response. The sense conveyed here is that a break from work and from reflecting can actually promote reflection later on. Cliff and Jerry spoke of vacations as having this effect. They felt as though they could think better at work by not thinking about work while on vacation. Health Co.'s Todd described how he frequently left the office at lunch or dinner in order to work out before returning to the office. While exercising he intentionally tried not to reflect on his work, which he felt helped clear his head and re-energize him to do better reflecting when he returned.

Third, off-line reflection was also associated more with complex, abstract, and especially troublesome issues, the types of issues that managers often found themselves reflecting on away from work even when they had not intended to do so. Reflecting off-line provided them with greater opportunity to delve into problems. Bob described how he reflected a lot off-line about whether to display an unconventional ingredient in his new beverage on the front of the bottle's label.

We did a lot of thinking about that. It's those conceptual things that tend to have more of that [off-line reflection]. The things where you're thinking through the production or the formula, it's there and it's more concrete, versus conceptually trying to see how this thing fits into the whole picture.

The research reported here indicates that reflection is not merely a debriefing exercise at the conclusion of an experience, as it is often viewed. Significant reflection occurs throughout experiences, both on-line when immediate action is called for and off-line when a manager has the opportunity to step away from the experience momentarily to reflect on what to do when action resumes. Both forms of active reflection are important in learning how to respond to a developmental experience.

The description of off-line reflection just given accurately portrays the experiences of most research participants. There were variations, however. Of all the managers interviewed, Pete, of Food Corp., was the only one who reported setting time aside to do nothing but reflect. He structured this 1-hour "think time," as he called it, into his daily routine, arising around 5:00 a.m. every morning. No multitasking was involved here. Pete did this during his Mexican assignment but was fairly consistent with it throughout his career, so it can be attributed to his disposition and lifestyle at least as much as to being in a developmental experience.

If Pete was the only manager who reported pure "think time," Health Co.'s Todd was the only one who shared nothing that would indicate involvement in off-line reflection. When asked directly about this, he replied that he intentionally tried not to think about work when he was not at the office. He explained how he felt "psychological breaks" from work were important if he was to be at his best when he was on the job.

Patrick also tried to forget work when he went home at night, although he occasionally reflected about work while wood carving in his shop. Two other managers who reported minimal off-line reflection attributed this to having young children at home. "When I go home," shared Phyllis, "I have two young children I want to spend time with, and try to focus my mind that way and not necessarily rehash work." Cliff felt the same way:

I don't want to be thinking about work things when I'm working in the yard and playing with the kids. I try to block out everything else. I find myself trying to suppress thinking about work when I go home. I'd rather go home and deal with the wife and children and enjoy it, rather than think about work.

Phyllis and Cliff expend effort to "block out" and "suppress" active reflection about work when they are at home, but they expend the energy apparently because their subidentities as family members (Hall, 1976) are as strong as their subidentities as managers.

Ted, in contrast, who also has children at home, described extensive off-line reflection. He also described the centrality of his work to his identity: "Indirectly my job is my hobby. I don't have any other real hobbies. I'm never off the job." This made it natural for him to reflect as easily at home as on the job. His extensive off-line reflection can thus be attributed to his personal orientation toward work. It can also be credited to an important element of the assignment he had. Ted's developmental experience, in contrast to Phyllis's and Cliff's, involved extensive travel. He spent much of his week on airplanes, in airports, and in hotels. Frequent opportunities to be alone made it easy for Ted to spend time reflecting. Off-line reflection thus appears to be traceable to both individual differences and situational causes.

The finding here that off-line reflection is common among managers contrasts with Schön's (1983) finding that it was rare. This may be attributable to the different types of managers studied in his research compared to the sample reported here (high-potential managers). A more likely explanation is simply that Schön's research did not provide much exposure to off-line reflection. Schön studied the reflection of people involved in coaching relationships; senior professionals demonstrated on-line reflection while they were working with junior professionals. It is difficult to know how much off-line reflection they engaged in, since that would have occurred when they were away from the junior person, something Schön did not examine closely.

INTUITIVE AND ANALYTICAL APPROACHES TO ACTIVE REFLECTION

Research participants approached reflection using logical analysis and intuition. Previous research on managerial reflection has framed it primarily as a logical cognitive process. The critical reflection and hypothesis testing of Robinson and Wick (1992) described in chapter 1 have strong rationalistic overtones. In his cycle of learning from experience, Lewin (1951) saw reflection as helping produce new insights through the mental analysis of experience. Kolb's (1984) reflective observation and abstract conceptualization stages of experiential learning involve applying observational and reasoning skills to experience. The rationality of reflection is clearly seen in all this work.

The Analytical Approach

Logical analysis was certainly evident in the active reflection of the managers in this study. Recall Bob's list of 200 questions. Since developing a new product from scratch was something Bob had never done before, he deliberately strove to think through every important issue in the new product development process.

One of the things I personally did originally was I went through every new product book I could find that had a checklist in it. And I pulled out every single question that was related to what we're doing. I had my secretary put them all in the computer. So I had a list of 200 questions on new products in general that we were using as we went through this. Are we hitting everything we're supposed to be hitting?

Bob used this list over the months he worked on the project to guide and stimulate his reflection.

Sarah also reflected analytically. Her challenging experience involved becoming director of a subsidiary of Health Co., a role in which she took on significant line responsibilities for the first time. One of the first tasks she faced was figuring out why costs were rising so sharply at the subsidiary. Confronted with this business problem, she found she had to learn accounting, especially cost allocation, to meet her new responsibilities. She did this by meeting with financial experts in the company and with people in each of the parent company's cost centers who were charging costs back to the subsidiary. Her plan was to collect relevant data, learn how to interpret it, analyze the source of the cost increase, and provide an explanation to senior management. Although sorting through 500 cost centers while simultaneously trying to learn basic accounting principles was confusing and overwhelming, she tried to be as systematic as she could in thinking the issue through. Sarah described her reflection as coming up with a "theory" to explain the costs and then looking for evidence to "support or blow" the theory.

All managers described active reflection that was analytical, but none of the managers reflected in a way that was entirely analytical. They also described reflection that was more intuitive; that is, they also inquired and interpreted in a less structured and preplanned manner. Jerry's description of how he learned the day-care business illustrates how reflection can be both analytical and intuitive:

I pull in this bit and I pull in that bit of information and even if I can't use it, I'll oftentimes hold it. And then as new pieces of information come in it starts to create a picture. Then what I've always done is try to validate if the picture, which really is a summation of my judgments and conclusions, is sound and rational. So then I start to compare and validate what I think the situation is with other information from other people or other descriptions. And sometimes I use rational facts, available data. And sometimes, when the information is particularly obscure, when the answers are obscure to the information, then I really start to tap my intuition. It comes out of no place but my own gut. I'm just finding as I get older and older that there's a well there that I really can rely on.

Managers' active reflection is more than a series of logical steps for acquiring new skills and solving problems. Rather it is the way they draw on both logic and intuition to make sense of the challenges they face.

The Intuitive Approach

Not surprisingly, managers had trouble articulating reflection that is more intuitive. The very fact that it is more intuitive made them less aware of it. This may also be the reason intuition has received little attention in previous studies of reflection: there is no straightforward way to investigate it. No claim is made here to have done that, but the existence of intuition is acknowledged and a basic description of it is provided. The research participants in this study used a variety of terms to describe an intuitive approach to reflection: "gut feeling, a subliminal thing, semiconscious, something hits you, intuitive feel, subconsciously assimilating, letting it work in your head a little bit."

According to Pete, "It's almost like a semiconscious thinking state. It's not sitting down and making a mental checklist." Pete was most likely to use this approach to reflecting when he was trying to understand issues that were, in his words, "shades of gray." Likewise, Jerry said he turned to his intuition when things were "obscure." Indefinite, unclear, and incomplete situations seem particularly conducive to an intuitive approach. Since these situations were common for managers in this study, reflecting intuitively was common. It was the natural response when logical analysis could take managers only so far on an issue.

Reflecting intuitively also seems to be related to off-line reflection in that intuition was more available when managers were not directly immersed in particular issues. Being free of an issue, even if just for a short period of time, enabled intuition to activate. Paul described this in explaining his evolving understanding of the relationship between Health Co. and the HCFA:

I mean I thought I understood HCFA and Medicare, and here was an element of it that I didn't. When you're thinking hard about a problem, it's almost like you're sitting at the side of a pond. As you're constantly clawing at the issue, the water becomes less and less clear because you keep introducing more thoughts into it. Then when you're doing something else the original issue becomes clear. It just jumps out at you. You don't even have to be looking at it. It's clear enough that you just sort of catch it out of the corner of your eye or the corner of your mind. I think that people have a subconscious that's constantly thinking things over. When you're lucky it sort of kicks a thought or an insight out.

Gradually Paul learned both the significance of HCFA to Health Co. and the politics involved in the relationship. He felt, however, that this came to him as much "subconsciously" as it did through intentional analysis.

Reflection was not either analytical or intuitive for managers; it was both. While analytical reflection was under managers' control, intuitive reflection seemed to happen to managers as much as they tried to make it happen. Intuitive reflection had attributes of a sensation or feeling. Use of terms like *gut* or *feel* to describe it give further credence to the notion that cognitive reflection is not independent of managers' emotions. Emotions that managers experienced in their developmental experiences as well as their relationship to active reflection are discussed next.

THE ROLE OF EMOTIONS IN ACTIVE REFLECTION

The final dimension of active reflection is cognition–affect. By definition, reflection is a cognitive process. Active reflection has been described here as an internal conversation of inquiry and interpretation that involves collecting and mentally processing information about an experience to gain insight into the experience and consider future action. But reflection does not happen in a cognitive vacuum. Just as it can be understood only in relation to action/behavior, so too it interacts with affect/emotion in producing a manager's response to a developmental experience.

Previous management investigators have dealt differently with emotion, and in general it has received minimal attention in the context of reflection. Schön (1983), for example, gives it but passing mention. Kolb (1984) includes learning from feeling as one of the four stages in his learning cycle. This stage, called concrete experience, involves sensitivity to feelings and people more than taking a systematic approach to problems and situations. In Kolb's model, concrete experience is posited as the direct opposite of thinking (abstract conceptualization). Both are seen as important to learning, but they are also viewed as dialectically opposing forces. The findings of this study, however, suggest that emotion and reflective thinking directly interact in important ways. This idea was first introduced in the previous chapter where it was shown that strong emotions can be both a cause and a consequence of being in a haze when a manager is trying to make sense of something new.

Anxious Attraction and Capability Expansion

Two emotions strongly expressed by managers in developmental experiences are here referred to as anxious attraction and capability expansion. They occurred at the beginning and at the end, respectively, of developmental experiences. Both "exciting and frightening" is how one research participant described his initial reaction to his assignment. The amount of this feeling of anxious attraction was abundant early in his experience, diminishing over time. In contrast, capability expansion—the sense that one had grown and was capable of doing things one could not do before—grew over the course of an experience.

If pragmatic curiosity was the cognitive response to the stimulation of a challenging experience, then anxious attraction was a common emotional response. When first faced with a new experience that promised to stretch them, managers typically responded with simultaneous attraction and anxiety. In such a case, the opportunity presented by the experience is seen as very appealing, yet there is concern about one's capability to meet the challenge. This results from recognition that current knowledge and/or skills are inadequate for the situation.

As day-care emerged as a real and an important project for Jerry, he began to experience the chill and thrill (or anxious attraction) characteristically produced by developmental challenges. He put it this way:

I'm an HR guy so you got to understand this was all new to me. I can't tell you how exhilarating this was, because it was tough. But for any of us that have undertaken some of these projects, you have to have your own concept of fear of failure. I think any normal human being would always weigh the consequences of something.

As a result of his involvement in restructuring one of Health Co.'s two major divisions, Matt found himself with several entirely new responsibilities. About these he said, "I think I can do it but I'm not going to say I know I can." He was concerned that he would be taking on a bigger area of the company and one with more production demands.

I'm looking forward to the challenge but I'm also, you know, it's something new so there's a little anxiety there. But not enough to say, "Oh no, what am I going to do?" It's more like, "Well here's a new challenge, let's see what we can do with it."

Anxious attraction stimulated reflection. Managers responded to it by engaging the challenge they faced behaviorally and cognitively. The anxiety was never so strong as to paralyze a manager, because the attraction was always stronger.

Anxious attraction would not necessarily produce this effect in a broader sample of managers. It is important to remember the intentionally selective sample of this study; only managers who had been placed by their company in challenging developmental situations were selected here. These managers were already very capable, and they received new challenges because they had successfully met other challenges earlier in their careers. It is conceivable that other managers, especially those with less of a track record of success, would respond differently to the feeling of anxious attraction.

Anxious attraction was most intensely felt at the beginning of an experience. As managers moved away from anticipating an assignment and adjusting to it during the initial few weeks, anxious attraction began to subside. Brad described his transition from private medicine to the health care insurance business: "It goes from concern to worry that you might not be able to pull this off. But as you start seeing it working, it's fantastic, fantastic." Anxiety gradually began to be replaced with a growing sense of capability expansion. As managers' feelings of competence increased, their anxiety decreased. Rick believed that emotions played an important part in his response to his challenge. During his second interview, he even pointed out that emotions had not been included in my model of active reflection. He described how he moved from anxious attraction to capability expansion:

I overcame self-doubt, fear of failure, by recognizing that what I'm learning is important. And I'm learning enough. My confidence quotient is increasing. Yes, I'm getting a handle on this situation. So one of the ways you overcome that fear of failure is that self-feedback during the learning process.

Thus, a feeling of having one's capabilities expand grew gradually over the course of a challenging experience. This feeling was expressed by those managers who had completed their assignment and who felt they had done so successfully. This represented only a minority of research participants, but those managers who did experience capability expansion felt it intensely. Capability expansion, therefore, is a potential emotional outcome of responding to a developmental challenge. For those who experienced it, capability expansion produced a sense of accomplishment that was tied directly to their having grown and developed additional skills and abilities. Capability expansion meant feeling that one's competence had reached a new and exciting level. The initial gap between what one could do and what was required, which initially produced anxious attraction, had been closed.

The notion of capability expansion is quite similar to the development of a more competent identity as described in Hall's (1976) psychological success model of career development. Research participants who experienced success felt competent and confident, and their self-esteem was enhanced. Central to the notion of capability expansion is the sense of having changed in some fundamental way as a person because one could now do something one could not do before. In short, one's repertoire of capabilities had expanded.

Jerry began the day-care project with a clear sense of anxious attraction, since he had never before been charged with meeting a payroll and turning a profit. But once he had established a financially sound day-care operation, he felt a deep sense of enjoyment. "That whole process of learning the dynamics of that business was a challenge for me. Now I can see why people become general managers, because it's fun." The previous chapter's discussion of narrative reflection showed how Jerry thought of himself differently as a result of the project; he now saw himself as a line manager, not just an HR person. Jerry also felt differently; he felt energized and capable of handling more sophisticated responsibilities. He concluded that being a line manager was both achievable and enjoyable.

Ted felt he grew significantly as a result of his move to a position with nationwide sales responsibility. Moreover, that growth brought him great pleasure.

I was as happy as I could be because I was gaining national scope. Prior to that I had regional scope. It was a challenging experience both physically and mentally, because of the amount of information I was gathering and trying to sort and store, so I could regurgitate it whenever I needed to. But I was so pleased that I was gaining that knowledge that it was worth it.

Why was Ted happy as he could be? Because he felt capable of handling things—a national market, a new product, and a salesforce of outside brokers—that previously he had only passing knowledge of. These new competencies were things Food Corp. needed and they were things he became capable of supplying to the company.

Research participants did not draw a sharp distinction between learning and performing. They framed the outcome of engaging a challenging experience with action and reflection as acquiring a new capability more than as having learned something. Learning was seen as a natural, implicit requirement of performing effectively in a dynamic work environment.

Capability expansion and anxious attraction were not uniformly felt by all research participants. Managers whose interviews occurred in the middle of their assignments expressed minimal capability expansion and in fact expressed some anxiety about their ability to meet their challenges. Mark is instructive here. After having a subordinate taken away from him (as described in the previous chapter), he felt significant self-doubt about his capabilities rather than a sense that they were expanding. Bob, whose new beverage product was not being continued by Food Corp., also felt some self-doubt. He hoped he had learned something from the failure of the product, but he was not sure what that was. A feeling of capability expansion was not produced, thus, when the outcome of an assignment was in doubt or when a manager was disappointed in the outcome.

In terms of anxious attraction, all managers felt strongly "attracted" to their assignments, but four did not express feeling anxious. To them the experience offered great interest but elicited no worry. Bob said, "It's like, if you've got to do it, you've got to do it, so you do it and don't worry about it." He claimed that his natural response to a challenge was to focus all his energy toward the work that had to be done, and that worrying interfered with that focus. The other three managers who did not report anxiety over their experiences were from Health Co. Tim and Meg said that anxious attraction described experiences very early in their careers but not now. Having faced and successfully met many challenges over the years, they had little doubt in their ability to handle their current challenges.

Finally, although Paul felt stretched by his experience, which involved moving from hospital administration to health care insurance, he felt little uneasiness over the move. This can be attributed to his moving from the position of CEO of a small hospital to a vice president's position at Health Co. Health Co. had over 5,000 employees compared to under 500 at the hospital, but his prior executive experience increased Paul's confidence going into Health Co.

A lack of anxiety when beginning a challenging developmental experience thus appears to be related to a history of prior career successes and the extent to which the assignment really involves something stretching. A manager's personal stance toward risk taking may also be involved, since some managers with established records of career success still felt anxiety upon beginning their assignments.

Other Common Emotions

Although anxious attraction was strongest early in an assignment and capability expansion, if it was felt at all, came toward the end, managers experienced significant emotions throughout their assignments. Both anxiety and attraction or excitement were common, although anxiety and excitement occurred independently of each other once managers were beyond the initial period of their developmental experience. Specific issues arose periodically that elicited either concern or enthusiasm. Frustration and anger were the two other most commonly felt emotions, both of which Doug felt as he struggled to integrate two computer systems (one of which was entirely new to him) at Health Co. On the positive side, Meg shared that "the emotion I feel when learning is the excitement of anticipating something that's going to be fun and challenging."

One participant at Food Corp. and two at Health Co. expressed very little emotion at all. Matt was one of these. When asked directly about emotions he gave an evasive response. He genuinely seemed not to be feeling much, so he had little to share. In situations where emotions were felt strongly, they were associated with active reflection. In these situations, information about emotions emerged from participants before I had to ask directly about them. Mark was one of these cases.

Mark experienced significant self-doubt after he had one of his subordinates taken away from him. "If I get dispirited or concerned then I get down on myself," he confided. Mark felt tremendous stress in his new assignment, and this stress manifested itself in physical ways. Mark brought a lower back pillow to our first interview because he said he was suffering from back pain. The pillow was gone 2 months later at our second interview. But during this interview Mark had to excuse himself to go to the bathroom because he said he was experiencing stomach problems. His worry was so strong that it was beginning to interfere with his ability to work.

Mark's second interview was almost entirely narrative reflection. He was unable to focus on task issues until he could resolve what his experience meant to him personally. But even doing that was becoming difficult. As he confided,

If you have hopelessness you don't learn from that. Because I have had feelings of hopelessness in recent months where I've said, the stress is never-ending, getting worse, with no hope of it improving. And that's when I just break down and don't do anything.

Mark expressed to me how much he appreciated his interviews. The interview process itself had been an opportunity for catharsis.

This too was the case for Steve, who experienced significant stress in what he called his "traumatic experience." Steve had been hired by Health Co. to replace a manager who was not performing acceptably, primarily because of very poor interpersonal skills. Steve took over the manager's responsibilities, but the manager remained in the department in a parallel position. The scheduled 90-minute interview with Steve actually went for more than 2 1/2 hours as Steve spent much of the time venting. As he put it, "I could take four days to talk to you."

Harry experienced very strong emotions during his experience and even had a heart attack during his assignment. He attributed this to the pressures of the assignment since just 2 weeks before the heart attack his weight, blood pressure, and heart rate were all determined to be excellent. Harry was a highly respected manager at Health Co. For his assignment, he transferred to a major division of Health Co. whose weak performance was attributed to the inadequate managerial and interpersonal skills of Bill, the division's senior vice president. Harry was given full authority and responsibility for revitalizing the division. But there was a catch: Harry came into the division as a vice president while Bill remained the senior vice president. The major obstacle to success in the division was Bill, yet Harry was expected to make changes while reporting to Bill!

Not surprisingly, this required, Harry learn interpersonal, influence, and political skills he heretofore had never imagined. The challenge was to make the changes that were needed without appearing insubordinate. This situation caused him tremendous anxiety. "A very, very, very trying time" is how he put it. He also said,

I've got to tell you, the first week in this job was the toughest in my career. Worse than starting a job for the first time! Particularly after the display at the initial meeting [where Bill had publicly humiliated a subordinate for a minor infraction]. It was like, oh my god, my worst fears are confirmed. What the hell am I in for here? There was a tremendous amount of anxiety to the point that for those two nights I didn't sleep probably more than an hour. So that was tremendously stressful for me.

Harry felt anxious attraction when he began his assignment. He was very worried about what might transpire, but he also knew it would be a phenomenal growth experience for him and the company if he could turn the division around. Once he was on board the feelings of attraction disappeared and were replaced with a steady sense of anxiety, frustration, and anger, which continued for over a year. Eventually Harry was able to persuade the president of Health Co. (and Bill's boss) that real change would never happen unless Bill was out of the picture. Bill was finally transferred to a "consulting" position.

This incident says a lot about the atmosphere at Health Co. The effect of that atmosphere on active reflection will be discussed in the next two chapters, where consideration is given to the impact of working conditions on reflection. For now, Harry's own words sufficiently capture what he felt was the effect on his reflection:

My thought process sucked. For the first time in my career I found myself not dealing with business issues in a quick, black-and-white, decisive way. I deliberated, I procrastinated. No doubt in my mind it affected my decision-making ability. I mean it actually made me tired physically. By the end of the day I was not capable of getting through some of the stuff that I needed to get through. I literally had myself to the point where I was sleeping about three hours a night, because the historical mode wasn't working and I couldn't figure it out.

Once Bill was removed from the division, Harry began to learn how to change a deeply entrenched culture. He gradually felt less anxiety and less frustration, and he recovered fully from his heart attack. His thought process also improved noticeably, but he continued to struggle with what was a very difficult assignment.

The Specific Role of Emotions in Active Reflection

Much about the relationship between emotions and reflection has been implied by the preceding examples. This is summarized in Figure 7-1. As illustrated at

Figure 7-1
The Role of Emotions in Active Reflection

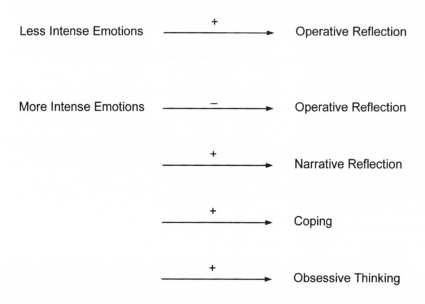

the top of the figure, results from this study suggest that less intense emotions stimulate operative reflection. Mild anxiety or frustration, for example, motivates managers to do something to reduce the anxiety/frustration. Actively reflecting on how to handle the task at hand brings a sense of control over the situation. Anxious attraction had the same effect. Attraction stimulated reflection because managers were intrigued by the situation and wanted to explore it. Anxiety stimulated active reflection because managers wanted to grasp the situation so as to reduce their fears.

When Meg became president of a Health Co. subsidiary, one of the things she had to do immediately was reorganize. While no employees would lose their jobs, some of her subordinates would have reduced responsibilities. She felt mildly apprehensive over this, but she also reported that this was a positive force for reflection in that it "really made me think." Likewise, when Steve faced something he had difficulty understanding to the point of being "bothered" by it, he found it caused him to reflect. "I stepped back and said, OK what could I do? What steps could I take? This has been less of doing and a hell of a lot more thinking."

Less intense emotions, whether they were negative (like mild anxiety) or positive (like interest), promoted operative reflection. In contrast, more intense emotions promoted operative reflection only if they were positive (strong excitement or attraction). But the vast majority of emotions felt most intensely were negative (deep anxiety, frustration, or anger were most common). These feelings inhibited operative reflection (refer to Figure 7-1). Mark felt very anxious and self-doubtful about his abilities as a manager, and it was difficult for him to reflect on his work tasks because he was so consumed with feelings of inadequacy. Harry and Steve, who felt substantial frustration, experienced trouble reflecting operatively as a result. Meg describes how emotions can so overwhelm a person that reflection is impossible until the emotions subside:

If something happens that is very irritating to me and I'm in a situation where I have to figure out how to respond, I set it aside until it passes. If my irritation lasts more than 20 minutes it's pretty unusual. But during that 20 minutes I don't even try to figure anything out.

If strong negative emotions inhibit operative reflection, they foster narrative reflection. Thoughts turn inward as managers try to figure out the personal meaning of their distress. Harry's "what the hell am I in for here?" captures this nicely. So does Mark's intensive examination of his abilities as a manager. Instead of thinking about the work he needed to be doing, he was preoccupied with thoughts about what his experience meant for him and his future.

Jerry had a similar experience during his day-care project. As construction was reaching completion on the million-dollar facility Jerry helped design, the building looked oddly out of proportion. Other managers were commenting at how large the building looked as it rose across the street from the company's main plant. The actual building looked very different to Jerry than it had appeared on paper. He became quite concerned that the day-care project could cost him his career at Food Corp. if the building turned out to be what he called a "white turkey." As his worry grew, he reflected more and more on himself and less and less on the project. (As it turned out, this situation had a happy ending. Once the building was fenced and landscaped, it looked fine.)

Strong negative emotions also produced a basic coping response as managers tried to deal with the stress they felt. By *coping* is meant not trying to reflect on the meaning of the situation, but simply trying to endure it. Venting and resignation were two coping mechanisms demonstrated by research participants. Venting to me in the interview (or to a friend or spouse) was common. Steve used the words *venting* and *purification* to describe this.

Resignation (in the sense of acceptance of the situation, not leaving the job) was another coping mechanism. Steve joined Health Co. with high expectations. Once it became clear that the company refused to confront the cause of the problem Steve was hired to fix (i.e., the problematic manager Steve replaced not only remained with the company but stayed in the same division), Steve resigned himself to operating in suboptimal conditions. His active reflection turned from determining the best solution to the situation to deciding how best to put up with it.

When coping was the least effective, stress manifested itself in physical ways—Harry's heart attack and Mark's back and stomach problems. According to Louis and Sutton (1991), feeling overwhelmed and threatened decreases active cognitive processing because it results in defensiveness. This is consistent with the finding of this study that intense emotions resulted in coping responses.

A final result of strong negative emotions is thinking to the point of obsession. When thinking becomes obsessive it ceases to be reflection and moves to an emotional stress reaction. Once again Mark is illustrative. His is the prototypical case of intense anxiety inhibiting operative reflection and leading to narrative reflection, coping, and obsessive thinking. He expressed feeling, in his words, "out of control" during the last 6 months of his assignment.

It's [the new job as director] so much of an information overload that I'm trying to find ways to cope with that right now as a new manager. I have forced myself to stop thinking all the time. I've got to get away from it some of the time, or I would be thinking about it 24 hours a day, 7 days a week. It's like the whole thing is so chaotic or uprooting. This change from being an individual contributor to a manager has intruded on my whole being.

Mark's sleep was being disrupted by thoughts of work. As he confided, "I've had sleepless nights over the pressure I feel in this situation. It's an intrusion on my ability to function normally." This intrusion clearly disabled his active reflection. Harry also experienced problems sleeping from obsessing over his assignment. He had moments when he just could not stop thinking about the assignment even though that thinking was nonproductive.

Steve became so obsessed with the issue of the former incumbent of his job still being around that he was unable to deal with any other issue. "I had been too damn focused [the former incumbent's presence]. It had become the cause célèbre. It was really frustrating." Thinking obsessively was caused by situations that elicited strong negative feelings. It was as antithetical to active reflection as was responding to a situation without thinking at all.

This discussion of Figure 7-1 has presented emotion as either inhibiting or stimulating different types of active reflection. Affect had these effects on the research participants in this study. But affect was also the consequence of active reflection, not just its cause. Capability expansion is an example here. Managers who in their own eyes successfully completed their assignments noticed how they had grown and developed new skills and abilities. This recognition caused them to feel good; specifically, it caused them to feel a sense of accomplishment and growth (i.e., capability expansion).

Active reflection could also lead to negative emotions. Occasionally, reviewing an experience left a manager feeling frustrated or disappointed. Ted and Pete are two examples. Both managers left the primary division of Food Corp. to accept assignments outside the core business. Ted went to a venture start-up group and Pete moved to Mexico. Although both felt positive about their experiences while they were happening, upon returning to the primary division they quickly became frustrated when their new ideas were not readily accepted. The more they reflected on this and on the differences between where they had been compared to where they were now, the more frustrated they became. Being unable to act on insights gained from active reflection was frustrating; Ted said it was like going to medical school but then not being allowed to practice medicine. Affect and cognition, then, mutually influenced one another in reflecting during developmental experiences.

SUMMARY

This concludes three chapters on how active reflection functions during developmental job experiences. These chapters answer the first research question explored in this work: What is the process of active reflection for managers undergoing developmental experiences? Put simply, active reflection was found to involve an internal dialogue of inquiry and interpretation (recall Figure 5-1). But the entire process is far from simple. It occurs amidst haze and elicits task-oriented reflection as well as reflection that is more personal. It happens on-line while managers are trying to respond to specific issues but also off-line when they are not directly involved in those issues. Active reflection is approached both analytically and intuitively by managers; it influences and is influenced by managers' emotional states. Active reflection begins with pragmatic curiosity, and can produce heightened insight into experience. Through it managers collect and process information to learn how to meet emerging performance requirements.

So far, active reflection has been viewed as an internal cognitive process; it takes place inside managers' heads. Understanding a manager's work environment, however, is also crucial to understanding the kind of reflection that occurs naturally during developmental experiences. This environment both provides the information that is reflected on and influences the degree to which active reflection transpires easily or with difficulty. This is so because managerial reflection occurs in a specific organizational context. By definition, managers' active reflection cannot be separated from the setting in which it happens. Exploring the contextual conditions that impact active reflection is the focus of the next two chapters.

Chapter 8

Influences on Active Reflection: An Overview

Managers' active reflection does not occur in a vacuum. It occurs in plush executive suites, dusty shop floors, and the winding corridors in between. It is one more activity of busy managers striving to exist in the demanding environments of today's business firm. The purpose of this chapter is to put active reflection—which was described in earlier chapters as an internal dialogue of inquiry and interpretation—into context. Attention will thus be turned to those forces that influence managers' abilities to actively reflect during developmental experiences. Doing this will provide answers to the second and third major research questions of this investigation: What range of contextual conditions influence active reflection in business organizations, and what psychological states give rise to reflection in managers?

Answers to these questions are introduced in this chapter and then elaborated upon in the following chapter. A condensed answer to the second research question was given earlier (Seibert, 1999). This chapter will review the notions of contextual conditions and psychological states, then briefly illustrate those constructs using the experiences of one research participant from this study. Detailed material from other research participants will be provided in the next chapter. These chapters should help the reader appreciate the relationship between active reflection and the rich work environment in which it occurs.

OVERVIEW OF INFLUENCES ON ACTIVE REFLECTION

The previous chapters on active reflection framed it as an internal cognitive process. During developmental experiences, this process interacts with action (or behavior) to produce learning. But active reflection is influenced by two important forces: external contextual conditions and internal psychological states. The relationship among all these variables is illustrated in Figure 1-1. Contextual conditions and psychological states refer not to the process of active reflection itself but to forces that significantly influence it. Like active reflection, psychological states exist inside a manager, but they result directly from conditions existing in the manager's work environment. These contextual conditions represent important influences on active reflection that exist outside a manager.

As has been emphasized throughout this book, the interaction between factors outside and inside managers is key to understanding their reflection. The reflecting a manager naturally did during a developmental experience was influenced by his state of mind (i.e., psychological states), which in turn was influenced directly by his immediate work environment. Thus, certain forces in an organizational work environment promoted a particular state of mind, which then enabled a manager to reflect. The specific concepts that will be shared concerning each of these influences were inductively developed from the data collected in this study.

The power of these forces is demonstrated by the finding here that all managers, regardless of their learning style (Kolb, 1985), engaged in substantial amounts of active reflection. Thus, the existence of contextual conditions conducive to reflection seemed to be a more powerful determinant of active reflection than were individual differences in learning styles. The general framework of external and internal influences is derived from Hackman's (1985) work on job redesign and Kahn's (1990) work on personal engagement, both of whom demonstrated the important role of work environments and the psychological experience of work on cognitive and behavioral outcomes.

More specifically, *psychological states* refers to a manager's personal experience of conditions in her immediate work environment that affect her inclination to reflect. Put simply, this involves a manager's state of mind (e.g., engaged or confused). Psychological states incorporate characteristics of both cognition and affect. Conditions in the work environment are experienced simultaneously both cognitively and emotionally. The manager experiences contextual conditions both cognitively in her head and emotionally in her stomach. Together these two reactions determine her state of mind or what is called here her psychological state.

Contextual conditions refers to characteristics of the manager's immediate work environment that affect her psychological states. Simply stated, this involves the manager's specific surroundings. Contextual conditions influence active reflection by affecting a manager's psychological states.

The research participants in this study described several psychological states and associated contextual conditions that enabled them to reflect during their experience. Obviously the terms *psychological states* and *contextual conditions* were not used in interviews with research participants, but they are used here to develop a conceptual model of the influences on active reflection. Influences that were discovered in managers' responses to interview questions are summarized in Figure 8-1.

The model presented in Figure 8-1 shows, for example, that a work environment characterized by feedback and access to other people enables a manager to

Figure 8-1
Specific Enabling Influences on Active Reflection

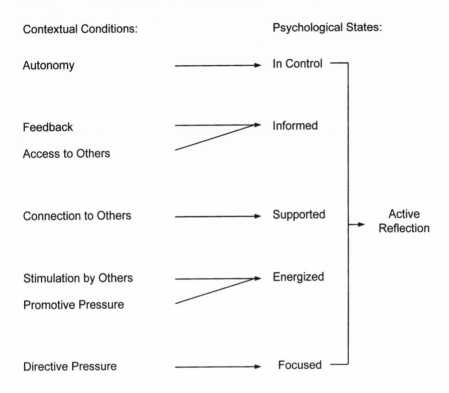

feel informed, which in turn promotes active reflection. The manager who felt not only informed but also in control, supported, energized, and focused was more likely to engage in active reflection (i.e., to inquire and interpret). The seven contextual conditions defined next describe a work environment that promotes active reflection. The five psychological states defined after the contextual conditions depict the state of mind that enables active reflection.

CONTEXTUAL CONDITIONS

Definitions of the contextual conditions are provided here. Each definition is followed by the psychological state its condition helps produce.

Autonomy—A work environment affording ample freedom and discretion in the performance of required responsibilities. (In Control)

Feedback—A work environment providing information on the outcomes of one's actions. (Informed)

Access to Others—A work environment offering encounters with knowledgeable and skilled workers. (Informed)

Connection to Others—A work environment providing caring interpersonal relationships. (Supported)

Stimulation by Others—A work environment offering encounters with people who provide new ideas and alternative perspectives. (Energized)

Promotive Pressure—A work environment characterized by significant performance demands on managers stemming from time limitations and/or very large amounts of information. (Energized)

Directive Pressure—A work environment of significant performance demands resulting from the visibility and importance of the work being performed. (Focused)

PSYCHOLOGICAL STATES

Each psychological state is defined next. Recall that these are experienced within the manager. Each state is followed by the contextual condition or conditions that produce it.

In Control—A sense of personal responsibility and having complete charge over assigned tasks. (Autonomy)

Informed—A sense of having at one's disposal the information one needs to accomplish one's objectives. Feeling well supplied with the "raw material" of active reflection. (Feedback, Access to Others)

Supported—A sense that other people are genuinely concerned with one's well-being. (Connection to Others)

Energized—A sense of being engaged, invigorated, turned on. Feeling well "fueled" for active reflection. (Stimulation by Others, Promotive Pressure)

Focused—A sense of concentration of one's faculties on the tasks at hand. Feeling attentive, absorbed, intense. (Directive Pressure)

The five psychological states, all positive in nature, together produce a state of mind that is conducive to inquiring and interpreting. The previous chapter revealed that certain negative emotions are also involved in stimulating active reflection. For example, mild anxiety is positively associated with operative reflection, and strong emotions, like deep anxiety or anger, are associated with narrative reflection. So while active reflection generally is associated with a positive state of mind, there are important exceptions.

AN ILLUSTRATIVE CASE

Before each condition and psychological state are explored in detail, the concepts of Figure 8-1 will be illustrated briefly by describing one manager from Health Co. Sarah, who was mentioned in previous chapters because her active reflection was typical of research participants, also demonstrates the forces that influence active reflection. Remember that Sarah's experience involved directing a newly created subsidiary of Health Co. that was responsible for processing claims for newly created health care insurance products. Her experience most closely resembles a "switch" according to McCall et al.'s (1988) typology of developmental experiences, although it also had elements of a start-up.

One of her initial challenges involved learning how to determine why Health Co. recently began allocating significantly more costs to the subsidiary than it had previously. Sarah reported engaging in considerable active reflection during this experience. She also described working in an environment that put her in a state of mind that was conducive to active reflection.

Interestingly, when asked in her first interview to identify a challenging situation that required her to learn and to think consciously about what she was learning, Sarah did not pick her current assignment, which was a promotion from the subsidiary to a major division of Health Co. Although she felt her current assignment was indeed a challenging one that required learning, it did not involve the same degree of reflection she experienced at the subsidiary. Much of this can be attributed to the fact that the contextual conditions listed in Figure 8-1 were largely missing in the environment surrounding Sarah's current assignment. In contrast, they were quite noticeable at the subsidiary. Although she did not feel particularly in control, informed, supported, energized, or focused now, she felt all those things strongly when she was at the subsidiary for the prior couple of years.

Sarah was given what she called great "independence" in her role as director of the subsidiary. Since the products being serviced were so new, there was no one to tell her how to do it, which she said gave her a strong sense of "accountability." Thus her immediate work environment provided autonomy, which led to a strong sense of being in control (see Figure 8-1). All of this promoted her active reflection because it required her to think things through on her own. She also felt well informed while at the subsidiary as a result of regular access to feedback and other people. This came from the chairperson of the committee that had ultimate responsibility for starting up the subsidiary and from the many financial experts Sarah sought out to help her understand cost accounting.

The chair of the committee, a well-respected female manager at Health Co., happened to be Sarah's mentor. This connection provided Sarah with a strong sense of support while she was at the subsidiary. Having a source of emotional support freed Sarah to concentrate her reflection on the work tasks she faced. Sarah also described what she called the "adrenaline" (energy) she experienced during this assignment. Most of this came from stimulating interactions with other employees or from the promotive pressure that resulted from the high volume of work she faced and the deadlines for presenting her findings regarding cost allocations to the committee. Finally, Sarah felt she was readily able to focus her attention during her assignment at the subsidiary. This enabled her to reflect on issues when she needed to. Directive pressure resulting from the high visibility of the subsidiary project among senior management contributed to her sense of focus. Knowing that these important people were keeping a close eye on the subsidiary made a sense of focus come readily to her.

Overall, certain contextual conditions promoted particular psychological states in Sarah, which in turn enabled her active reflection. She was led to inquire and interpret issues in her experience by the type of work environment in which the experience was embedded.

COUNTERCASES

Before this chapter is concluded, it is instructive to briefly consider the contextual conditions experienced by the four managers who did not fit the model of active reflection presented here. Gill and James of Food Corp. and Coleen and Loretta of Health Co., for reasons presented in chapter 5, did not fit the model of active reflection developed based on the experiences of the other twenty research participants. As explained earlier, this was essentially because they ended up not being in truly challenging developmental experiences.

Their lack of engagement in active reflection can also be attributed to the fact that their work environments did not enable reflection. In particular, stimulation by others, promotive pressure, and directive pressure were minimal or nonexistent. Recall that James viewed himself as a "caretaker" during the year he switched jobs with Patrick. His experience lacked the conditions that produced the psychological states of energy and focus in other managers.

Coleen's and Loretta's promotions, even though they were genuine promotions in terms of title and salary grade, required the same basic job duties the women had already been performing for several months. If feeling energized is really the fuel of active reflection, these managers' fuel tanks were empty. If the model of contextual conditions and psychological states presented in Figure 8-1 is valid, one would expect the absence of the conditions listed there to disable active reflection. This is confirmed by the countercases provided by these four managers, giving further evidence of the power of contextual conditions on active reflection.

SUMMARY

There is a long history of research demonstrating the potent effect of work environments on employees. Empirical evidence demonstrates their impact on motivation, among many other things (Hackman & Oldham, 1980), and on the extent to which people express and employ their personal selves at work (Kahn, 1990). Leading researchers of learning in the workplace like McGregor (1960), Argyris (1976), and Hall (1976) have long emphasized the importance of organizational working conditions to individual learning. It is only natural, then, to propose that environmental conditions will impact the active reflection of managers.

The research reported here reveals that a challenging developmental experience provides the opportunity for active reflection. But such reflection is most likely to appear when that experience unfolds in an environment rich in autonomy, feedback, interactions with other people, and pressure. These conditions make managers feel in control, informed, supported, energized, and focused. When managers are in this state of mind, active reflection comes easily and in abundance.

This chapter introduced the contextual conditions and psychological states that enable active reflection. The next chapter will discuss each of these concepts in detail.

Chapter 9

Key Influences that Enable Active Reflection and Learning

The previous chapter introduced the notions of external contextual conditions and internal psychological states, forces outside the manager and processes inside a manager that interact to produce active reflection (recall Figure 1-1). A basic model of the operation of these influences was presented in Figure 8-1. Active reflection can be understood only when it is considered in light of these important influences. This chapter provides detailed descriptions of the external contextual conditions and internal psychological states found in this research to enable active reflection in managers. Like previous chapters, this chapter includes selected quotes from research participants that illustrate the influences on reflection and that represent variations to prevailing patterns.

THE IMPACT OF CONTEXTUAL CONDITIONS AND PSYCHOLOGICAL STATES

Ted, from Food Corp., illustrated the power of contextual conditions and psychological states on active reflection. As described earlier, Ted moved to a venture start-up group of Food Corp. with national sales responsibility for a product that was new to the company. The venture group was working to capture some of the frozen snack food market. The frozen fruit bars it introduced were the only product of Food Corp. that needed refrigeration, which required the company to learn different production, marketing, and distribution techniques. It also introduced the venture group to an entirely new group of competitors. Ted's assignment was to develop a national sales network from scratch to give the new product maximum visibility in grocery stores from coast to coast.

Ted will be used to elaborate on all of the concepts in Figure 8-1. Quotes from other managers that either reinforce examples provided by Ted or provide notable variations will also be shared. Formal definitions of each contextual condition and psychological state were provided in the previous chapter.

Autonomy → In Control

Autonomy means operating in a work environment that affords ample freedom and discretion, in which the manager has the authority to act independently to attain generally defined results. Bob operated under this condition while developing a new beverage for Food Corp. The chairman of the company had charged him to operate like an "independent entrepreneur." Bob believed this was much more conducive to active reflection than previous work situations where, as he put it, he felt like a "puppet" or someone operating according to a "cookbook."

Operating with autonomy contributed to the psychological state of feeling in control. That is, managers felt personally responsible and in charge of doing things so as to accomplish results. This feeling was conducive to reflection because it required managers to think for themselves. There is nothing like knowing that one's destiny is in one's own hands to cause a person to seriously reflect about that destiny.

Ted had substantial autonomy in his role as national sales director at the venture start-up, for several reasons. First, there was minimal staff at the start-up, so all staff were expected to take responsibility for themselves. Second, no one at Food Corp. had ever had responsibility for creating a national sales force for a frozen product. No one could tell Ted what he should do because no one knew any more than he did. Finally, being a brand-new organization, the start-up did not have the well-established structure and rules that governed behavior at Food Corp. Ted put it this way:

We had to do things our own way because we were selling a product in the frozen section of grocery stores. We had the chairman of the board's blessing to go out and do business any way we had to. And to throw away the rules; not do it the way Food Corp. does it, but do our own thing.

The autonomy Ted was afforded gave him a strong sense of control, or what he called "responsibility." This resulted in a "tremendous opportunity for me to personally grow." It also contributed to his reflecting on questions of purpose (as defined in chapter 6), since the very reason for the start-up's existence was still evolving. He thought long and hard about the purpose of frozen products in Food Corp.'s overall product mix.

Having control over the start-up's sales activities also prompted Ted to reflect seriously about the best way to construct a sales force for a product that had yet to generate any sales. Here Ted's inquiries involved questions of approach. Initially Ted had assumed he would need to build an in-house sales force from nothing. Once he learned the projected sales revenues for the frozen juice bars' first year, however, it became clear the numbers were too low to support a full-time sales staff.

Ted had never thought about managing sales in any way other than through an in-house sales team. Did other approaches exist? In asking and answering this question for the first time in his career, Ted learned of the existence of "sales brokers," independent salespeople who sold products from established producers on a contract basis. After analyzing the advantages of this type of arrangement, Ted gradually came to view his role as one of coordinating the efforts of external sales brokers rather than managing a team of internal sales employees. Thus, the feeling of being in control of sales at the start-up, which resulted from the condition of autonomy, facilitated Ted's reflection.

Notable variations

Reflective inquiry by research participants at deeper levels (i.e., formulating questions of purpose and of approach) was clearly associated with autonomy, producing a sense of being in control. An important variation to this condition was also evident in participants' responses. Three managers operated under conditions of autonomy, but the autonomy existed by default, not design.

These managers were not intentionally given their independence. Instead, they were allowed to drift aimlessly on their own by bosses who initially gave them little direction and who then showed minimal interest in their assignment. The manager had autonomy but rather than feeling empowered, felt adrift. This produced anxiety that tended to disable reflection. According to Christine, "I wasn't sure what I was supposed to be doing. Things fell between the cracks." This frustrated her and confused her about just what her new role entailed, which made it hard for her to reflect on what she was supposed to be learning.

If autonomy by default disabled reflection, so did a lack of autonomy. Having to function in a confining environment limited feelings of control, which decreased the sense of the need to actively reflect. When things were beyond a manager's control, active reflection seemed less useful. Steve found this to be the case when he worked with limited autonomy. "I don't have direct accountability, which causes me a lot of meandering around."

Ted experienced autonomy at the start-up, which enabled his reflection. But he lost that autonomy when he returned to Food Corp.'s major division after his assignment at the start-up, which disabled his reflection for two reasons. First, he felt less of a need to reflect because things were now, as he said, "beyond my control." Second, he was frustrated by feeling so limited back at Food Corp., which disabled his operative reflection. (The reason this happened was described in the section of chapter 7 on emotions. Also, for reasons discussed there, his narrative reflection increased.) Ted put it this way:

It [the autonomy at the start-up] was a positive and now it's negative [being more confined at Food Corp.]. I had the cake and now I don't have the cake anymore. You come back into a huge organization like this, it's been so structured and it has such a history and everybody has clearly defined tasks. It inhibits a person's ability to think.

Ted illustrates both how autonomy enables active reflection and how confinement disables it. His experience also demonstrates the power of contextual conditions on active reflection. Ted was basically the same person at the start-up as he was back at Food Corp., yet he reported engaging in significantly less active reflection at Food Corp. Although he had not changed dramatically, his work environment had, and the change in conditions adversely influenced his reflection.

Feedback and Access to Others → Informed

The contextual conditions of feedback and access to other people both worked to produce the psychological state of being informed.

Feedback

Feedback involves a work environment that provides sufficient information on the results of one's actions so that one can assess one's progress. Feedback is information resulting from action. When action produces feedback, managers have something useful to reflect on to make sense of their actions. Sources of feedback for the managers in this study included other people (i.e., formal and informal feedback from superiors, peers, subordinates, clients, customers, and suppliers) as well as the task itself (e.g., financial data, increased sales, the completion of a building under construction).

Operating with feedback contributed to the psychological state of feeling informed. Feeling informed is a sense of having at one's disposal the information needed to accomplish one's objectives. This includes feeling a sense of purpose and direction, feeling adequately supplied with technical data, and being aware of the consequences of one's actions. Information is the "raw material" of active reflection. When it is readily available, managers have much to draw on in order to reflect; when it is scarce, their thinking is sterile.

At the venture start-up, Ted reported working in an environment that provided sufficient feedback. This feedback came from several sources: sales agents, his supervisor, and the increasing number of stores willing to carry the frozen juice bars. The sense of being well informed helped Ted engage in active reflection because the information he needed to process was readily accessible.

Rick called feedback the "breakfast of champions" in describing its role in helping him reflect while learning a technical aspect of his assignment. Christine explains the way feedback enabled her active reflection:

I get knocked off balance a lot, where I have to go back through the same things again, even after I think I've got it figured out. I know how to approach it, everything's working, and then I realize there was a piece I didn't understand, and then I've got to go back to square one again. A lot of the way I realized it wasn't working is by reactions that people have to me. Then I tend to go back to them and try to process it even further to understand what's going on. Then it can become very complex in terms of trying to understand, OK, just what was it that didn't work? Was it this? Was it that?

People's "reactions" to Christine were a source of feedback to her. They provided input she then tried to "process" by engaging in reflective inquiry ("What didn't work? Was it this? Was it that?"). Much of the way managers learned from experience was by trial and error. When they tried something, whether it worked or not, the result of their action provided input for reflection.

Jerry's immediate environment was rich in feedback that made him feel well informed throughout his day-care assignment. His two primary sources of feedback were people and the outcomes of the work itself. Here is how he explained it:

Bob and Susan [his superiors] and even Ben [the CEO] were supportive through this. And that would occur verbally almost on the fly. I had repeated contact with Ben and his staff. The other feedback I got was from the hard work. That is, the numbers would start coming in and the parents who use the day-care said, "Oh, this is great. I hope you can do it."

Thus, the people he worked for as well as the tasks he was learning to perform— financial analysis, market surveying, focus group interviewing—all provided useful feedback, information that became fodder for active reflection.

The managers in this study rarely mentioned formal performance appraisals as a source of feedback. One other formal source of feedback was mentioned, when Christine shared how she received very useful feedback on her management style from attending a session at the Center for Creative Leadership in North Carolina. Despite the lack of formal feedback, managers were able to get adequate feedback informally during their experiences. The one exception was Pete.

Notable variations

Pete was the Food Corp. manager whose challenging experience involved serving as operations director for the company's Mexican plant. Pete worked with very limited feedback, a problem exacerbated by his difficulty with the Spanish language. Pete said he got "zero official feedback" and little more when he solicited it informally. The only feedback he did get was not constructive. As he put it, "The only feedback I got was, 'Tell Pete he'd damn well better learn Spanish quick.' And you know, it's just not that easy. At least for me it wasn't."

Operating in conditions that can be described as "information-poor" resulting from both difficulty with the language and the lack of feedback, Pete felt uninformed, which disabled his active reflection. Absent sufficient input, reflection did not come easily. A condition of information poverty, then, appears to disable active reflection for managers.

Access to others

As shown in Figure 8-1, two distinct conditions contributed to the psychological state of being informed. In addition to functioning with adequate feedback, managers who felt informed had ready access to other people who had expertise the manager needed. Meaningful interactions with others were an important contextual condition. Indeed, Figure 8-1 shows that three of the seven conditions involve some form of interaction with people. This is consistent with existing research demonstrating the importance of relationships (including mentoring, sponsorship, networking, and colleagueship) to career development (Kram, 1988; Hall and Associates, 1996).

The term *interaction* is used to describe these conditions instead of the word *relationship* since two of these conditions—the first and the third—involve encounters with people that, although very meaningful, never developed the depth typically associated with relationships. Despite this, specific types of contact with other people were some of the most important enabling conditions of reflection. This study found that significant active reflection transpired for research participants through conversations with other people.

Active reflection, therefore, involves dialogue with other people, not just cognitive activity within a manager's head. Moreover, the reflection in that dialogue appears to be less a case of managers formulating their thoughts in order to communicate them than it is a case of managers formulating their thoughts through the process of communicating. As Jerry said, "You hear yourself talk, and so you may learn something from the experience of talking yourself."

Access to others was the second condition contributing to managers' sense of being informed. This condition means managers work in an environment offering encounters with people who are knowledgeable and skilled in their field. When managers arrived at an unfamiliar situation, their initial reaction was how much they did not know. Access to a variety of other people helped provide necessary cognitive input. Superiors provided a broad sense of where a manager should be going and why. Customers, consultants, functional experts, and suppliers were important sources of task-related information (on products, other customers, new technologies, etc.). Thus, access to others provided managers with raw technical data, which helped them feel informed.

Ted began his assignment with a host of questions about frozen snack products, various regional grocery store chains, national market conditions, and the possible use of sales brokers. Access to others gave him the information he needed to reflect about these issues. For example, he offered the following:

I traveled about 70 to 80 percent of the time. I would go into the marketplaces and I would sit down and talk to our food brokers, and we'd have a meeting for a while. Then we'd actually go out into the marketplace and walk into the various grocery stores. And I would ask, probably, more questions than they've ever been asked before on the different operations of the different customers throughout the country. The hired sales force [brokers] were experienced salesmen. They were my eyes and ears in the field and they were with me on most of my initial visits to those markets. They had working knowledge of those markets and customers. My day didn't end at 5:00. We'd go back to the hotel and go out to dinner until 9:00 at night. So my questions continued until 9:00 at night.

If intentional inquiry is a key element of active reflection, then access to others is clearly a crucial enabling condition of inquiry. The many experts Ted had access to greatly facilitated his ability to collect the information he needed to understand the frozen snack food business and, as he put it, to form a mental "M.O." of various markets. Ted's boss, who was hired from outside the corporation because he had experience in this business, also helped Ted feel informed. As Ted said, "He was the expert, the teacher, and I was the student."

Having access to other people who can provide managers with information parallels the "career" function of developmental relationships (Kram, 1988). These functions, which include such things as sponsorship and coaching, tend to be task-oriented, assisting junior employees in their professional development. These functions differ from access to others, however, in their breadth. Whereas career functions help employees advance in their overall career, access to others has the more narrow effect of helping managers learn particular job skills required by a specific developmental experience.

Notable variations

Access to others was a consistent condition across all managers' experiences with the exception of Pete. Many of the people he wanted to talk to in Mexico could not speak English and he could not speak Spanish well. He used an interpreter on occasion but still found the language issue to be very limiting.

General discussions with people, you know, you obviously do a lot of learning just by talking to people. I talked to the people I could talk to in English. Although a frustrating part was that there were a lot of people that I wanted to learn things from that couldn't speak English, and I couldn't speak Spanish, so I was in a hell of a mess.

Pete had neither feedback nor sufficient access to others and as a result he felt uninformed while on his Mexican assignment. In contrast, Ted had both conditions, which helped him feel informed and facilitated his active reflection. Whether having either feedback or access to others, but not both, would be sufficient to generate a sense of being informed is an important question. Unfortunately there are insufficient data from this study to answer the question, since none of the research participants had one but not the other. The answer awaits further research.

Connection to Others → Supported

The fourth contextual condition, and the second one involving interaction with people, is connection to others. This condition means managers are in an environment that provides caring interpersonal relationships. Here the encounter with someone transcends the mere transactional type of interaction described in the previous section. This encounter involves much more than "access" to someone; it entails being "connected" to someone through a meaningful relationship.

If the interaction described in the previous section provided managers with information and direction concerning their tasks, the interaction described here provided managers with personal support, in the form of encouragement, confirmation of managers' values, and just having a sympathetic "sounding board" (in one manager's words). These interactions were with bosses, peers, mentors, and/or spouses. This type of interpersonal interaction parallels closely the psychosocial functions of mentoring (Kram, 1988), including counseling, friendship, and acceptance–confirmation. Among other things, they help a developing professional feel supported.

Managers in this study who felt supported sensed that others were genuinely concerned with their well-being. This provided the emotional security and help that managers needed when faced with feelings of anxious attraction upon confronting and working through situations in which their existing capabilities were insufficient. Support facilitated active reflection because it provided an emotional anchor in the turbulence of a challenging developmental experience. Reduced anxiety enabled managers to concentrate their thoughts on the tasks they faced.

Connection to others was the one condition that Ted did not have in abundance during his developmental experience. He did report having the support of his family: "My family supported that effort, which allowed me not to worry much." He did not, however, report having any relationship at work that provided support. The only interpersonal interaction at work he did talk about (other than those that provided access to or stimulation by other people) was one that caused him distress. This relationship was with his boss. From a purely technical standpoint the relationship was fine; his boss was a very useful source of information on frozen food products. The problem came when Ted's boss expected Ted to help cover up an affair he was having. Ted did not feel comfortable lying to his boss's wife when she called inquiring about his whereabouts. Obviously this situation made it difficult for any trust to be built between Ted and his boss. Ted put it this way: "You lose respect for people that do that because if they're going to lie to their wife, they certainly won't have any problem lying to you." Far from providing an environment of trust and support, Ted's boss fostered one characterized by doubt and suspicion.

Ted would have liked to have had more support at work, but it was not there for him. When I began to close our second interview, he volunteered how thankful he was for the opportunity to talk to me, which indicated his need for support and its lack of availability. "I appreciate having a bi-partisan person," he said, "that I could talk to about this. It's almost like having a psychiatrist of sorts." He was not completely without support, thanks to his family, but he would have felt more supported had he been able to connect with someone at work.

Jerry, in contrast, was connected to others during his day-care project in ways that helped him feel supported. This enabled him to reflect by giving him the assurance that others knew his situation and cared about him. The team Jerry had formed to tackle day-care was a primary source of support.

I'm starting to realize I know people all over this corporation, and I know something about them and that's been invaluable. I could call any of them and say, "Hey, I have this problem, could you help me?" I think any of them would help me.

In addition to having the support of the informal task team, Jerry received suport from senior management. He described one of his superiors this way:

He would encourage me. He's good at offering a challenge to you, but he's also a caring person. He'll informally just ask, "How's it going? How's the day-care coming? Do you have any problems? How's this? How's that?" There are some in this company that go around and have the capacity to personally connect and touch with people and make them feel good and important about what they do. And Bill is good about that. That was very supportive to me.

Christine illustrates that reflection can happen through the dialogue that takes place in supportive relationships. She described a "network" of peers whose express purpose was to support one another in difficult times. She also had an especially close relationship with one colleague.

One woman I ended up sharing experiences with was Ellen. I'm up at corporate head-quarters a lot and in between meetings I'd need a place to sit. And John was nice enough, he had an extra office, so he would allow me to use his office. Ellen sits right next door, so we just started talking and I felt a need to share all this stuff I was going through [when she started up a new function and assumed significant managerial responsibilities for the first time]. I felt I could trust her, so we talked, and she shared some of her challenges. She also manages a department. There was mutual sharing, I mean it just wasn't me sort of saying everything and her just saying, "Uh huh, uh huh." She could come back with her own examples and was willing to confide in me. So I felt we were confiding in each other. That sort of helped me to feel more comfortable, that I could trust her, in terms of keeping it to herself. That's one person who was an important part of my network.

Two things stand out in this example. First is the "sharing" by which both managers were able to vent and gain insight into their experiences. Later Christine said, "Some of the ah-ha's I get come through conversations with people where I had an insight I wouldn't have had if I hadn't been talking." Second is the fact that trust was an important ingredient in the relationship, and it was nurtured by sharing that was "mutual." The relationship was not just one-way. For Christine, as well as most managers, being able to talk about experiences with a person she trusted was an important mechanism for active reflection.

Notable variations

There was an important variation to the condition of connection leading to the psychological state of support. Four managers—Matt, Steve, Christine, and Ted—had relationships that not only were not supportive but actively under-mined the support the manager felt. Matt dealt with other vice presidents on a reorganization team who regularly "attacked" his ideas, making him feel "defensive."

Christine's work environment produced a mix of this condition. As described, she was connected with Ellen in a way that made her feel supported. But

Christine also worked in the context of relationships that she said produced a "negative undercurrent." These interactions involved subordinates. After a reorganization, Christine, who was at the director level, had people reporting to her who had previously reported to a vice president. Some were openly resentful of this. They "challenged" (her word) her by using jargon that forced her to ask what certain terms meant, or they indirectly suggested that the only reason she got her job was because she was female. Far from feeling support from these interactions, instead she felt uncomfortable and defensive.

Christine reported that these adverse relationships stirred up a lot of negative emotions for her that she had to deal with. Her response to strong negative emotions was one of coping and engagement in narrative reflection. This response is consistent with the effect of emotions on active reflection as described in chapter 7.

Christine illustrates how a sense of support enables operative and narrative reflection. Feeling attacked by subordinates enabled narrative reflection too, but it disabled operative reflection. The emotions elicited as a result of being questioned made it hard for her to think about the work tasks at hand. Her mental focus became limited to herself and her role in the situation. Working in conditions where managers are under attack, then, disables operative reflection.

Another condition that disables operative reflection is working in isolation. Once again, Pete's experience in Mexico is illustrative. Food Corp. gave him minimal assistance in his move to Mexico, most Mexicans expected that he should be able to quickly pick up Spanish, and he worked for a boss who was suspicious of his intentions at the plant. He described himself as a "loner and a pioneer" in his Mexican assignment, and he felt largely unsupported as a result of being isolated. All this contributed to the difficulty he had reflecting on the work he needed to do there.

One of the difficulties of developmental assignments is that they typically take managers to an entirely new part of their company, so that existing supportive relationships are often severed or become much more difficult to maintain. Although Rick reported receiving support from his new colleagues, he also missed the people he used to work with. His old "golfing buddies" had even stopped calling him to join them on outings since he no longer had time for golf. The loss of these relationships came at a time when the support of others was needed most—at the beginning of a stretching, stressful, and often even intimidating assignment. Thus, the time when emotional support is greatly needed is also the time when it is least available.

Finally, the expression of strong emotions was most apparent in developmental experiences that lacked supportive connections to other people. Recall Mark's back and stomach problems, Harry's heart attack, and Pete's troubles adjusting in Mexico. None of these managers had a support network, and all of them demonstrated strong emotional reactions to their experiences that negatively impacted their ability to reflect.

In contrast, managers who were connected to others in ways that gave them support did not suffer this problem. Even those who had a mix of adverse and supportive relationships (like Christine and Ted) seemed significantly less stressed emotionally by their experiences. It seems that the availability of supportive interactions allowed for emotional issues to be addressed within the caring relationship. In the absence of such relationships, however, unexpressed emotions overwhelmed managers and interfered with their ability to reflect on their work.

Interaction with other people is an important enabling condition of active reflection. "Access to others" provides a sense of being informed, while "connection to others" helps managers feel personal support. A third and final contextual condition involving interactions with other people enables reflection by arousing managers' thinking. "Stimulation," the third condition involving others, is described next.

Stimulation by Others and Promotive Pressure → Energized

The psychological state of being energized, of feeling mentally invigorated and turned on, was produced by two contextual conditions: stimulation by other people and a particular type of pressure. Each of these conditions will be discussed in turn.

Stimulation by others

Stimulation by others means that there is a work environment that offers encounters with other people who freely share new ideas and alternative ways of looking at things. Other people were rich sources not only of basic information and emotional support but of fresh ideas and different perspectives as well. Given that managers were in unfamiliar, developmental situations, this input arrived at a time when they were hungry for cognitive input. This led to the psychological state of feeling energized; that is, interested, invigorated, and mentally turned on.

If information is the raw material of active reflection, then stimulation is the fuel. Managers began to actively reflect and then persist at it ultimately because they were turned on affectively, behaviorally, and cognitively by the experience itself. As new employees engage in "sense making" as a result of being "surprised" by what they find in their new organization (Louis, 1980), in similar fashion, managers in a developmental experience engage in inquiry and interpretation (i.e., they reflect) as a result of being "stimulated" by their surroundings.

Ted's exposure to people with backgrounds in areas that were brand new to him—frozen snack foods through his boss and contracted sales teams through food brokers—provided a source of stimulation that he found very invigorating. This led him to reflect about his work in ways he had not done for years in his old, routine job. Sales representatives in the field were much more than just a source of facts and figures for Ted; they also provided an excellent forum for the exchange of ideas.

I was constantly talking to our regional manager or the broker of specific markets. If I had an idea I'd bounce it off of them. And then they started bouncing ideas off of me. And I knew which customer they were talking about, the way they operated, and it became very effective. And I was happy as I could be because I was gaining national scope.

Through the earlier discussed condition of "access to others," Ted became informed by getting basic information like which competitor's products a particular grocery store carried and how those products were displayed. "Stimulation by others" helped him move beyond basic fact-finding to idea-generation. Here he was working with the brokers to learn effective sales strategies and marketing plans to help Food Corp. establish a foothold in the competitive frozen snack food industry. These exchanges with brokers were one form of fuel for his reflection.

Another form of stimulation by others that made Ted feel energized involved employees at the start-up's home office. Employees in the start-up's sales, marketing, and production departments were all very interested in what Ted was learning out in the field. They needed this information to perform their jobs effectively, so they would pump Ted for information on Fridays when he was in the office after a week on the road. Ted's anticipation of these weekly inquiries provoked his active reflection while in the field. He had quite the opposite experience when he came back to Food Corp.'s main division, where people were uninterested in anything he might have learned from a business trip. He explained it this way:

Over here [at Food Corp.'s main division], you can take a trip and come back and nobody will ask you one thing about what you learned or saw. And that [people expecting to hear from him after trips at the start-up] definitely makes you feel good, confident, and growing when people are interested. When they're not interested, it just, you just slowly pretty much evaporate. If you know that you're not going to be asked about anything when you come back, you're not going to ask the questions and you're not going to do the thinking. As opposed to when you know somebody's going to ask you when you come back, you're going to learn more.

Stimulation by others was universally experienced by the research participants of this study. Bob found it to be critical in developing the new beverage for Food Corp. When he felt his reflection was not producing the ideas he needed to understand how to market the drink, he asked and then answered his own question:

Do I need more fuel or more stimulus to play with in my head? [If so] I basically go to people I know who'll look at this differently, and try to see how they'd see it to give me more depth to my thinking. They used to tease me that I did "grandmother research" [because he even asked the opinions of family and friends]. But I was just trying to get more perspectives on things.

Likewise Jerry benefited from the "totally different perspectives" of the people he had assembled on the day-care team. He described the effect they had on him as a "treat" and a "great kick." Another useful illustration of the power of interactions with others to stimulate reflection is the discussion Jerry had with the consultant that led Jerry to consider becoming a line manager (described in chapter 6). That discussion prompted Jerry to reflect on his abilities and to begin to see them as broader and deeper than he previously had.

Stimulation by others could happen through a meaningful relationship. But the interaction with someone else could also be much more superficial yet still make a manager feel energized and therefore inclined to reflect. Cliff, for example, participated in a project assignment implementing a new distribution technique—called Quick Response—at Food Corp.'s largest division. His interactions with consultants, academics, and other manufacturers at a national conference on Quick Response provoked his thinking about how the technique could be applied at the company. Prior to this he knew what Quick Response was, but he did not have enough ideas about how it might actually work at Food Corp. to be able to reflect on it. Once he attended the conference, his mind became filled with potential applications at the company:

I came back [from the conference] knowing that people were really doing this [i.e., Quick Response]. I made good contacts with our major customers that were there, you know, Wal-Mart and Finast and others. So I came back with a greater sense of urgency to our mission.

Being in stimulating interactions with others thus enables active reflection by prompting managers' thinking and providing an impetus to keep it moving along. It also facilitates the asking of deeper questions—questions of purpose and approach. One of the most useful ways other people stimulated managers was by encouraging them to ask these types of questions (bosses were particularly helpful in this regard) or by presenting them with alternative viewpoints, which forced managers to examine their own assumptions (customers and consultants were especially useful here). In contrast, interactions that merely provided access to other people tended to elicit more basic questions of fact and of function.

Notable variations

Stimulation by others was a condition that all managers in this study experienced. Three participants operated in situations where they were stifled in addition to being stimulated by others. This meant that there was little receptivity to managers' ideas. Facing such a situation caused managers to shut down and feel frustrated, which disabled active reflection. Remember that people had little interest in Ted's ideas after he returned to the main division of Food Corp. He put it this way:

It's frustrating [being back at Food Corp.] because you had a different way of doing business [at the start-up]; but people don't want to hear it. Because they never left. They've never seen that it's effective. So it's not really acceptable to sit there and say, "But, you know, at our business we tried this." There's nobody that wants to listen to that. They'd say, "Yeah, but they're not making much profit and those guys are goof-balls." That's the perspective of the people that are in the cocoon.

Rather than being excited and energized at Food Corp., he felt frustrated and deprived. "When you've had that chocolate cake and you can taste it, it's difficult not to have it." Active reflection, then, could be disabled by stifling conditions as well as by a simple lack of stimulation.

The psychological state of feeling energized is brought about by more than stimulation by others. A second contextual condition, and the sixth in the model in Figure 8-1, also contributed to a sense of being vitalized. That condition is described next.

Promotive pressure

Pressure implies that force or influence is applied by one thing upon something else. The descriptor *promotive* is used here to indicate the positive nature of the pressure discovered in this study. Promotive pressure refers to a work environment characterized by significant performance demands stemming from time limitations (due to very heavy workloads and/or tight schedules) and/or very large amounts of information (i.e., the need to process substantial volumes of new data). Being faced with limited time or seemingly unlimited information encouraged managers to actively reflect in order to respond quickly and effectively to the demands they faced.

This finding is contrary to the popular view that reflection requires large amounts of time, time that is simply unavailable given the rapid pace of business. The managers in this study actively reflected because they had to in order to survive. Their existing knowledge and skills were inadequate for handling the challenges they faced, challenges that required quick and decisive action if managers were to succeed in their duties. Thus, working with time limits forced managers to reflect, and do so quickly and soundly, in order to act.

As Health Co.'s Steve said, "It was the realization that I can't spend any more time on this." Four managers even claimed that the busier they were, the more they reflected. According to Patrick, "It's probably easier for me [to reflect] when I'm busy because then I've got the pressure." Promotive pressure energizes managers to reflect. The common ingredient here was necessity; managers had to think and act deliberately and efficiently in order to survive. Not surprisingly, this reflection was highly concentrated and of brief duration, often lasting for a few minutes or less.

Ted felt busier than at any other time of his career. Although this did produce considerable stress, on balance Ted saw the situation as positive. He accepted the situation because of the ultimate benefits it produced in terms of active reflection, learning, and career growth. He viewed it as similar to going to school. "I always equated it as going to graduate school. I was doing my thesis. That's the way I looked at it." In terms of workload, he shared the following:

I did a tremendous amount of trip reports on airplanes. Primarily I would write my trip reports on Sundays. I'd come in the office and I would go through my in-box. So if I didn't work on Sunday I couldn't accomplish my job. It was so challenging. Because of the amount of information that I was gathering and trying to sort and store; it was a challenging experience both physically and mentally.

Ted traveled Monday through Thursday. As mentioned earlier, his days on the road often lasted until 9:00 at night. He was in the office primarily in meetings all day Friday, then he went back to the office on the weekend to work alone.

Although Bob's project assignment developing a new beverage took much more time than his normal job responsibilities, he actually believed this promoted his active reflection. He described how he thought through what to name the product and how to position it in the market:

It's one of those where there were mutually exclusive alternatives. We didn't have time or money to go down the wrong road and double back. We just didn't have the time or money to turn around. So it had to be right. So we did a lot of thinking.

Bob saw time pressures as especially useful in forcing him to quickly think through the more straightforward issues (like how to test market the drink). Here is how he described it:

I think [being busy] is very positive. It causes you to place your thinking quicker. I'm more organized in the way I'm storing the information and I'm able to process it much quicker. You're just forced to do that because you've got to move on. We're literally at all times facing ten issues, and you need to process those and do what you need to do. Especially ones that are concrete, black and white. They're in and out and over with.

Managers' lives did not provide long periods of uninterrupted time that could be devoted to reflection, but this did not mean that managers did not reflect. Challenging developmental experiences require reflection, and needing to do many things efficiently actually seemed to help managers reflect.

For Jerry, the pressure of the day-care project, which he had voluntarily taken on in addition to his other job responsibilities, captured his attention and then maintained it until the demands of the project were under control. He used brief windows of opportunity to do off-line reflection during his experience:

There are tremendous demands placed on me here, which I enjoy. I love the pressure, but it's rare that I have an hour or two or three to sit down and think or write. My schedule is just, it's wall to wall. I'm in meetings all day long; typically, that's my week. I have a very crammed schedule, which is fine. So that requires me to think while I walk. I take, I shouldn't tell you this, but if there's anything I can do to read or think about when I'm going to the john, I don't waste a minute. If I'm walking to a meeting you'll see me reading papers while I'm trying to cross the street!

Jerry succinctly captured the relationship between the condition of promotive pressure and the psychological state of feeling energized when he added, "A touch of urgency is exhilarating."

Notable variations

If substantial work demands facilitate active reflection, does even more pressure produce yet greater amounts of reflection? The answer to that question appears to be no. Rather, the results of this study suggest that promotive pressure has a curvilinear relationship with the psychological state of feeling energized. Too little pressure and managers are understimulated and bored. Ease produces complacency, not energy, and complacency does not enable active reflection. This was the case for one research participant in this study, at least early in his experience.

Paul was hired from outside Health Co. to join a team charged with turning around a struggling but vital division of the company. Once he became a fully functioning member of the team, he began to feel energized as he became immersed in the pressure-filled environment of the struggling division. However, he spent his first 3 months on the job in essentially an observational role. Having left a position as CEO of a community hospital, this was quite an adjustment for Paul. The lack of pressure those first months left him feeling underutilized and mentally lethargic.

The other extreme is too much pressure. There does seem to be a point at which performance demands become overwhelming and therefore debilitating, not enabling of reflection. Three managers at Food Corp. and half those at Health Co., in addition to describing conditions of promotive pressure that energized their reflection, also spoke of periods when the pressure exceeded the point where it was useful. Again, Ted is illustrative:

It was a very demanding job, and I sat on planes many nights wondering how much longer I could do this. Because it was so physical and mental that it was outweighing the joy I was getting from the learning experience.

For Ted, this was the cumulative effect of traveling 4 days a week for over 2 years. The pressure also seemed to build up over time for some other managers. For still others, brief episodes of intense pressure flared up on occasion. Tim referred to these as the proverbial "fires."

One manager, Mark, reported having only too much pressure. Mark exhibited back and stomach problems during his interviews and verbally expressed the difficulty he was having coping with his transition into a managerial role. Not only did he find the transition to management difficult (which is not uncommon), but one of his subordinates had just been taken away from reporting to him. On top of all this, he was working in truly exceptionally demanding circumstances.

When Mark received his promotion he was supposed to have four direct reports. During his first 3 months on the job, one of his subordinates was beginning maternity leave, another missed a lot of work because her husband died unexpectedly of a heart attack, the third had minimal experience in the department, and the fourth position was open. This job, which took 3 months to fill, was the job Mark had been promoted from. Thus, upon his promotion, he continued to do his old job in addition to assuming the new responsibilities he had as a manager. "Those were 80-hour weeks," he said, "And they'll kill you." Mark reported that this pressure was "debilitating" and made him feel "hopeless."

The extreme pressure Mark felt obviously disabled rather than enabled active reflection. It went beyond energizing managers to incapacitating them. The two opposite extremes of promotive pressure, then, were disabling—either excessive pressure or too little pressure. Conditions of overload or of ease produced feelings of debilitation or boredom, respectively, and neither resulted in productive reflection. In contrast, promotive pressure—significant but manageable pressure—enabled active reflection by putting managers in an energized state of mind.

Promotive pressure—significant pressure stemming from heavy workloads—was one of two types of pressure that enabled active reflection. Along with "stimulation by others," promotive pressure contributed to the psychological state of feeling energized. Jerry referred to this type of pressure as "exhilarating." Jerry also worked in conditions that provided a second type of pressure, directive pressure, which contributed to a different type of psychological state. Jerry spoke of this type of pressure this way: "It's got to be important to the person. I like pressure if you have something that's important."

Directive Pressure → Focused

If promotive pressure promotes reflective activity, then directive pressure directs or channels it. The condition of directive pressure describes a work environment of significant performance demands that come from the visibility and importance of the work being performed. Directive pressure means that managers felt under pressure because they knew the work they were doing counted for something. Their assignment was of major significance to themselves; they personally viewed it as important. But it was also of major consequence to their company. Their success or failure had direct implications not only for their personal career advancement but for the future of their business as well. As such, their assignment had high visibility in the organization. Many of the assignments examined in this study had direct ties to the CEO of Food Corp. or Health Co. and/or were widely visible to employees throughout the corporation.

Harry's assignment was typical: turning around a major division of Health Co. The division was a source of significant revenue for the company and a source of jobs for thousands of employees. Harry operated under substantial directive pressure. He knew how important his assignment was as well as the visibility it held with executive management and employees alike. Operating under this kind of pressure quickly helped managers feel focused. So important was the challenge that managers could not help but orient their thinking toward it.

"Focus" was the psychological state that resulted from the contextual condition of directive pressure. Focus entails concentrating one's faculties on the task at hand, both the work that has to be completed and the learning that has to happen to make that possible. Focus means feeling attentive, involved, absorbed, and intense. A focused state of mind enables active reflection by helping managers filter out extraneous influences and devote their full attention to cognitively processing their experiences. It also helps them identify and center in on core issues.

Ted felt directive pressure because executive management hoped that the venture into frozen snack foods would prove profitable for Food Corp. The company had been slow to introduce new products, and the venture start-up was expected to change this. Ted said:

This was a pet project of the chairman of the board, so we had his blessing to go out and do business. And to do it any way we had to, but to do it. The venture group takes risks, they do things different. That was new to me, and it was hard.

Although the expectations of the chairman and the risk-taking culture of the start-up added pressure, since Ted viewed himself as an "eternal optimist," he saw his assignment as a wonderful opportunity to learn and grow.

The general manager of the start-up also put pressure on Ted. Ted knew he had to keep on his toes to be ready to answer questions the general manager frequently directed to him.

You tend to learn and spend more time on things you feel are important, and that somebody will ask you a question on. The more time you and I spent together, I would know more what you are interested in. When I'm out learning something I'd make sure I have all the answers to that particular thing, because when I come back, you're going to ask me about it. The general manager was that way. Once I got to understand him, I knew what kind of questions I had to ask, because I knew the kind of questions he would ask me. So I would spend more time focusing on his questions, because when I came back, I didn't want him to ask me a question and have me say, "Well, I don't know," because then he's disappointed in me. I looked at it as a positive. I enjoyed that because here's a man that was interested. And he relied on me. So I tried to please him. So it did help me because I did more probing and more understanding and asked more questions. And I benefited from it because I did acquire a better knowledge. On top of that I acquired knowledge of him, of his thinking process.

Knowing that the general manager was sure to ask him questions prompted Ted to focus his active reflection on the types of questions he thought the general manager would ask. Ted was motivated to do this so as not to disappoint the boss. The fact that the boss was asking the questions produced the pressure. Knowing other people would be asking managers questions was discussed earlier under the condition of "stimulation by others." When those questions came from a boss or executive, as was the case for several research participants, the condition moved beyond stimulation to pressure. This pressure enabled active reflection by helping focus managers' attention.

A common event that produced directive pressure was being required to make a presentation on the status of one's project to senior management. Sarah, among nine others, was somewhat intimidated by this but also recognized how valuable it was in making her focus her reflection on the vital issues of her assignment. The time preparing for these presentations, and even the discussion generated at the presentation, was productive reflection time. In this regard, Bob shared, "You can think so much quicker when things have to happen. Your thought process and everything's working so much better. Concentration's a big part of this."

Notable variations

There were no instances in the data of too much directive pressure. Managers' workloads could become excessive, and there could be too much promotive pressure, as discussed previously. However, managers in this study never had projects with too much visibility or importance. It was possible, on the other hand, to work under conditions of too little directive pressure. Rick faced a situation where the directive pressure he initially experienced was removed, with the predictable response that he lost focus. Rick's assignment moved him from the position of director of marketing for a major Food Corp. division to a spot on the human resource development team of the corporate staff. Overall his was a challenging and worthwhile experience, but there was one exception.

As part of his assignment, Rick became certified in facilitating a variety of managerial training workshops. His boss arranged for him to receive yet another certification, this one in negotiating skills, which had been an important part of the management skills curriculum. Rick was excited about the opportunity to receive 3 days of training in Boston. His reflection was focused on negotiating skills during the days preceding the trip. He even bought a book on negotiating to supplement the instructor materials for the workshop. He began reading the book on the flight out and gave a lot of thought as to how best to train negotiating skills. He had planned to finish the book and consolidate his reflection about negotiating on the flight home.

The evening after the first night of the certification workshop, Rick checked his voice mail. To his chagrin his manager had left a message encouraging him to continue in the workshop and try to get something out of it even though the negotiating skills class had just been dropped from the curriculum. Needless to say, Rick's intense focus on negotiating skills was quickly lost:

I don't care how good I am. I'm sure that directly impacted what I picked up and what I learned on Friday. Where's an interest level? How important is this? Is the importance subject to change? I didn't read the book on the way back. On the way back I read the *Wall Street Journal* and *USA Today*, whereas my plan had been to finish reading that book.

What had been something of importance became meaningless, and the directive pressure evaporated. His focus was lost and he became distracted easily by other reading material. Thus, a lack of directive pressure disabled active reflection by causing managers to become unfocused and easily distracted.

SUMMARY

This chapter has provided detailed qualitative data on the impact of external and internal influences on managers' active reflection. It is important to remember that active reflection is a means to an end. Managers do not engage in reflection for the sheer pleasure of reflecting; they do so to help them learn how to respond to the performance demands they face. Moreover, managers are more inclined to reflect when certain conditions are present in their immediate work environment. Work environments characterized by autonomy, feedback, meaningful interactions with other people, and pressure to perform that is noticeable but not overwhelming help managers achieve a state of mind where they reflect readily.

This research identified external contextual conditions that led managers to feel in control, informed, supported, energized, and focused. Experiencing these internal psychological states enabled active reflection to happen naturally. Not experiencing these things, as illustrated in the discussions of notable variations, made it harder to reflect. The organizational context, therefore, is critical not just in providing raw material for learning but also in enabling or disabling active reflection.

The findings of the study reported here suggest that at least a majority of the seven contextual conditions are needed to enable active reflection. Thus the existence of some conditions can compensate for the lack of others. It appears as though the psychological state of being energized as a result of a pressure-filled and stimulating work environment is particularly important for promoting reflection. The data are inconclusive, however, regarding the relative importance of each condition and state to active reflection.

This chapter answers the second and third research questions of the theory-building study introduced in chapter 4: What range of contextual conditions influence active reflection in business organizations, and what psychological states give rise to reflection in managers? It also clearly demonstrates that the cognitive process of active reflection—of inquiring and interpreting in an effort to develop insight—can be understood only in relation to certain important internal and external factors.

PART III

A Deductive Examination of Proactive Reflection at Tech Inc.

Chapter 10

An Experimental Study of Proactive Reflection

The purpose of this chapter is to describe the research methodology and design used to study proactive reflection. The literature review presented in chapter 2 demonstrated that education takes a prescriptive orientation to reflection, emphasizing methods or interventions for developing learners' skills in reflection. This orientation is reasonable given that education's fundamental purpose is to help people become better learners. Given this natural emphasis on teaching learners, considerable attention has already been given in the field of education to the internal process of proactive reflection and to specific interventions designed to facilitate it.

The primary gap in the education literature involves the *link* between the interventions and the proactive reflection they are intended to produce (refer to Figure 2-1). Three types of interventions are well known, but their relative effectiveness at promoting managers' reflection is unknown. Addressing this gap is the purpose of the experiemental research reported here.

SPECIFIC RESEARCH QUESTION AND DEFINITIONS

This experiment addressed the following question: Which of three types of proactive reflection interventions—individual reflection, peer group discussion, and tutor guidance—are most effective for enhancing learning from developmental experiences of managers in business organizations?

Brief conceptual definitions of key words used in the research question are listed below to facilitate understanding of how they are used in this study.

Proactive Reflection—The act of stepping back from an experience to carefully and persistently ponder its meaning to the self through the development of inferences.

Proactive Reflection Interventions—Activities that promote proactive reflection. These can be grouped into three categories: (1) those involving individual reflection, such as learning diaries; (2) those involving peer group discussion, such as participation in structured discussion groups; and (3) those involving guidance from someone, such as a one-on-one meeting with a tutor.

Learning—The creation of meaning from past or current events that serves as a guide for future behavior.

Enhanced Learning—An increase in the amount of meaning created from past or current events that serves as a guide for future behavior.

Managers—Exempt employees who direct the activities of other people and who have responsibility for formulating policies and directing the operations of work at the department, division, or corporate level.

Developmental Experiences—Any of the five types of assignments identified by McCall et al. (1988) that create developmental challenges: (1) building something from nothing; (2) fixing/stabilizing a failing operation; (3) discrete projects and temporary assignments done alone or as part of a team; (4) significant increases in numbers of people, dollars, or functions to manage; and (5) moving from line operations to corporate staff roles.

Effective—A statistically significant increase in learning as measured by comparing the scores from the treatment group questionnaires to those from the control group.

METHODOLOGY

Since the research question used to guide this study attempts to measure the relative effectiveness of three different reflection interventions, an objective methodology that provides quantitative statistics that can be compared is required. The methodology chosen to answer this question is a field experiment that allows subjects to experience different reflection interventions under controlled conditions. Since it is hoped that the results of this study will change the way corporations approach the development of their managers, it is critical that the conclusions be derived from a careful study of managers' current experience rather than their perceptions of previous experience. An overview of this study was previously reported elsewhere (Daudelin, 1996a).

Eichelberger (1989) provides support for this choice of methodology: "It is important to know whether conclusions, such as those in your professional field, are based on empirical information that has been systematically collected and carefully analyzed, rather than on edicts or unexamined truths from some authority or from a person's distilled experience" (p. 5). However, Reimer (1993) acknowledges its limitations as being "the lack of observation over time, the removal of subjects from their natural environment and, ethically speaking, the inability to treat subjects as collaborators in the research effort" (p. 56). While these concerns are noted, it is believed that this research methodology provides the best way to answer the research question posed here.

POPULATION/SAMPLE

The population from which subjects were drawn is made up of 732 non-officer-level managers in a U.S. Fortune 500 corporation. "Tech Inc." (not its real name) is an international research, design, manufacturing, and sales organization with approximately 10,000 employees. Its headquarters are located in the Northeast United States.

Managers, as defined earlier, were the chosen population for three reasons: first, this replicates the population used in recent studies of experiential learning at work (e.g., McCall et al., 1988; O'Neil and Marsick, 1994); second, the proactive reflection of a management population had not previously been studied; and third, the researcher's position in the Leadership Development Department of the firm provided access to subjects and opportunities to experiment with new designs.

Invitations to participate were sent to the 732 managers. Of the 290 who returned their responses by the deadline, 159 managers agreed to participate in the study. A random table of numbers and the list of those who agreed to participate were used to assign 15 different managers to each of the three treatment groups and a control group. This assignment of subjects followed guidelines suggested by Kerlinger (1973) for probability samples.

Due to postassignment cancellations, the original sample of 60 was reduced to 48, with 10 managers in the individual group, 14 in the peer group, 11 in the tutor group, and 13 in the control group.

SETTING AND INTERVENTION

The study was conducted in corporate classrooms that are removed from the day-to-day activities of the business and are conducive to relaxed learning. Two locations that are used for company retreats and special meetings were chosen. Both locations have large, well-equipped classrooms as well as many small, comfortable break-out rooms. They are located in areas bordering fields and woods, providing a relaxed atmosphere conducive to proactive reflective activity.

Overview of Intervention

The intervention (or treatment) consisted of a one-time, 1-hour proactive reflection session. The intervention occurred separately with the three different groups of managers to test each of the three specific proactive reflection interventions. The sessions had three major parts. The first part was an introduction, which reviewed the purpose of the study and provided an overview of the process. The second part was the treatment, which led participants through a four-stage reflection activity that applied seven proactive reflective questions to a subject's chosen developmental experience. This basic approach, which is shown in Exhibit 10-1, was used with the three different treatment groups. The peer group intervention was videotaped. The third part of the general intervention was the completion of the posttest.

Exhibit 10-1
Experimental Treatment: Proactive Reflection Activity and Proactive Reflection Questions

---

Four-Stage Reflection Activity:

  I. Articulation of a problem or challenge

  II. Analysis of the problem or challenge

Seven Proactive Reflection Questions:

  1. What happened? (What did you see, what were you feeling, what was the most important thing?)

  2. What is the fundamental likeness of this problem or challenge to others?

  3. What is the fundamental difference?

  4. Why was that significant to you?

  5. Why do you think it happened?

  6. How can you do it differently next time for different results?

  7. How can you use this information? (What concepts and principles will guide your future approach?)

  III. Tentative theory to explain the problem or challenge

  IV. Action to be taken in the future

In addition, each subject completed a follow-up survey 1 week following the intervention to determine if there had been any new learning or any difference in the type of learning reported on the posttest.

Individual Intervention

Individual proactive reflection sessions were held on six different dates to meet the scheduling needs of the subjects and the researcher. In sessions with more than one subject, directions were given to all participants together. Subjects were asked to choose one challenging work experience to focus on from the list of five developmental experiences (defined earlier). If none of the five applied, they were instructed to choose one of their own, following specified criteria.

Subjects then moved to separate spaces within the training facility to complete the 1-hour proactive reflection process. At the conclusion of the reflection period, posttest questionnaires were distributed and explained to all subjects together. The researcher circulated throughout the facility several times during the 1-hour reflection period. This informal observation showed that all subjects wrote on the reflection worksheets or the reflection question handout, as advised. Subjects referred to these notes when completing their posttest questionnaires.

Peer Group Intervention

The peer group was randomly divided into three subgroups: Group A, with five members; Group B, with five members; and Group C, with four members. The groups met on separate days to facilitate scheduling.

After instructions were given and subjects chose a work experience to focus upon, the researcher started the video camera and left the room. At the end of the 1-hour proactive reflection session, the researcher returned, stopped the video camera, and administered the posttest questionnaire.

A review of the videotapes showed that all groups spent the first 5 or 10 minutes introducing themselves and the work experience they chose to reflect upon. After a brief silence, one person in each group volunteered to begin talking in more detail about their experience, and a free-flowing discussion followed. In all cases, the subjects followed the general direction of the conversation rather than the structure provided by the proactive reflection questions and worksheets. Only one of the fourteen participants took notes and none appeared to reference the handouts provided by the researcher.

Tutor Intervention

Six of the eleven subject/tutor pairs attended one large meeting; the remaining participants met in separately scheduled sessions. As instructed, all subjects brought someone to guide them through the proactive reflection session.

In the large group, instructions were given to all subject/tutor pairs together. As in the other two interventions, subjects were asked to choose a work experience from the list of five, or one of their own. Tutors did not participate in the choice. Pairs then dispersed to find quiet, comfortable areas in the training facility to begin the 1-hour proactive reflection process.

Informal observation by the researcher showed that subjects began the reflection activity with a brief description of their chosen work experience. Subjects and their tutors then discussed this experience using the reflection questions as guides, while making occasional notes on the reflection worksheets.

At the conclusion of the 1-hour proactive reflection activity, tutors departed and subjects completed the posttest questionnaire.

RESEARCH DESIGN

The design chosen for this research was one of those described by Campbell and Stanely (1963) as "true experimental designs." It is their Design 6, the posttest-only control group design. It was chosen because, according to

Campbell and Stanely, it addresses all eight potential sources of internal invalidity (i.e., history, maturation, testing, instrumentation, regression, selection, mortality, and interaction of selection and maturation) and is among the most successful in addressing external validity, primarily by controlling the interaction of testing and the treatment. The decision was made to use this design rather than the more popular pretest–posttest control group design because answering questions about the developmental experience before the treatment would inappropriately influence the results. The very act of thinking about the experience for the pretest would have been a sort of reflection that could have influenced results on the posttest. Campbell and Stanely claim that a pretest is not essential to true experimental designs as long as treatments are randomly assigned to experimental groups, which they were here. In this study, which includes three treatment groups and a control group, the design is diagrammed as follows:

$$
\begin{array}{lll}
R & X_1 \text{ (Individual)} & O \\
R & X_2 \text{ (Peer)} & O \\
R & X_3 \text{ (Tutor)} & O \\
R & & O
\end{array}
$$

INSTRUMENTATION

The major instrument used in this study was a questionnaire that served as a posttest. In addition, a set of reflective questions facilitated reflection in each of the treatment groups. These questions were developed and described in the literature review (see chapter 2). The posttest questionnaire is discussed in detail next, including a general description, how it was developed, how it was used in the study, and how validity and reliability were ensured.

Posttest Questionnaire

The posttest questionnaire has five parts. In Part I, managers were asked to identify the challenging developmental experience they focused on for this study. Part II asked managers to describe this experience (using a five-point scale) on three dimensions: how long they had been involved in this experience, how important it was to their career, and how positive or negative the experience had been thus far. Part III asked managers first to list what they had learned from the experience and then to indicate how it would influence future action. Part IV asked subjects to evaluate the learning listed in Part III in three categories: amount of learning, quality of learning, and impact of learning. Part V, completed only by those in the treatment groups, asked questions about the impact of "amount of time" and "performance of others" on the quality of the reflection experience.

As discussed earlier, Part I of the instrument was developed based on the research reported by McCall et al. (1988) describing the types of experiences most likely to be developmental in nature.

Part II used the "temporal" category from Kottkamp's (1990) work to measure how long a manager had been involved in the activity. The other two categories of Part II—importance and the positive or negative value attached to the experience—were created by the researcher based upon general distinctions appearing throughout the literature.

Part III provided the primary data for use in analysis: the amount of learning derived from the developmental experience as a result of the reflection session (or, in the control group, the amount of learning derived without the assistance of a reflection session). This section was developed using the operational definition of learning that resulted from the review of the literature. Since a key element of that definition is the use of learning as a guide for future behavior, this section has two parts: the identification of the learning and the description of how it will be used to guide future behavior.

Parts IV and V were included to provide additional quantitative and qualitative information important to the interpretation of the learning listed by subjects in Part III of the questionnnaire. The identification and description of the experience in Parts I and II provided additional data that were used in analyzing the learning measured in Part III: type of experience, length of experience, importance of experience, and negative or positive nature of experience.

The data from Part III of the posttest questionnaire were used in two ways: to measure the amount of learning that occurred and to determine differences in type of learning between treatment groups. The researcher counted the number of meanings that the participant determined would influence future action. Therefore, each manager had a score based upon the number of meanings. These scores were used to compare the number of learnings from members of each treatment group to the control group results. In addition, a coding system was developed to analyze participants' descriptions of their learning. This system used guidelines set forth by Bogdan and Biklen (1982) for developing coding categories.

Parts IV and V provided additional quantitative and qualitative data to be used in interpreting the results of the study. Part IV, the subjects' responses to questions about their satisfaction with their learning, provided data to be used in interpreting the responses recorded in Part III. In Part V, responses to questions regarding the amount of time and the impact of the performance of others helped determine the impact of the perceived quality of the reflection experience on the results obtained.

Because of the open-ended and subjective nature of the posttest questions, it was difficult to determine a measure of stability over time that would ensure the reliability of the instrument. However, pilot sessions with managers from the general population were conducted to ensure that the measure did consistently produce a list of learnings over time. Concerns with construct validity were addressed by using the research-based operational definition of learning derived from a review of the literature. Concerns with content validity were addressed through interviews with those participating in the pilots to collect information about their interpretations of the questions and their rationale for the types of responses they recorded.

TREATMENT OF DATA

According to Pedhazur (1982), regression analysis seeks to answer the question, "What are the expected changes in the dependent variable as a result of changes (observed or induced) in the independent variables?" (p. 5). Since this is the basic question this study seeks to answer, regression analysis was the primary statistical technique used to analyze the data produced by the research design.

The central focus of this research involved studying the effect of reflection, the independent variable, on learning, the dependent variable. If the analysis were limited to the effect of this one independent variable, simple regression analysis would be called for. However, more powerful results were obtained by using information on the other variables collected on the posttest questionnaire: the type of experience, the length of time involved in the experience, the importance of the experience to the manager's career, and the relative positive or negative nature of the experience. Thus, this study also examined the impact of these moderator variables on learning from experience. Since these variables may be intercorrelated, or may interact in their effects on the dependent variable, multiple regression analysis was employed.

This study dealt with both continuous variables (amount of learning, length of time, importance, relative value) and categorical variables (types of reflection and type of experience). Typically, designs with categorical independent variables are analyzed by analysis of variance (ANOVA). However, according to Pedhazur, there are distinct advantages to treating these variables as a special case of multiple regression.

Additional statistical tests were employed to determine the significance of findings resulting from data analysis beyond the effect of the independent variables on the dependent variable. They are described in the following procedures.

PROCEDURES

The following procedures were followed:

- Randomly assign fifteen managers to each one of the three treatment groups and fifteen to a control group.
- Send a letter to treatment group subjects announcing the date and time of their session. Those in the tutor treatment group were instructed to bring someone to serve as a personal guide through the proactive reflection process and were provided with tips on how to select an appropriate person.
- Send a letter to all tutors reviewing their role in the study.
- Conduct the intervention, including introduction, 1-hour proactive reflection session (videotaping the peer group), and administration of posttest questionnaire.

- Administer the posttest to the control group over the telephone.
- Transcribe the control group responses.
- Send follow-up survey to subjects 1 week after their session.
- Analyze the data from the posttest questionnaire, videotapes, and follow-up survey:

Step 1:   Record number of learnings (the number of insights that had a corresponding meaning for future action) for each subject.

Step 2:   Assign dummy codes to the two categorical variable: type of proactive reflection and type of experience.

Step 3:   Record the type of proactive reflection assigned and the type of experience chosen for each individual.

Step 4:   Record scores for length, importance, and negative/positive nature of the work experience for each participant.

Step 5:   Calculate totals, means, ranges, and standard deviations for the raw data described above.

Step 6:   Calculate mean number of learnings by treatment group.

Step 7:   Use ANOVA to determine whether the overall difference in mean number of learnings by treatment group was significant.

Step 8:   Compare means between treatment groups using a Scheffé F test.

Step 9:   Use ANOVA to calculate the effect of type of experience on amount of learning.

Step 10:   Use analysis of covariance (ANCOVA) to calculate the effects of each of the remaining independent variables (length, importance, negative/positive nature of experience) on amount of learning when combined with type of proactive reflection.

Step 11:   Calculate the combined effects of all independent variables on amount of learning using multiple regression analysis.

Step 12:   Record scores for each subject's level of satisfaction with the amount, quality, and impact of learning.

Step 13:   Record scores for each subject's level of satisfaction with the amount of time for proactive reflection, the performance of the researcher, and the performance of others.

Step 14:   Calculate totals, ranges, means, and standard deviations for the raw data from Steps 12 and 13.

Step 15:   Use ANOVA to determine whether significant differences occurred between treatment groups and between peer subgroups for level of satisfaction with the learning and the process.

Step 16:   Analyze written comments under each of the scale questions to explain quantitative results.

Step 17:   Analyze subjects' descriptions of learning to determine differences in type of learning between treatment groups.

Step 18:   Determine whether differences in type of learning were significant using a chi-square test.

Step 19:   Analyze subjects' descriptions of learning to determine differences in quality of learning between treatment groups. No tests of significance were employed (see explanation in the next chapter).

Step 20:   Analyze videotapes for explanations for quantitative results.

Step 21:   Analyze follow-up data to determine (*a*) differences between treatment groups in mean amount of time spent reflecting since the session (via ANOVA), (*b*) differences between treatment groups regarding conversations with others after the proactive reflection session (via chi-square), and (*c*) differences between treatment groups in number of additional learnings (no test was conducted since numbers were so low).

LIMITATIONS OF THE STUDY

Individuals vary considerably in their ability and comfort levels with written and oral communication. Since the intervention in this study depended on both types of communication, different levels of learning may be attributed to this difference in ability or comfort. The process of randomization partially addressed this limitation by spreading the difficulty equally among treatment groups.

Another potential limitation to the study was that individuals who volunteered to participate may not be typical of the general population. They may begin with a greater natural interest in and ability to reflect upon experience.

An additional possible limitation is one attributed to Saretsky, called the "John Henry" effect (Eichelberger, 1989). "In this situation the control, or comparison, group works unusually hard to show that the experimental or innovative program is not better than (or not as good as) the regular program or procedure" (p. 170). The possible solution of not revealing the true nature of the study to the control group was not an option, given the researcher's desire to conform with the ethical standards of good research and the cultural expectations of Tech Inc.

Another limitation was the fact that no previously designed instrument was found to measure the dependent variable: amount of learning. It was therefore necessary to develop a special instrument that did not have the advantage of use over time with many different sample groups.

In addition, the subjects' ability to engage in meaningful proactive reflection sessions depended, in part, upon the behavior of others involved in the process: the researcher, as I directed the intervention; peers, as they discussed their learnings with each other; and tutors, as they guided participants in the process of reflection. My extensive experience facilitating similar learning events should resolve the first part of the concern. I conducted all sessions to ensure consistency in how the task was presented and facilitated. To address peer group and tutor behavior, a portion of the introduction in the second and third treatment groups consisted of guidelines for effective coaching. In addition, data were collected through the posttest questionnaire to determine what effect, if any, the behavior of others had on the results.

Finally, the interpretation of results was subject to my biases, so I employed standard procedures to limit bias in interpretation. These included blind questionnaires, standard coding procedures, videotaping, and audiotaping. It was especially important to keep the identity of the treatment groups from influencing coding results in the interpretation of learnings. This was accomplished simply by copying Part III of the questionnaires (which did not contain the treatment group label) and using only that section to code responses.

This procedure was effective when used with the three treatment groups; however, it was not possible to fully disguise the learning statements of the control group. The descriptions of learning for the control group were in the form of typed transcripts from audiotapes of a telephone interview, identifying them as different from the hand-written responses of the subjects in the three treatment groups. However, individual identities in the control group were disguised. While the procedures described limited the amount of bias on my part, one extra safeguard—the use of additional scorers—was not employed. The use of two or three trained scorers is recommended for future research to establish interrater reliability.

SUMMARY

The method used to conduct this study of proactive reflection was a field experiment. This experiment tested the use of three specific proactive reflection interventions under controlled conditions to determine their relative effectiveness in enhancing learning from managers' developmental experiences. The three interventions were individual reflection, peer group reflection, and tutor-guided reflection. The proactive reflection interventions were conducted with three different, randomly assigned groups of managers. A posttest-only control group design was used to conduct the experiment. The major thrust of the analysis was the effect of each proactive reflection intervention (independent variable) on the amount of learning (dependent variable).

In addition, the effect of four moderator independent variables was analyzed: type of experience, length of time involved in the experience, importance of the experience, and negative or positive nature of the experience. A follow-up survey was conducted 1 week after the intervention to detemine changes in learning that occurred following the intervention. Multiple regression was employed to determine the interactive effects of the independent variables on the dependent variable. Qualitative data were studied to interpret the findings. Finally, limitations of the study were raised and methods to address them were discussed.

Chapter 11

How Reflecting Alone and with Others Enhances Learning

This chapter reports the results of data analysis designed to reveal which of three types of proactive reflection interventions—individual, peer group, and tutor—are most effective in enhancing managers' learning from experience. These results were first reported in abbreviated form elsewhere (Daudelin, 1996a). Both findings and conclusions are reported, with the discussion organized into three sections. The first section reports the results of quantitative analysis of the effects of the independent variables on the dependent variable. The second section analyzes additional quantitative and qualitative data to explain findings from the interaction of the variables. The third section reports the results of an analysis of the videotapes and the follow-up survey. Each section begins with a description of the raw data and how it was analyzed.

QUANTITATIVE ANALYSIS OF MAJOR VARIABLES

This section analyzes the effect of the five independent variables on the dependent variable. A description of the data used in this analysis by the type of variable follows.

Description of Variables

Type of proactive reflection intervention

As described in detail in the preceding chapter, fifteen managers were assigned to the three proactive eflection intervention groups and the control group. Thus, type of reflection was an assigned categorical variable with each subject having one of four possible designations: control, individual, peer group, or tutor. The type of reflection intervention assigned to each individual was recorded by subjects on their questionnaires. Actual numbers, after cancellations, were thirteen in the control group, ten in the individual group, fourteen in the peer group, and eleven in the tutor group.

Type of experience

In Part I of the posttest questionnaire, subjects were asked to identify the experience they focused on during their proactive reflection intervention. Type of experience was, therefore, a categorical variable, chosen by the participants, with each subject having one of six possible designations. These designations, and the total number of participants who chose each one, were the following: (a) building something from nothing, fifteen; (b) fixing/stabilizing a failing operation, eleven; (c) participating in a project assignment, fourteen; (d) managing a significant increase in people, dollars, or function, four; (e) switching from line to staff role, three; (f) and other, three.

Length, importance, and negative/positive nature of experience

Data for these variables came from Part II of the posttest questionnaire. Subjects were asked to rate their responses to three questions on a 5-point scale: (a) How long have you been involved in this experience? (b) How important is this experience to your career? (c) Rate the relative negative or positive nature of the experience. Thus, each subject had a score between 1 and 5 for each of these variables, with mean scores of 4.3 for length, 3.1 for importance, and 3.6 for negative/positive nature of the experience.

Amount of learning

The data for this variable came from Part III of the posttest questionnaire. A total score for each subject was obtained by counting the number of lessons listed that had a corresponding meaning for future action. Scoring was facilitated by requiring subjects to link meanings to lessons and separate them with numbers, letters, or bullets. Subjects' scores ranged from 0 (one control group member) to 15, with a mean score of 4.8. All of the subjects except one control group member were able to list a corresponding meaning for future action for each insight listed.

Type of Proactive Reflection and Amount of Learning

The control group reported the fewest number of learnings ($M = 1.69$, $SD = 1.03$). Of the three treatment groups, the individual treatment group had the highest number of learnings ($M = 8.60$, $SD = 3.69$), followed by the tutor group ($M = 6.09$, $SD = 2.63$). The peer group reported the least learnings of the three reflection intervention groups ($M = 4.14$, $SD = 1.79$).

An ANOVA was conducted to determine whether the overall difference in means was significant. This procedure showed that the overall difference between groups was significant [$F(3, 44) = 17.554$, $p = .0001$]. A Scheffé F-test was then conducted to compare the means between groups. These results are shown in Table 11-1.

Table 11-1
Comparison of Learnings between Treatment Groups (Analysis of Variance)

Comparison	Mean difference	Scheffé F-test
Control vs. individual	−6.908	16.093*
Control vs. peer	−2.451	2.415
Control vs. tutor	−4.399	6.879*
Individual vs. peer	4.457	6.915*
Individual vs. tutor	2.509	1.968
Peer vs. tutor	−1.948	1.395

* Significant at .05 level.

The analysis summarized in Table 11-1 shows that both the individual and the tutor treatment groups had a significantly greater number of learnings than the control group. However, the peer group did not have significantly greater learnings than the control group. Regarding the comparison among the three treatment groups, the only significant difference was between the individual and peer groups; the differences between the individual and tutor groups and the peer and tutor groups were not significant. Conclusions and possible explanations for these results will be discussed later in this chapter.

Impact of Moderator Independent Variables

In terms of the categorical variable "type of work experience," the means and standard deviations for the number of learnings for each type were as follows: building something from nothing ($M = 3.57$, $SD = 2.34$); fixing/stabilizing a failing operation ($M = 4.70$, $SD = 4.69$); participating in a project assignment ($M = 5.08$, $SD = 3.07$); managing a significant increase in people, dollars, or functions ($M = 4.00$, $SD = 1.00$); switching from a line to staff role ($M = 8.20$, $SD = 4.21$); and other ($M = 5.67$, $SD = 1.16$).

Mean scores and standard deviations derived from responses on a scale from 1 to 5 for the three continuous moderator variables were: length of work experience ($M = 4.29$, $SD = 0.92$), importance of work experience ($M = 3.13$, $SD = 1.20$); and negative/positive nature of work experience ($M = 3.60$, $SD = 1.25$).

The impact of the four moderator independent variables was examined using three separate procedures. First, the effect of type of experience (a categorical independent variable) on amount of learning was examined using ANOVA, and no significant results (at the .05 level) were found [$F(5, 42) = 1.55$, $p = .1956$].

Second, an ANCOVA was conducted to examine the combined effects of type of reflection (the major independent variable) and each of the remaining independent variables on amount of learning. The overall model showed a significant difference (p = .0001), as expected, since a significant difference was previously found between means in type of reflection. However, when type of reflection was controlled for in each ANCOVA, the differences were no longer significant. Table 11-2 summarizes these results.

Table 11-2
Effect of Type of Proactive Reflection and Other Independent Variables on Amount of Learning (Analysis of Covariance)

Source	DF	Type I SS	Mean square	Adjusted F value (p)	Original F value (p)
Type of experience	5	25.408	5.082	0.90 (.4913)	1.55 (.1956)
Type of reflection	3	235.534	78.511	13.89 (.0001)	17.55 (.0001)
Length	1	2.338	2.338	0.41 (.5239)	0.18 (.6775)
Type of reflection	3	294.476	98.159	17.34 (.0001)	17.55 (.0001)
Importance[a]	1	10.678	10.678	1.95 (.1694)	3.84 (.0562)
Type of reflection	3	263.292	87.764	16.05 (.0001)	17.55 (.0001)
Negative/positive	1	0.363	0.363	0.06 (.8021)	0.10 (.7545)
Type of reflection	3	293.390	97.797	17.13 (.0001)	17.55 (.0001)

[a] Scores on this dimension were highly skewed to the positive end of the scale.

Finally, multiple regression analysis was conducted to examine the interaction of all variables together, except type of experience. Type of experience was eliminated from the multiple regression analysis for two reasons: first, the addition of a second categorical variable containing six options required complex dummy coding, which would have increased the risk of multicolinearity problems; second, since the subjects in each treatment group had six choices, no one option had more than three data points. Since the ANOVA showed no significance separately, the impact of removing this variable from the multiple regression analysis is minimal.

As expected, given the results from the above two procedures, the only significant effect was between the major independent variable (type of reflection) and the dependent variable (amount of learning). The overall model, with type of reflection included, was significant (p = .0001; R^2 = .5668). The overall model, with type of reflection excluded, was not significant (p = .3018, R^2 = .0788). Table 11-3 summarizes the results of the analysis.

Table 11-3
Effect of All Independent Variables (Except Type of Experience) on Amount of Learning (Multiple Regression Analysis)

Source	DF	Type III SS	Mean square	Adjusted F value (p)	Original F value (p)
Type of reflection	3	263.553	87.851	15.40 (.0001)	17.55 (.0001)
Length of experience	1	0.661	0.661	0.12 (.7353)	0.18 (.6775)
Importance of experience	1	9.084	9.084	1.59 (.2141)	3.84 (.0563)
Negative/positive	1	0.614	0.614	0.11 (.7446)	0.10 (.7545)

Conclusion

It can be concluded from this analysis that both the individual and tutor reflection groups provided greater amounts of learning than no reflection at all; however, the peer group reflection intervention provided no greater learning than no formal reflection intervention. In addition, the individual group had a significantly greater number of learnings than the peer group, but not more than the tutor group. Finally, the additional, moderator independent variables studied had no effect on amount of learning. Neither the type of experience nor its length, importance, or negative/positive nature had any effect on the amount of learning, when examined separately and together.

The remainder of the analysis, therefore, focuses on two issues: (a) what might explain the low number of peer group learnings and (b) whether differences exist between groups in dimensions other than amount of learning.

ADDITIONAL DATA COLLECTED VIA POSTTEST QUESTIONNAIRE

Quantitative Data

Information regarding the subjects' satisfaction with both the learning they recorded and the reflection experience was collected. Using a 5-point scale, subjects rated their satisfaction with the learning they recorded in three areas: amount, quality, and impact of the learning. Subjects then rated their satisfaction with the reflection experience in three areas: the amount of time spent reflecting upon their own experience, the performance of the researcher, and the performance of others. No significant differences between treatment groups were found for level of satisfaction with either the learning or the reflection experience (see Table 11-4). However, differences between groups in subjects' level of satisfaction with the impact of their learning approached significance ($p = .058$). Further studies with larger sample sizes are called for to see if the higher scores for the tutor group become significant.

Table 11-4
Mean Level of Satisfaction with Learnings Recorded and Proactive Reflection Experience by Treatment Group

Level of satisfaction	Total	Treatment group			p
		Individual	Peer	Tutor	
Learnings recorded					
Amount[a]	3.8	4.1	3.4	4.2	.8293
Quality[a]	4.0	4.1	3.6	4.3	.4686
Impact[b]	2.6	2.5	2.1	3.4	.058
Reflection experience					
Amount of time[c]	2.7	3.0	2.4	2.9	.2013
Performance of researcher[a]	4.1	4.2	3.9	4.4	.3563
Performance of others[a]	4.2	—	3.9	4.7	.0816

[a] scale: 1 = very dissatisfied, 2 = dissatisfied, 3 = neutral, 4 = satisfied, 5 = very satisfied.
[b] scale: 1 = little impact, 2 = moderate impact, 3 = significant impact, 4 = major impact, 5 = critical impact.
[c] scale: 1 = much too short, 2 = a little short, 3 = just right, 4 = a little long, 5 = much too long.

On average, subjects were "satisfied" with both the amount and quality of the learning (3.8 and 4.0, respectively), and rated the learning as having "significant impact" (2.6). They felt the amount of time was "just right" (2.7), were "satisfied" with the performance of the researcher (4.1), and "satisfied" or "very satisfied" with the performance of others (peer group = 3.9 and tutor group = 4.7).

In addition, responses for each of the three peer groups were analyzed to determine any significant differences between peer groups for the same variables. A Kruskal–Wallis ANOVA showed no significant differences between peer groups (see Table 11-5).

Table 11-5
Mean Level of Satisfaction with Learnings Recorded and Proactive Reflection Experience by Peer Subgroups

Level of satisfaction	Total	Peer subgroup			H value[a]
		A	B	C	
Learnings recorded					
Amount	3.4	4.0	3.8	3.3	1.522
Quality	3.6	4.0	3.4	3.5	2.289
Impact	2.1	2.4	2.2	1.8	1.265

Reflection experience

Amount of time	2.4	2.4	2.4	2.3	0.294
Performance of researcher	3.9	4.0	3.8	3.8	0.774
Performance of others	3.9	4.4	4.0	3.0	4.071[b]

[a] Critical value at .05 level, 2 $\underline{df}$ is 5.99; thus, none of the values are significant.

[b] This relatively high value is the result of one score of 1 by a subject who reported a personality conflict with one other member of the group.

Qualitative Data

The posttest questionnaire provided two sources of qualitative data: the written comments under each scale and the description of learning from Part III.

Written comments

Content analysis of the written comments under each scale provided four possible explanations for the insignificant peer group results. These possible explanations are listed next along with two sample comments for each explanation. These comments are typical of those used to develop the explanations.

- *Explanation #1:* The search for similarity among experiences caused subjects to place less emphasis on learning that was unique to themselves. *Sample comments:* "I enjoyed hearing others talk about fighting the same battles, and strategies they used to remain effective and sane." "We tended to identify common frustrations we all have in trying to work in the Tech Inc. system."

- *Explanation #2:* The tendency to do what several members labeled "playing 'ain't it awful'" (i.e., complaining about general corporate decisions or management philosophies) used up valuable time that was not used to discuss learning from their specific experiences. *Sample comments:* "We played 'ain't it awful' for too long, but when we got back on track the discussion was good." "It seems to me that this is what Tech Inc. salaried people talk about all the time—someone called it 'recreational complaining' at an offsite function."

- *Explanation #3:* The need to discuss several different subjects' experiences discouraged the group from detailed probing that may have elicited more learning. *Sample comments:* "Not enough time for all to be fully explicit." "It requires multiple sessions to fine-tune thoughts."

- *Explanation #4:* The lack of a facilitator made participation by all members difficult and allowed members to digress. *Sample comments:* "One member of the group shared nothing about her experience." "Set-up was fine, but the group definitely needed a facilitator during the conversation to halt the negativity and begin a dialogue." However, one comment suggested the group was pleased with its ability to facilitate the process: "All of us were included either by one or more facilitating the conversation." Given this contradiction, the videotapes were explored to determine whether the lack of a facilitator was dysfunctional.

These explanations were developed by analyzing the most frequently occurring peer group written comments. They were then tested by examining the individual and tutor groups' comments to see if they were indeed unique to the peer group. No comments regarding, for example, a tendency to "play 'ain't it awful'" were recorded in the other groups. However, comments regarding time for detail and facilitation were found in the other groups.

Comments regarding sufficient time for detail were found in the individual and tutor groups; for instance, one subject from the tutor group reported, "This whole process let me explore in greater detail my journey as a person, a team member, and a shareholder of this great company" and one person from the individual group reported, "This forced me to look a little deeper than I would have."

Comments regarding facilitation from the tutor group included many about the helpfulness and skill of their tutor: "She was excellent—good listener and offered brief insights that were helpful and allowed me to go wherever my feelings and emotions took me" and "My mentor was able to help me with cause versus effect: what did I learn from each activity in the process and what could I do differently the next time." However, several also felt their tutor could have done more: "He could have asked a few more probing questions," and "He's just as clueless as I am about how to use this learning in a positive way." Again, a contradiction appears over the role of facilitation.

Thus, the first three explanations appear to be possible reasons for the difference in amount of learning between treatment groups. The fourth explanation, the lack of facilitation, will be investigated further using the videotapes.

Descriptions of learning

The subjects' descriptions of learning entered in Part III of the posttest questionnaire provided data supporting significant differences in type of learning between treatment groups. Four categories were used to explore the type of learning that occurred: task, interpersonal, intrapersonal (i.e., the self), and cultural (i.e., corporate culture and its impact on subjects' learning). Each insight and its corresponding meaning for future action were placed into one of these categories. Examples of statements coded into each category are listed next.

Task:

- "Be more conservative on estimates."
- "Develop overall strategy, business plan."

Interpersonal:

- "Many employees are very willing to help if you ask."
- "Treat others as you wish to be treated."

Intrapersonal:

- "I've become even more aware that I need details to function—I need to know how things work and why in order to be satisfied."
- "I spend too much time 'caretaking' other people's problems, not enough on my own."

Cultural:

- "In our culture/society action is rewarded more than planning (ready, fire, aim)."
- "Similarities with other events in the history of the company that were not positive."

Table 11-6 summarizes the total number of learnings in each of these four categories by treatment group. This analysis shows that most of the learning in the individual and tutor groups fell in the intrapersonal category, while most of the learning in the peer group fell in the interpersonal or cultural category. A chi-square test found these differences to be statistically significant [$X^2_{obs} = 25.1 > X^2_{crit}(9 \underline{df}) = 16.9$].

Table 11-6
Number of Learnings by Type of Learning and Treatment Group

| Types of learning | Treatment group | | | |
	Individual $\underline{n}$ (%)	Peer $\underline{n}$ (%)	Tutor $\underline{n}$ (%)	Control $\underline{n}$ (%)
Task	13 (14.4)	6 (10.3)	16 (22.9)	3 (16.7)
Interpersonal	22 (24.4)	20 (34.5)	12 (17.1)	8 (44.4)
Intrapersonal	41 (45.6)	12 (20.7)	31 (44.3)	6 (33.3)
Cultural	14 (15.6)	20 (34.5)	11 (15.7)	1 (5.6)
Totals	90	58	70	18

An attempt was made to search these descriptions for differences in quality of learning. Several criteria were used, including new learning versus reinforcement of old; learning that was specific and implementable versus general and unimplementable; learning that could change behavior; and impact at the corporate versus department versus individual level. An attempt was then made to code each statement with a general quality code (high, medium, or low) and an impact code (corporate, department, or individual level). However, it became apparent during this process that a determination of quality was inappropriate or impossible for several reasons.

The nature of proactive reflection and its resulting learnings are highly personal; therefore, the subject is the only one who can truly judge the quality level of a particular insight or its personal meaning. Additionally, each criterion was found to have inherent flaws when applied to these data: general learning may be just as powerful as specific; "implementable" cannot be proven until action is taken; changes in behavior can only be predicted at this point; and impact at the individual level may be just as powerful as impact at other levels. Finally, an attempt to proceed created such a small numbers in each category that tests of significance could not be conducted.

Thus, the subjects' ratings of their level of satisfaction with the quality and impact of their learning (as reported in Table 11-4) are judged to be more useful than the researcher's attempts to judge their written descriptions.

Conclusion

An analysis of the additional quantitative data found that all treatment groups were equally satisfied with the amount, quality, and impact of the learning they recorded. In addition, all treatment groups were equally satisfied with the amount of time spent reflecting on their own experience, the performance of the researcher, and the performance of others.

Analysis of the written comments found four possible reasons for the insignificant number of peer group learnings: (a) the search for similarity among experiences, (b) the tendency to "play 'ain't it awful,'" (c) the lack of detailed probing of subjects' experiences, and (d) the lack of a facilitator.

An examination of the subjects' descriptions of learning found significant differences in the type of learning between groups. Most of the learning in the individual and tutor groups was intrapersonal (about themselves), while most of the learning in the peer group was either interpersonal (about others) or cultural (about the corporation).

ADDITIONAL DATA FROM OTHER SOURCES

In addition to the posttest questionnaire, two other sources of data were analyzed: videotapes of the peer group sessions and follow-up surveys.

Videotapes

The videotapes of the peer group sessions were analyzed to validate the four possible explanations for the differences in the peer group scores. Each of the three peer group sessions was examined for evidence supporting the four possible explanations with the following results.

Explanation #1

The search for similarity among experiences caused subjects to place less emphasis on learning that was unique to themselves.

Evidence from the videotapes supports this explanation. In all three groups, the majority of time was spent finding and discussing common issues. In Group A, one member actually summarized the discussion with a list of common learning. The interactions in Group B were characterized by statements such as this: "Listening to you, Paul, a similar thing happened to me..." and "There's a common thread here...." In Group C, one member in particular played a role of linking one comment to another before adding his own interpretation.

Explanation #2

The tendency to do what several members labeled "playing 'ain't it awful'" used up valuable time that was not used to discuss learning from their specific experiences.

Evidence from the videotapes supports this explanation. Group A spent approximately 30 of the 60 minutes engaged in this sort of activity. It was finally stopped by a comment by one member who said, "We're playing 'ain't it awful.' I think we're off track here." Group C spent approximately 20 minutes doing this, and Group B approximately 10 minutes.

Explanation #3

The need to discuss several different subjects' experiences discouraged the group from detailed probing that may have elicited more learning.

Evidence from the videotapes supports this explanation as well. In Groups B and C, efforts to ensure that all members had a chance to talk caused members to shift focus before developing much depth. In Group A, the group's tendency to focus on global corporate issues first limited the detailed probing that may have led to greater learning; however, once the focus changed to individuals' learning, the same phenomenon took place.

Explanation #4

The lack of a facilitator made participation by all members difficult and allowed members to digress.

Evidence from the videotapes does not support this explanation. In each group, one or more members played the role of facilitator. Although this was done in different ways and with varying degrees of expertise, in all cases these efforts caused the group to refocus, get back on track, or include nonparticipating members. The efforts in Group A were made by two individuals, primarily in service of moving from global generalizations to more specific discussions of members' learnings. In Group B, almost all members played process facilitation roles throughout the session. Three of the five members asked clarifying questions regarding others' experiences (e.g., "Were you involved with outsiders?"), one person regularly engaged in paraphrasing (e.g., "Sounds like it wasn't done in a vacuum") and the interactions were, in general, characterized by affirmations of others' contributions (e.g., "You just said something important").

In Group C, one individual (a senior human resources administrator) took on a fairly formal role of group facilitator for the entire session. She asked deeply probing questions of all members (e.g., "How were you feeling..."; "How would you do it differently next time"; "I hear a very big 'should' in that statement"). In addition, she monitored the time and made process comments when the group appeared to be straying from its task. A second person also made an effort to include a nonparticipating member.

This difference in type of facilitation observed across the groups prompted a reexamination of the three peer groups' descriptions of learning to see if any differences emerged as a result of the different facilitation strategies. Group B had three specific instances of a comment from one member being recorded as a learning for another. The learnings recorded by Groups A and C did not show such obvious evidence of direct influence from other members. A possible reason is the nature of the facilitation that occurred in Group B, in which all members of the group were supportive agents of each other's learnings. In the videotape, they appeared to be good listeners and to relate others' statements to their own situations. Their written comments provided evidence that this was indeed the case.

During the videotape analysis, two additional differences between the peer group and the other groups emerged. First, the peer group tended to focus on whatever topic emerged during the discussion, rather than on the previously chosen specific developmental experience. This contrasts directly with the concentrated focus on the chosen experience that seemed to occur in the other two groups. Second, although worksheets for notes were provided, and advice was given to capture learnings as they occurred during the discussion, only one person of the fourteen in all three peer groups took notes and no one referenced the reflection questions or worksheets. This is in direct contrast to the individual group, where subjects progressed through the guidelines and questions before recording their learnings; and to the tutor group, where my informal observation noted repeated reference to the reflection questions. Therefore, a fifth explanation emerges.

Explanation #5

The tendency in the peer group to concentrate on the discussion kept members from following reflection guidelines and questions and from recording learnings during the process, thus limiting the total number of learnings recorded after the session. Having the additional task of interacting as a group member limited the attention that could be given to reflection. Since the reflection questions and guidelines were developed to ensure a level of vigorous critiquing of assumptions, the tendency to focus on the group discussion eliminated the process of vigorous critique, shown earlier to be an important part of critical reflection.

Follow-Up Surveys

A follow-up survey was conducted as part of the research design based upon pilot results which indicated that reflection takes place over time and learning is not limited to what occurs in one 1-hour session. Follow-up questionnaires were sent to all participants 1 week after their reflection session. Subjects were asked to report *(a)* how much time they had spent reflecting on the work experience they chose or the learnings they recorded since the session occurred; *(b)* whether they talked with anyone about the experience or the learnings, and the relationship of those people to the subject; and *(c)* what additional learnings they had had.

From highest to lowest, the mean amount of time spent reflecting since the session was 133 minutes (2.2 hours) for the tutor group, 103 minutes (1.7 hours) for the individual group, and 43 minutes (0.7 hours) for the peer group. Although the raw data indicate that the tutor group spent more time reflecting on the session than the individual or peer groups, ANOVA showed the difference to be statistically nonsignificant ($p = .1317$).

An analysis of the data regarding conversations with others about the experience showed that all but one member of the peer group and all but one member of the tutor group talked with others about their experience after it was over. Slightly over half of the individual group subjects talked with others. One may be tempted to conclude that subjects who talked with others during the intervention tended to continue talking to others after the experience, while those who did not talk with others were not as likely to talk with others after the session. However, a chi-square test found the difference to be statistically nonsignificant [$X^2_{obs} = 5.3 < X^2_{crit}(2 \underline{df}) = 5.99$ at the .05 level].

When subjects did talk to others, the peer group, on average, talked to more people about their experiences than the tutor group, and the tutor group talked with more people than the individual group. Fifty-eight percent of the peer group talked with more than one person, 50 percent of the tutor group talked with more than one person, and 38 percent of the individual group talked with more than one person. Subjects talked most frequently with spouses and co-workers; less frequently mentioned were friends, supervisors, and children. No differences between groups were found.

Contrary to the expectation established as a result of the pilot study, very few additional learnings were recorded. The mean number of additional learnings was less than 1 for each group (individual = 0.4, peer = 0.2, and tutor = 0.6). However, subjects did report a general reaffirmation of previous learnings and an awareness of the value of reflection as a process. Comments made in reference to the time spent reflecting since the session indicated that many people spent that time reflecting about the process they went through rather than the developmental experience or the learnings that emerged from the process.

Conclusion

An analysis of the videotapes suggests that possible reasons for the insignificant peer group results include *(a)* the search for similarity among experiences, *(b)* the tendency to "play 'ain't it awful,'" *(c)* the lack of detailed probing of subjects' experiences, and *(d)* the lack of note taking during the process. The lack of a facilitator did not appear to be a viable explanation.

An analysis of the follow-up survey showed no statistically significant differences between treatment groups in the amount of time spent reflecting since the treatment or the tendency to discuss the results with others. In addition, almost no additional learnings were recorded after spending, on average, an hour or two thinking further about the learning. This may be explained by the fact that the majority of the reflection time was spent thinking about the process rather than the work experience or the learnings from the experience. Subjects did report, however, a reaffirmation of the learning recorded during the session.

SUMMARY

According to the education literature, forces external to a learner are needed to bring about the internal process of reflection on experience (recall Figure 2-1). The literature suggests that three interventions—individual, peer group, and tutor guidance—are useful external forces for facilitating proactive reflection, carrying the potential to stimulate a particular form of reflection. Proactive reflection is a formal, structured form of reflection that helps learners step back from an experience to carefully and persistently ponder its meaning.

Results are reported in this chapter pertaining to the use of these three interventions with a sample of managers of a major corporation. The findings and conclusions offered are the result of analysis of both quantitative and qualitative data collected using a posttest questionnaire, videotapes, and a follow-up survey. Overall, it was found that the individual and tutor proactive reflection interventions produced more learning than no reflection at all, but the peer group intervention did not.

In addition, the only significant difference between treatment groups was between the individual and peer groups. All treatment groups were equally satisfied with the learning recorded and the proactive reflection experience. None of the following moderator variables had any effect on the amount of learning recorded: type of work experience, length of work experience, importance of work experience, and negative or positive nature of the work experience. However, an analysis of the qualitative results showed that the type of learning produced did differ between groups. Most of the learning in the individual and tutor groups was intrapersonal, whereas most of the learning in the peer group was either interpersonal or cultural.

Follow-up data showed no difference between treatment groups in the amount of time spent reflecting after the intervention or in subjects' tendencies to discuss their results with others. Also, subjects reported virtually no additional new learning after the session but did report a reaffirmation of previous learning. This was most likely because they spent their additional reflection time thinking about the intervention rather than about their experience or the learning.

The results of the experimental research reported here answer a critical question. These findings show that individual and tutor-guided proactive reflection interventions are most effective for enhancing learning from developmental experiences of managers in business organizations.

PART IV

A New, Holistic
Perspective of Reflection

Chapter 12

An Integrated Model of Active and Proactive Reflection

Previous research as well as the research described in this book demonstrates that reflection is critical to how managers learn from experience. Reflection involves the cognitive activity of taking an experience from the outside world, bringing it inside the mind, filtering it through past experiences, examining it, and trying to make sense of it. If this activity is effective, managers develop inferences about possible ways to respond to the demands of their experience. In other words, they learn.

The findings from the two studies described here substantiate that two different but complementary modes of reflection exist. The first mode, here referred to as active reflection, derives from the way the management literature has framed reflection as a natural cognitive response of managers facing on-the-job learning challenges. Given the minimal prior research on this managerial phenomenon, an inductive theory-building study aimed at exploring active reflection was conducted. This research found that active reflection involves alternating moments of inquiry and interpretation, and that managers are most inclined to reflect when they are in a work environment characterized by certain enabling conditions.

The second mode of reflection, which we call proactive reflection, has its roots in the education literature, where reflection is framed as an induced activity that helps managers extract from experience the lessons it offers. There is a long history of research into reflection in the field of education. Previous research indicates that three different approaches or methods have been used to help learners reflect: answering a series of reflective questions alone, in a group of one's peers, or with the assistance of a tutor. What prior research has not established is the relative effect of these three methods as well as their applicability to a managerial population. A deductive experiment that was described in earlier chapters of this book found that individual and tutor-based proactive reflection interventions resulted in significantly greater learning from experience for managers than did a control condition in which managers were not exposed to a reflection activity.

The two research investigations reported here were conducted independently. Each study provides very useful insights into an aspect of reflection as it affects the way managers learn from experience, but each study alone provides an incomplete picture of reflection. By combining the findings of the two studies, it is possible to offer an integrated and holistic framework of managerial reflection, which does not presently exist in the literature. Presenting this framework is the purpose of this chapter.

The combination of active and proactive reflection is referred to as managerial reflection. The essence of a framework of managerial reflection is the two complementary modes of managerial reflection: active reflection, which refers to managers' spontaneous inquiring and interpreting during a developmental experience, and proactive reflection, which involves managers deliberately stepping back from an experience to ponder, carefully and persistently, its meaning to the self.

According to the framework proposed, the two modes of reflection are best understood in relation to two dimensions: factors and character. Factors of reflection refer to the key elements that must be examined in order to understand reflection. These include the internal cognitive process of reflection and the external forces outside of managers that influence their inclination to reflect; a holistic understanding of reflection is possible only when it is examined inside and out. The character dimension refers to the ultimate nature of managerial reflection. This involves whether reflection happens naturally for managers or whether it must be induced in managers. An integrated understanding of reflection requires giving attention to both its natural and induced aspects. Taken together, factors of reflection and the character of reflection provide a comprehensive way of understanding the role of reflection in the experiential learning of managers.

The framework and dimensions will be expanded in the next section of this chapter, and then the two modes of reflection will be compared and contrasted in detail. The chapter will conclude with a case example that applies the framework to a manager undergoing a developmental experience at work.

AN INTEGRATED MODEL OF MANAGERIAL REFLECTION

The framework is presented as an integrated model of reflection in Figure 12-1. The model depicts the relationships among the significant elements involved in how managers learn from experience, excluding action/behavior. Certainly managers also need to engage experiences behaviorally in order to learn from them, but the focus here is the mental aspect of learning from experience.

The model shows how managers do not learn directly from experience but through the intervening processes of two modes of reflection, each of which is in

Figure 12-1
Integrated Model of Active and Proactive Reflection

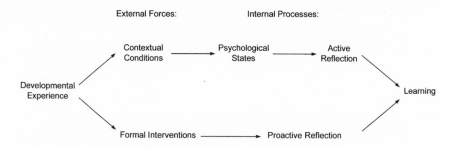

turn affected by significant external forces. For managers to actively reflect in the midst of a developmental experience, they need a work environment that provides conditions conducive to active reflection. Likewise, for managers to step back and engage in proactive reflection about a learning experience, they need some form of formal intervention into their experience. Reflection is not entirely within managers' control; it depends upon important forces external to the manager. Moreover, learning, the desired outcome of a developmental experience, is maximized only when both modes of reflection occur.

As indicated earlier, the management literature introduced the concept of active reflection but has not explored it in depth. Each item in the top row of Figure 12-1 is understudied, especially contextual conditions, psychological states, and the connection between them and active reflection. These gaps were what the theory-building research reported here was designed to explore. That research produced detailed descriptions of the active reflection, psychological states, and contextual conditions of twenty-four managers at two companies. It also developed dynamic models of how the three concepts interact during developmental experiences.

In terms of the bottom row of Figure 12-1, much has been written in the education literature about various reflection interventions as well as about the process of proactive reflection itself. What is missing in that literature is rigorous experimental tests of the relative efficacy of various interventions: the gap involves the *link* between formal interventions and proactive reflection. This gap is more limited than those in the management literature, but it is equally important. The experimental study described here was expressly designed to address this gap. This research provides hard evidence as to the comparative effectiveness to managers of three common reflection interventions.

The integrated model of active and proactive reflection presented in Figure 12-1 clearly demonstrates the need for balance when considering reflection in managerial learning. As originally designed, the two studies reported here took different but equally narrow views of reflection. Their imbalance reflects the imbalance that exists in the current literature on reflection. Whether the issue is gaining a theoretical understanding of active reflection in experiential learning, conducting experimental research of managers' proactive reflection, or working in business to facilitate managers' reflective learning, a balanced perspective is essential. This requires recognizing the equal importance of two distinctly different but complementary modes of managerial reflection as well as giving balanced attention to the internal processes and external forces of reflection. Prior research has been too one-dimensional to give justice to the reflection construct.

A Two-Dimensional Matrix of Active and Proactive Reflection

A two-dimensional matrix of active and proactive reflection is provided in Figure 12-2. This matrix must be examined in light of Figure 12-1; that is, the context of the matrix is a developmental experience that is intended to produce learning through a combination of action and reflection. The matrix integrates the findings from the two studies reported here and displays them according to the dimensions of factors of reflection and character of reflection.

Reflection is at once both a natural and an unnatural act for managers. On the one hand, during developmental experiences, managers cannot help but reflect,

Figure 12-2
Matrix of the Specific Variables Involved in the Two Modes of Reflection

Factors:	Enabling External Forces		Internal Processes
Character:			
	Contextual Conditions:		Active Mode:
Natural	- Autonomy - Feedback - Interactions with Others - Pressures	An Activated State of Mind	- Inquiring and Interpreting - Inbriefing

Induced	Formal Interventions:
	
	- Individual Reflection Session
	- Tutor-Guided Reflection
	  Session
	- (*Any* questioning about
	  experience)
			Proactive Mode:
			
			- Pondering the meaning of
			  experience
			
			- Debriefing

while on the other hand, managers involved in developmental experiences tend not to reflect. The paradox is resolved, of course, by recognizing that two different modes of reflection exist for managers, one that occurs spontaneously and one that must be induced by something outside the manager. Reflection is natural for managers in the sense that their minds become automatically engaged as they seek to respond to new and puzzling information during developmental experiences.

The internal cognitive process of natural reflection, which is reflection in the active mode, involves consciously inquiring and interpreting over the course of the experience. Although this reflection happens naturally, it is significantly enhanced when a manager experiences an activated state of mind; that is, when he has the internal sense of being informed, in control, supported, energized, and focused. In this frame of mind, inquiring and interpreting come readily. The term *inbriefing* is introduced in the matrix to capture the essence of active reflection.

Internal processes of inbriefing and debriefing

When a manager is faced with the unfamiliarity, ambiguity, and tension of a developmental challenge, her mind shifts into drive. Immediately upon encountering new challenges she attempts to understand them. How are they like previous encounters? How are they different? Which stimuli are important and which can be ignored? What current skills can be applied to the situation? What new skills will be needed? As the manager acquires information that is relevant to these inquiries, it is organized and examined. Assumptions are made, which may or may not be critically evaluated. Conclusions are drawn and actions are planned. All of this happens as the manager confronts the experience. There may be time later for more contemplative thinking, but for now she must inbrief and respond or else be swept along by the rising tide of the experience. Reflecting and acting are swift and staccato. In time, hopefully, an increasing sense of clarity will develop.

Such is the hectic and turbulent experience of inbriefing, or active reflection. In stark contrast, a second, proactive mode of reflection exists. This mode is much more orderly and controlled than the active mode, and it happens only if deliberate effort is extended to make it happen. Proactive preparation is required to induce this mode of reflection in a manager. If inbriefing captures the essence of active reflection, then the term *debriefing* can be used to describe the heart of proactive reflection. To debrief is to occasionally step back from an experience to ponder its meaning. Debriefing is also an internal cognitive process, but it is one whose character is induced rather than natural.

When a manager is confronted with the performance demands of a challenging developmental experience, his attention is focused mostly on meeting the challenge and less on personal development. New things will have to be learned, but attention must be turned to getting the job done as soon and as well as possible. Thus the manager throws himself into the assignment, which, since it is a business assignment, is driven largely by the technical demands of the task. The work is completed, hopefully more successfully than less, and before the manager has a chance to put a new filter in his coffee maker, the boss is breathing down his neck about the next project, so it is back into the fast lane again. Weeks or perhaps months later, or perhaps never, the manager reflects on the original developmental experience to consider what might have been learned from it.

Debriefing, or proactive reflection, is designed to counteract the "ready, shoot, aim" mentality of management. To debrief is to stop, look, and listen, but mostly it is to ask questions. This is done by getting away physically and temporally from the demands of the moment; once away, the manager can turn his attention beyond the thoughts of the moment. Using standardized worksheets and guidelines, the manager tries to push his thinking deeper and wider; to explore difficult issues and search uncomfortable reactions; to allow contradictions to surface and to resist the tendency to force ideas into structured patterns; to surface new awareness of assumptions, values, and beliefs; even to try to access dreams, memories, and metaphors.

Specific problems or issues in the experience are analyzed in relation to previous similar situations, and tentative explanations of the problem are developed. Explicit lessons learned from the experience are articulated, and the implications of the lessons for future behavior are considered. In short, the manager systematically and seriously probes the experience to try to identify the most important issues that can be learned from it. He realizes that debriefing requires time away from the fray of the battle (although it does not require much time), yet to not debrief would be shortsighted and foolish. Valuable lessons would be lost in a misguided desire to sacrifice contemplation for combat.

We propose that the potential to learn from experience is greatest when managers *intentionally* engage both modes of reflection—when they inbrief throughout their experiences while stopping periodically to debrief as well. As important as inbriefing and debriefing are to managerial reflection, they represent only one dimension of the reflection puzzle, the cognitive or internal half.

Enabling external forces: contextual conditions and formal interventions

Equally important to understanding managerial reflection in business organizations is the other, external half. The factors dimension of the matrix in Figure 12-2 includes not just the internal cognitive processes that describe what managers do when they reflect in the active and proactive modes, but also the forces external to managers that enable them to reflect. Both enabling and disabling external forces exist, but we chose here to focus primarily on enabling forces. For active reflection, the relevant forces are the work conditions in the immediate environment in which a manager's developmental experience unfolds, whereas for proactive reflection, the pertinent forces are the formal interventions designed to interrupt that experience to allow the manager to contemplate the meaning of the experience.

Active reflection happens naturally for managers in the context of their normal work setting. This research demonstrated that a work environment that has certain contextual conditions is most conducive to active reflection. Managers like Pete, whose work environment had a minimal amount of these conditions, labored to actively reflect. In contrast, active reflection came most easily and was most productive for managers like Jerry and Ted, whose work environments were rich in these conditions. The environment most conducive to active reflection had a blend of pressure and support and of independence and accountability.

Managers felt various and substantial (although not overwhelming) pressure. There were heavy demands on their time and on their capacity to process large volumes of new information in new and creative ways. They operated under a spotlight of sorts, with others in the company having an intense interest in their work. Their environment provided a steady stream of information that not only had to be deciphered but that also helped them deepen their understanding and gauge their progress. The weight of responsibility for their performance was on their shoulders; they could not accomplish the assignment alone, but it was up to them to drive results. Finally, their environment provided access to emotional support. A trusted colleague, friend, mentor, or spouse was available to offer encouragement or even just a sympathetic ear. Such conditions produce a fertile environment where active reflection flourishes.

Proactive reflection is even more dependent upon forces outside the manager. The research here demonstrates that a relaxed, contemplative review of experience occurs only when it is induced in managers by formal reflection interventions structured by someone other than the manager. Without specific tools and guidelines, proactive reflection rarely occurs. With them, not only does the likelihood of reflection increase but important lessons from the experience surface. Two interventions are particularly productive in this regard: providing managers with tools to reflect in writing on their own, and providing managers and a tutor with tools to reflect on the manager's experience together.

To productively reflect alone, a manager needs an hour away from the developmental experience, a specific set of steps to follow to reflect, a list of questions to answer, and worksheets to record emerging insights. Providing a safe (nonevaluative and confidential) and comfortable setting enhances this mode of reflection. A similar process produces productive reflection with a tutor as long as the manager is able to choose the tutor and the tutor is committed to assisting the manager. Insights still need to be recorded in writing, not just discussed. Reflection is most productive when tutors pay close attention to what the manager is communicating and help make sense of the manager's experience by offering their own nonjudgmental ideas. Most of all, tutors need to listen.

A very powerful finding of the experimental study reported here is that *any proactive reflection enhances learning from experience*. The peer group reflection intervention did not produce statistically significantly more learning than the control group, but it still produced an average of four lessons per peer group participant. And surprisingly, even the control group, which had only a brief phone conversation with the researcher, produced two lessons per control group member. Thus simply being questioned by someone else about a developmental experience stimulates proactive reflection, which produces learning insights. Indeed, out of the forty-eight managers who were subjects in the experiment, only one—a control group member—was unable to produce any meaning for the learning that resulted from a developmental experience. Does proactive reflection using formal interventions work? The unequivocal answer based on the research reported here is a resounding yes!

The two sets of enabling external forces just described—contextual conditions and formal interventions—are as important to understanding managerial reflection as are the contrasting internal processes of inbriefing and debriefing. The reflection matrix presented in Figure 12-2 integrates the findings of the theory-building and experimental studies reported here and illustrates the importance of examining both the active and proactive modes of managerial reflection from both the inside and the outside. Further comparison of the two basic modes of managerial reflection appears next.

COMPARING THE TWO MODES OF REFLECTION

Active Reflection as Ongoing, Unplanned, and Immersed in Experience

Three central characteristics of active and proactive reflection illustrate the contrasts between these two different ways managers think about learning experiences. Active reflection is ongoing, unplanned, and immersed in the experience that produces it. Ongoing means that active reflection happens throughout an experience. It is triggered by perplexing or novel situations, and since developmental experiences are replete with such situations, it happens regularly. An aspect of active reflection that is relevant here, and one that is not reported in Schön's (1983) descriptions of reflection-in-action, is that active reflection happens away from work as well as at work. Managers frequently reported engaging in active reflection while performing other tasks that required minimal conscious involvement, like traveling, commuting, exercising, showering, waking up at night, doing lawnwork or housework, or engaging in a hobby. Active reflection transcends traditional workplace boundaries.

A second characteristic of active reflection is that it is essentially an unplanned activity. It arises and continues spontaneously when a manager is intrigued by something. The managers studied here virtually never deliberately set aside time just to think about an issue. Rather, active reflection occurred as the issue arose or recurred in the manager's mind. Finally, active reflection occurs while managers are immersed in their experience. To be removed from the experience means that active reflection is no longer possible. Even off-line active reflection like the kind that happens away from work still occurs while the experience is a central part of a manager's life. The term *inbriefing* captures the essence of active reflection by emphasizing that such thinking happens *in* an experience. Moreover, that inbriefing occurs spontaneously away from work points to how immersing and all-encompassing challenging developmental experiences are.

Proactive Reflection as Episodic, Planned, and Detached from Experience

In contrast to active reflection, proactive is episodic, planned, and detached. Unlike active reflection, which happens regularly throughout a developmental experience, proactive reflection occurs in a clearly defined event for a specified period of time. In the study reported here, there were three different types of proactive reflection interventions: 1 hour spent reflecting alone, with peers, or with a tutor.

Proactive reflection by definition is a planned activity; it happens as a formal intervention using tools and guidelines, either alone, with one other person, or in a small group. Further, proactive reflection is detached from a developmental experience. Learners are intentionally removed in time and space from their experience in order to reflect upon it in a more thoughtful way. Just as active reflection requires immersion in an experience, proactive reflection requires detachment from that experience.

Other Comparisons Between the Two Modes

Due to its immersion in particular issues of a developmental experience, active reflection is focused on response to the immediate demands of a situation. Active reflection helps managers see the "trees" of their experience (versus the "forest"). The outcome of this reflection is an interpretation in the short-term and increased insight over the longer term. When they are actively reflecting, managers make little distinction between learning and doing. Since their experience exposes them to new things, the need to learn is taken for granted. Managers are mostly concerned with being able to perform and focus their attention there. Learning is an important but an *implicit* part of that performing.

In contrast, proactive reflection, precisely because it is detached from experience, helps managers make *explicit* what they are learning from an experience. The outcome of proactive reflection is what is more conventionally thought of as the outcome of learning. Specific lessons from the experience and their meaning for future action are formally articulated through proactive reflection. Through this mode of reflection, managers are enabled to see the forest of the experience (versus the trees). The broader and more general lessons the experience offers become apparent.

There is an element of seeing the forest and the trees in each mode of reflection, but differentiating active reflection as having a more micro focus and proactive reflection as having a more macro focus also has validity. This difference in emphasis of each mode of reflection is further evidence of the importance of maintaining a balance between both types when considering how managers learn from experience. The primary time when active reflection is more macro in focus is when it happens off-line. Indeed, off-line active reflection is rather similar to proactive reflection in that it is removed in both time and space from the immediate demands of the experience. They still are not the same types of reflection, of course, since off-line, active reflection happens spontaneously, informally, and without any tools or guidelines. But their similarities speak to the issue of why they produce insights at a similarly more macro level.

The results of the theory-building and experimental studies presented here also suggest that pressure has a differential effect on managerial reflection depending on whether that reflection is active or proactive. Active reflection is focused when managers face directive pressure. Knowing that their experiences are of vital importance to their companies and their careers focuses managers' minds in a way that enables active reflection. In contrast, the experiment's moderator variable measuring the relative importance of the experience to the manager's career did not affect the amount of learning subjects reported. At first glance these findings seem contradictory.

A reasonable explanation for this difference is that active and proactive reflection are indeed two qualitatively different modes of reflection and thus are subject to different forces. In the midst of a challenging experience, it is understandable that feeling pressure is important to activating reflection. The bored manager is unlikely to be turned on cognitively, whereas the pressured manager is. It is equally understandable that removing managers from their experiences in order to proactively reflect would lead to productive thinking regardless of the importance of the experience. Stepping out of an experience allows a manager to pause to consider what can be learned from the experience, even if on the surface it is not apparent that the experience is a particularly important one to the manager. Even if he was bored by the experience, a manager in a structured reflection session may generate some important insights, including, perhaps, why he was bored by the experience.

The relationship of pressure to managerial reflection is an interesting and paradoxical one. Virtually all managers today work in a pressure-filled environment that simultaneously promotes active reflection and inhibits proactive reflection. The same pressure that causes active reflection by forcing managers to think through situations quickly so they can respond effectively actually makes it harder for them to proactively reflect, because they cannot fit proactive reflection into their schedules. Pressure is thus something that managers need to embrace *and* resist. It should be embraced in the midst of responding to a challenge with the realization that the pressure is helping stimulate active reflection. It should be resisted in the sense that an occasional break from pressure must be taken to reap the benefits of proactive reflection. Fortunately, a break of as little as an hour can produce positive results, as this research shows. Once again the challenge is to find the right balance, this time between embracing and resisting pressure.

If pressure is an external force that affects active and proactive reflection differently, both modes of reflection are affected in similarly positive ways by the interactions of other people with the learner. Whether through the informal process of active reflection or the structured activity of proactively reflecting with a tutor, the involvement of others facilitates reflection. That the peer group did not produce significant results in the experiment seems to be more a function of some inadequacies in the design of that intervention than of any inherent problems with using peers to reflect (see Daudelin, 1996a). The weight of the evidence indicates that managerial reflection is as much a social–psychological phenomenon as it is a purely cognitive one.

Finally, both modes of managerial reflection are in full agreement that questions are at the core of reflection. In active reflection, questions of fact, function, approach, purpose, and self come naturally to managers as they inquire into and seek to understand their experiences. In proactive reflection, the careful posing of questions intentionally designed to extract learning from experience drives the process of reflection. But whether questions come from within or without, it is through considering important questions that managers attempt to discover the meaning of challenging work experiences. Indeed, grappling with significant questions is what ultimately unites the two modes of reflection in the manager's quest to know.

The preceding discussion shows that two different but complementary modes of reflection exist for managers. A practical example of the operation of those modes is provided next.

A CASE EXAMPLE

The integrated model of active and proactive reflection presented in this chapter will now be illustrated through an example of a manager undergoing a developmental experience. Although the case is based on an actual manager and an experience that really occurred, the account given here has been dramatized to adequately demonstrate the concepts discussed previously.

The Manager and Her Experience

Jean was a 39-year-old commercial loan officer at a major midwestern bank. Her developmental assignment was primarily a line-to-staff switch, although it also had elements of a project assignment (McCall et al., 1988). Jean was sent on a 2-year stint in the bank's corporate human resources division. Her first year would be spent standardizing the bank's compensation system across the entire corporation. The major task would be to integrate ten recently acquired affiliate banks' systems into the corporate system. Jean had no prior human resources experience and no experience outside of the commercial lending function of the bank.

Jean's Active Reflection

Jean's work environment was generally conducive to active reflection. (Explicit connections will not be made to the material in Figures 12-1 and 12-2, because it is assumed that readers should be able to make those connections.) Other than the directive from her new boss, the corporate vice president of human resources, that full integration must be completed in 12 months, all Jean was told was, "Get it done anyway you can; just get it done." Jean's interaction with compensation experts was varied, which was important because Jean knew nothing about compensation administration. The four corporate compensation people she worked with were very knowledgeable as well as willing to assist her. But the compensation managers at the affiliate banks were suspicious of her intentions and resentful of her interference, especially since it was clear to all parties involved that Jean knew very little about compensation.

As the project progressed, Jean received emotional support from a trust officer who had done a similar stint in human resources the year before. Jean met Donald by chance one morning on the elevator. Upon discovering their similar human resources experiences, they began a professional relationship that involved periodic lunches where they would swap war stories. One of the frustrations Jean shared with Donald was the difficulty she had getting feedback during the project. Other than a rare "keep up the good work," her boss said nothing about the project, and the affiliate compensation managers almost seemed to deliberately conceal information on the status of their banks' conversion to the corporate system.

Jean did not complain about the pressure of the assignment, which was noticeable but not severe. The deadline for the project was a challenging one given the volume of work involved. There were over 5,000 employees and several hundred different jobs at the affiliate banks, all of which had to be evaluated for compensation purposes. Jean's corporate compensation colleagues were a great source of ideas for how to pull the conversion off. Her boss was helpful in that the few comments he made to her about the project were usually pointed and probing questions that caused her to consider issues from fresh angles. Her boss also served as the liaison between Jean and the lead bank's president, who was very interested in the project. He was quite concerned about compensation costs and was counting on a standardized system to reduce those costs. Jean was required to make quarterly progress presentations to the president that included projected cost savings.

Jean's work environment led to an activated state of mind. She experienced the psychological states of control, support, energy, and focus based on the context within which her experience was imbedded. She often felt less informed than she wanted to be, but on balance the conditions surrounding her experience enabled active reflection.

Jean's active reflection centered on questions about a myriad of challenges that were new to her. As the experience unfolded she inquired into the intricacies of the corporation's point factor job evaluation method and its labor market pricing procedures, in addition to the idiosyncrasies of the ten affiliate banks' compensations systems. At times she felt overwhelmed and confused by the eleven different compensation systems she was seeking to understand. Jean was clear on the overall purpose of the project, so most of her thinking involved trying to understand the different approaches taken by the affiliate banks and how their compensation systems actually functioned.

Jean came to understand that she had originally oversimplified the conversion to the corporate system. It was not simply a matter of converting all the affiliate banks' systems to the lead bank's. One standardized system was required, but that system needed to consider the local labor market conditions and pay trends of each affiliate bank. The frustration caused by the affiliate compensation managers' minimal cooperation actually promoted her active reflection into the technicalities of compensation systems. She knew it was essential for her to gain an intimate knowledge of compensation issues.

In addition to some frustration, Jean also felt significant anxiety during her assignment over its potential effect on her future commercial lending career. She was worried there might not be a space back in lending for her when the line-to-staff switch was complete. This caused her to think a lot about herself, her future career options, and how this assignment fit into her life. On a personal level, her active reflection gave her insight into the types of settings she likes to work in, including how uncomfortable she is when she feels there are not adequately objective measures of her performance. On the technical level, Jean gained important insight into the significance of compensation systems. Previously viewing them as largely irrelevant to the primary purpose of the bank, she now appreciated the central role they played in influencing both employee motivation and the bank's cost structure.

Jean's Proactive Reflection

It took 3 weeks longer than planned and some last-minute software revisions, but the corporate-wide standardization of compensation systems was successfully completed. Jean took a well-deserved week off before returning to work to begin her second human resources project. But before she began that project, the corporate human resources vice president and the senior vice president of commercial lending met with Jean to ask her to complete an hour of formal reflection on her compensation experience. They explained that they wanted her to debrief the experience to identify significant learnings as well as pinpoint what those meant for her next human resources project and eventual return to commercial lending.

Being the high achiever she was, Jean was anxious to move on to her next assignment as quickly as she could. She recognized, however, that an hour of reflection could be productive. But how should she do that? The bank's corporate training and development director took Jean to the management training center and gave her materials to work through by herself in one of the break-out rooms. Jean grabbed a cup of coffee, sharpened her pencil, and reclined in a comfortable chair. At first she felt uncomfortable because she was *too* comfortable. After all, this was a Monday morning: there must be reports that need writing and customers that need serving. But as she began to peruse the reflection guidelines she had been given, thoughts and feelings of the last year of her life began to overtake her.

She worked through the steps and questions before her. What was a really important issue she faced during the assignment? How was it similar or dissimilar to other issues she had faced in her career? Why was it significant to her? Why did things happen the way they did? How could she explain what occurred? Could she have done things differently? What could she learn from this experience that could make her more effective in the future? Jean began jotting down several key issues she could examine. After a few moments she decided to focus on why she worried so much during the human resources assignment about its effect on her future career possibilities in commercial lending.

She tried to let her ideas flow freely. Knowing that no one would see her responses, she was able to record ideas that were a bit strange and even threatening. After what seemed like only a few minutes there was a knock at the door. The training director told her that the hour was up and it was time to summarize her thoughts. He gave her a sheet with two columns. The left one was marked "lessons learned" and the right column was marked "meaning for future action."

As a result of her thinking and note making, it was easy to write down several lessons and corresponding meanings for future behavior. For example, Jean had learned that she was uncomfortable working in situations with a lot of ambiguity. She had not really perceived herself this way before, but it certainly was the case during the compensation assignment. The ambiguity over the career implications of the assignment, the lack of feedback while she was working, and the affiliate compensation managers' ambivalence toward her had all been quite bothersome to her. Jean realized that in the future she needed to be more deliberate about seeking out information to relieve ambiguity when information was not readily available. She also understood that in many situations she would never be able to totally eliminate the ambiguity, so it was important to increase her tolerance level for it.

Another lesson Jean learned was that her personal career concerns were legitimate and that she should not bear them alone. Her natural tendency was to operate as a lone ranger in managing her career, because she did not want to appear dependent on anyone else. The implication of this lesson was the importance of maintaining existing relationships while developing new ones. The senior vice president of commercial lending could have easily allayed Jean's fears about returning to the lending division after her assignment if only she had talked to him about her concerns. The sense that she was too self-reliant in dealing with personal career issues was a deep intrapersonal learning for Jean and one that she believed would help her dramatically in managing her career in the future. Jean was excited by these insights, and she decided to meet with Donald the next week to probe more deeply the meaning of these insights to her current and future work.

Active reflection and proactive reflection both contributed in significant ways to Jean's learning during and from her developmental experience. In interaction with enabling external forces, these internal cognitive processes helped Jean make the most of her experience.

SUMMARY

The purpose of this chapter was to bring all of the material from earlier chapters together into a coherent whole. In particular, an integrated model of active and proactive reflection was presented. Taken together, these two modes of reflection capture the kind of reflection that is available to managers involved in developmental job experiences. Differences between the two modes were discussed and summarized in a 2 × 2 matrix (Figure 12-2). Finally, the operation of active and proactive reflection was demonstrated with a case example.

The capacity for continual growth and development throughout the lifespan is a fundamental attribute of what it means to be human. But there is no guarantee that this inclination will be realized. Several things are prerequisites to lifelong development. There must be an awareness of the need to continually learn, which is something managers today have. There must be an intentionality about learning, which today's managers are beginning to acquire. There must also be awareness of the importance of reflection to learning, something most managers do not possess today. Finally, reflection must be approached in a balanced way. Maximizing the benefits of managerial reflection means balancing the attention given to natural, active reflection *and* induced, proactive reflection as well as balancing internal and external dimensions of reflection.

Whether one is concerned with the practical issue of enhancing managers' learning from experience or the scholarly issue of theorizing and researching the phenomenon of managerial learning, balance must be maintained. The next two chapters will give specific attention to the scholarly and practical implications of the ideas about managerial reflection presented so far.

Chapter 13

Implications for Theory and Future Research

The two studies reported here were designed to investigate important unexplored areas of managerial reflection. They were intended to produce significant contributions to current theory and research in the fields of management and adult education. This chapter reviews the contributions of these studies and their implications for theory and research. Since the two studies were conducted independently and because one was exploratory in nature whereas the other was confirmatory, the issues that emerge from each will first be considered separately. Finally, the implications of an integrated view of managerial reflection will be offered, since we believe a genuine understanding of reflection is possible only when it is viewed holistically.

THE THEORY-BUILDING STUDY OF ACTIVE REFLECTION

The grounded theory study presented here was designed to explore inductively the process of natural managerial reflection during developmental job experiences. Because its purpose was to develop theoretical concepts, not to test or validate them, its findings are admittedly tentative. Even so, they make several important contributions to existing knowledge.

Contributions and Limitations of the Theory-Building Study

Prior to this work, a comprehensive and empirically based model of active managerial reflection did not exist. The two most unique aspects of this study are its detailed focus on naturally occurring reflection and its attention to contextual conditions that affect reflection. This study provides the most thorough description available of the nature of managers' reflection during developmental experiences in business organizations. What little writing already existed in the management literature emphasized prescriptive techniques for helping managers reflect (e.g., Robinson and Wick, 1992) or, if it looked at natural reflection during experiences, deemphasized the role of conditions in the work environment.

This research demonstrated that managers are not purely rational reflectors (and by inference, learners), just as prior research demonstrated that they are not purely rational decision makers. The intuitive aspect of managers' reflection was described here. Intuition is well recognized as a dimension of managerial decision making (Brockmann and Simmonds, 1997), but it is not usually associated with reflection. This is a deficiency in current thinking about how managers reflect. Schön (1983) recognized that there is an intuitive flavor to natural reflection, but much more needs to be understood about this important aspect of reflection.

Schön's (1983) writing on reflection-in-action comes closest to the natural view of reflection taken here. Schön studied professionals' reflection during their workdays; however, his overall framework was professions, not organizations. He studied only four cases of managers (because he also studied architects, psychotherapists, scientists, and town planners), and the people he studied were serving as coaches to apprentices to their profession. Thus, what he really describes is reflection-in-action in the course of a coaching relationship, which is a noticeably different context than that studied here.

Additionally, in contrast to Schön's findings that managers are disinclined to reflect separately from direct engagement in action, the results of this study point to the prevalence and significance of off-line reflection. Off-line reflection, which is not described elsewhere, is a seemingly potent means by which managers in developmental experiences try to make sense of their work and their learning. It certainly deserves attention in future research, as does narrative reflection and the impact of emotions on reflection, which are dimensions of managers' reflection that Schön does not describe.

The second unique aspect of this research is the focus on the contextual conditions in organizations that influence reflection. Schön refers to managers' organizational environment as a "learning system" that can help or hinder reflection, but he does not draw any generalizable conclusions about the effects of that environment on reflection. The investigation reported here explicitly examined the relationship between conditions in managers' work environments and their active reflection. As argued earlier, giving attention to the work environment is essential to fully understanding natural managerial reflection.

Kolb's (1984) theory of experiential learning is also relevant to the theory-building study described here. The contribution here in relation to Kolb's work results from the primary focus on reflection here and from the very different approaches taken to understanding learning. Kolb began with the notion of individual differences in learning styles and then used that framework to study behavior. In contrast, this study began with behavior (specifically, managers engaged in developmental experiences) and then described managers' natural reflection. Using a grounded theory, inductive approach, this study discovered how managers actually reflect rather than applying an existing framework to managerial behavior. Using this approach provides unique insights into how managers reflect while learning.

As is often a goal in qualitative research, this work also contributed to Food Corp. and Health Co. and to the lives of the participating managers. Representatives from both companies expressed gratitude for the feedback they received on their managers' reflection and on the conditions in their organization that affect reflection. Additionally, the research participants were thankful for the opportunity to reflect on their experiences and their work environments. Finally, this research is relevant to other companies and the way they manage developmental job experiences. The practical implications of the study will be presented in the next chapter.

Although this research makes important contributions, it is certainly not without limitations. The sample included just twenty-four managers, only twenty of whom were in challenging developmental experiences. This is an appropriate sample size for a grounded theory study, but much would be gained by studying more managers. This sample was also all white with only six women. Women were disproportionately represented among those managers whose experiences were not stretching ones. This was the case for two of the six female research participants (33 percent), while it occurred for only two of eighteen male participants (11 percent). The most plausible explanation for this is simply the paucity of women in challenging developmental experiences. Historically, such experiences were provided primarily if not exclusively to men, and progress is slow. Ruderman, Ohlott, and Kram (1995) found that women are promoted at a slower rate than men and only after they have already proved they can do the new job.

The sample used here was also narrow in the sense that it was intentionally limited to managers in developmental assignments. At best, therefore, the results can be generalized only to managers in similar situations. This limitation must be remembered whenever we refer to "managerial" reflection.

The interview methodology of the study produced self-report data. Although efforts were made to interview managers during or shortly after their experiences to minimize the effects of selective recall and reconstruction of responses, some of this surely occurred. Additionally, managers likely were inclined to a certain degree to provide socially desirable responses when answering interview questions.

This study was also limited to two sites. Although Food Corp. and Health Co. are reasonably representative of large food producers and health care insurance firms, respectively, they differ in important ways from companies of other sizes and in other industries. If conditions in the immediate work environment influence active reflection, then it is also reasonable to hypothesize that more macro-level forces like organizational culture and industry structure will impact reflection.

A final limitation involves the provisional nature of the findings reported here. This research represents an attempt at theory building, and the outcome of the research is not the verification of a model of active reflection but rather the development of such a model. That model requires testing in future research to establish its validity, although this does not make the findings reported here any less worthwhile. Using the grounded theory methodology ensured that the theoretical concepts proposed are solidly grounded in data and are not just the product of the researcher's ruminations. But as an inductive, theory-building study, it does mean that the findings must be treated as tentative.

Specific Implications for Theory and Research

Many implications of this research for theory and future research have been implied in the preceding discussion. Some additional comments will be made here with respect to theory, followed by several specific recommendations for further research. This research has implications for several related bodies of literature. The management literature has been interested in learning since the early work of Lewin (1948) and McGregor (1960). This interest has continued in the more recent work of Schön (1983), Kolb (1984), and Hall and associates (1996). The work reported here builds on existing theory to provide a much-needed conceptual model of an important element of learning from experience. The focus of the model presented here is individual managers in the context of their immediate work environment.

A more recent body of writing deals with the notion of organizational learning (Garvin, 1993; Levitt and March, 1988; Senge, 1990; Tobin, 1996). The idea is that organizations themselves are capable of learning from experiences they encounter, which entails moving from individual learning processes to collective learning dynamics. Although the research here dealt with reflection at the level of individual managers, the kinds of contextual conditions conducive to individual reflection may also support learning at more macro levels. Examination of this idea awaits further research.

The research reported here has indirect links to adult development theory (Merriam and Caffarella, 1991) and direct links to career theory (Arthur et al., 1989). An important issue in career theory is the impact on employees of fundamental changes in the nature of work in organizations. The intense competition and turbulence facing business organizations today has caused life within those organizations to become chaotic. Job descriptions change regularly, requiring employees continually to do new and different things. In addition, job security has become a thing of the past, as the implied contract between employers and employees of long-term employment in return for loyalty has quickly disappeared (Hall and associates, 1996). This has left employees feeling frazzled and fearful. It has also led to the realization by organizations and employees alike that life-long learning is a necessity for survival today. People must be able to develop continually and must be able to learn from new experiences they regularly encounter on the job. Doing this requires that they actively reflect and that their organizations recognize and support this.

The original impetus for the theory-building study reported here was organizations' increasing use of developmental assignments to build the skills of high-potential managers. But the findings presented here become relevant to all managers, if not all employees, as more and more find themselves, whether by design or default, in challenging and stretching experiences of the kind described by McCall et al. (1988). If "permanent white water" (Peters, 1992) really does describe the world of work today, then the ability to harness one's reflective abilities in the interest of learning from experience has universal applicability. All this implies that reflection needs a more prominent place in career theory.

A final body of theory for which this research has direct implications is cognition in organizations. Surprisingly few direct links exist between the organizational literatures on cognition and learning, which is odd given the inherently cognitive nature of much of learning. Active reflection—a process that is integral to learning—is obviously a cognitive phenomenon. This work, then, can add to cognition theory by describing one important cognitive process. In addition, this work could be enhanced by further integration with the cognition literature. For example, active reflection as described here resembles stimulus-driven (versus schema-driven) cognitive processing of information (Sims and Lorenzi, 1992). How are they similar and different? Questions such as this deserve attention in future research.

Several other areas of research should be fruitful using this study as a springboard. One is the issue of testing the conclusions drawn from this investigation. Survey research with larger samples could be undertaken to assess the validity of the models presented here. This requires developing operational definitions of active reflection and the contextual conditions and psychological states described here so that they can be measured and correlated. Does the model of active reflection presented here (see Figure 5-1) accurately describe the internal process of natural reflection? Do the influences proposed (see Figure 8-1) really enable reflection?

Since the purpose of this exploratory study was to provide a broad overview of active reflection, deeper examination of selected findings would be useful. These include off-line reflection, intuitive reflection, the reflection–affect relationship, and conditions that are disabling to reflection other than those presented here.

There would also be great value in research that examined the active reflection of other types of employees (nonmanagers and managers who are not in explicitly developmental situations) as well as more women and persons of color. The possibility of ethnic and cultural differences in active reflection is not only real but is potentially significant given the increasing level of diversity in the U.S. workforce and the rising influence of the global marketplace. Additionally, research on active reflection in different types of organizations and in various industries is also called for. Finally, action research with companies interested in deliberately promoting active reflection would provide an opportunity to assess the practical applicability of this study's findings.

THE EXPERIMENTAL STUDY OF PROACTIVE REFLECTION

In contrast to the theory-building investigation just discussed, the experimental study presented here was designed to confirm deductively the effects of three different proactive reflection interventions. Its purpose was to conduct a rigorous comparative test of the three interventions, to provide hard evidence on whether proactive reflection promotes learning from experience.

Contributions of the Experimental Study

The results of this research provide new ways to interpret theoretical work that was presented in chapter 2. This includes the work of Mezirow, Hall, and the three theorists who provided the conceptual framework for this study: Piaget, Lewin, and Dewey.

Mezirow (1991) believed that reflection results in new meaning schemes that he called "meaning perspectives." Although each member of the three treatment groups was able to develop specific meanings for each lesson listed as a result of his or her proactive reflection intervention, all but one control group member were also able to develop meanings for the limited amount of learning they reported. Thus, it appears that formal, structured reflection is not necessary to develop meaning perspectives. Even very brief reflection episodes, such as those the control group experienced, will produce meaning perspectives.

Mezirow did, however, define a special kind of reflection he called critical reflection—"the bringing of one's assumptions, premises, criteria, and schemata into consciousness and vigorously critiquing them" (Mezirow, 1985, p. 25). In this study, it was found that vigorous critiquing did not take place in the peer group: videotape analysis showed no vigorous critiquing of any assumptions or premises by subjects. The individual and tutor groups used the reflection questions and guidelines in their process, and these questions were developed to ensure probing and critique. In contrast, the unfacilitated peer group ignored these questions and guidelines. Therefore, it may be concluded that the process of critical reflection took place in the individual and tutor groups but not in the peer group.

The distinctions between task and personal learning described by Hall (1986a) were used to analyze the descriptions of learning in Part III of the posttest questionnaire. In the process of this analysis, the personal learning category, described by Hall as "socio-emotional" learning, was further divided into interpersonal learning (socio) and intrapersonal learning (emotional). In addition, the category "cultural" was added to describe comments that related to the corporate culture and its impact on subjects' learning.

Finally, the results of this study offer insight into the work of the three theorists who contributed to the conceptual framework for this study: Piaget, Dewey, and Lewin. As discussed previously, Piaget's contention that reflection is a cognitive, not a social, process provided the basis for the creation of an individual reflection group. Dewey's position that expert advice is important to reflection and therefore to learning provided the rationale for the design of a tutor reflection group. Finally, Lewin's argument for social interaction provided the basis for the creation of a peer reflection group. That both the individual and mentor groups had significantly more learning than the control group supports the positions of Piaget and Dewey. However, the low number of learnings reported by the peer group, when compared to the control group, calls into question the arguments proposed by Lewin when applied to the context and audience of this study. Further study of learning in peer groups is thus called for.

The results of this study contribute in important ways to prior empirical research conducted by McCall, Brooks, and Killian and Todnem. The five types of experiences that McCall et al. (1988) found to be most likely to promote learning in managers were used in this study as the focus for the proactive reflection activities. The results confirm the value of these experiences in promoting learning in managers. All subjects, including those in the control group, were able to identify lessons from one of these experiences and were satisfied with the amount, quality, and impact of this learning. In addition, there were no differences in amount of learning by type of experience: all were equally likely to produce learning.

Brooks (1989) found that proactive reflection promotes positive changes in organizations. This study further defines the level of potential organization impact as being at the individual or departmental level. This is likely because the experiment described here examined the experiences of individual managers.

Killian and Todnem (1991) found that managers typically will not engage in proactive reflection unless given the time, structure, and expectation to do so, and this study confirms their finding. During the intervention, subjects were given the time, structure, and expectation to reflect, and they all did so for the entire hour. In contrast, the follow-up survey showed that very few subjects reflected on their learning after the intervention, when no specific time, structure, or expectation to do so was given. This happened even though they all reported satisfaction with the reflection process and satisfaction with the learning they derived from it.

This study is certainly not without limitations, as presented in chapter 10. In spite of these limitations, this study makes important contributions to prior theory and research. It confirms the theories of Piaget and Dewey and the research of McCall et al. and Killian and Todnem. Results of this study also provide additions to or reinterpretations of the theories of Mezirow, Hall, and Lewin and further definition of the research by Brooks. Most importantly, this study provides the first experimental validation of the efficacy of individual and tutor proactive reflection interventions in promoting the learning from experience of business managers.

Specific Implications for Research

Several directions for future research, suggested by the results of this study, are discussed next.

Effect of additional variables

Additional variables that may affect the amount and type of learning include subjects' gender, seniority, job level, and personal style. The first two, gender and seniority, were suggested by research subjects. Analyzing the impact of gender was suggested by one of the female managers in the study, who contended that women are, by nature, more proactively reflective than men and would surface more personal learning than men. Several participants referred to the impact of seniority, stating that their many years in the corporation influenced the way they viewed their learning.

In the original design for the study, it was assumed that randomization would equally distribute level of management throughout the sample groups. However, it was discovered that all senior executives had participated in an intensely reflective management development experience immediately preceding the intervention, so this senior-level group was eliminated from the sample. This modification may have influenced the level of impact of the learning, which was at the individual or departmental level, and not at the corporate level. In contrast, Brooks (1989), who included levels all the way to the chairman of the board, found impact at the corporate level. It would be important to see if including top-level executives would add higher level impact to the learnings in this study.

The previous suggestion considered the impact of job level within the management ranks. Another suggestion for future research concerns the addition of nonmanagement employees to the research sample. The focus on management-level employees was important in this study since it was built upon prior research conducted at the management level. However, proactive reflection is not limited to the management level in corporations, and additional research should be conducted at all levels of corporations.

Finally, the current body of knowledge would be expanded by an analysis of the impact of personal styles on the results of this study. Several inventories widely used in corporations could be used to collect this data. The Myers-Briggs Type Inventory (MBTI) would provide data on four contrasting personality dimensions: introversion versus extroversion, sensing versus intuition, thinking versus feeling, and perceiving versus judging. The Hermann Brain Dominance Instrument would provide data on left-brain versus right-brain dominance. Kolb's Learning Style Inventory (LSI) would provide data on the four different learning styles he identified.

Quality of learning by treatment group

As discussed in chapter 11, the researcher determined that the subjects' ratings of satisfaction with the quality of their learning were more useful than the researcher's assessment. However, further examination of objective methods to assess the quality of subjects' responses is suggested for future research. One option is an independent panel of experts who would develop criteria as a group and judge each description according to those criteria.

Focus on peer group reflection intervention

Since organizations place great emphasis on team learning, it is important to investigate further the statistically insignificant amount of learning from the peer group compared to the control group. This would involve replicating the study while controlling for the explanations for the peer group's performance discussed in chapter 11. Specifically, the peer group could be instructed to resist playing "ain't it awful," to focus on the original developmental experience chosen, to refer periodically to the proactive reflection questions, and to take notes on the worksheets. A member of the group could be appointed to enforce these conditions.

In addition, these results suggest further examination of peer group discussions when used as a tool for reflection. In this study, participants discussed predominantly unshared experiences from the recent past. The results might have been quite different if the groups had shared a common experience. Existing work teams rather than groups artificially created for a proactive reflection intervention may be more conducive to proactive reflection.

Finally, the possibility that formal peer group discussion might actually interfere with proactive reflection on prior experience should be explored. The process dynamics of group formation and development may interfere with the content work required to do proactive reflection in 1 hour. Research in this area could be linked to existing theory and practice in the areas of group dynamics, team building, and group-centered psychotherapy.

Additional follow-up

Although a follow-up survey was conducted 1 week after the proactive reflection intervention, a longer term and more formal follow-up process would provide data about reflection over time. Two possibilities are an additional reflection intervention administered several weeks after the first, and an analysis to determine whether stated implications for future action resulted in behavior change on the job.

Focus on the process of proactive reflection

The follow-up survey showed that subjects spent more time thinking about the process they went through during their intervention than about the experience they chose or their learning from it. A formal analysis of this process from the subjects' point of view, through observations, document analysis, and interviews would add valuable insights into the role of reflection in learning from experience.

THE INTEGRATION OF ACTIVE AND PROACTIVE REFLECTION

Although much can be gained by studying active and proactive reflection independently, even more will be gained by examining them together. As has been argued throughout this book, the soundest approach to managerial reflection is a holistic one. Many issues are relevant here. Is the thinking that occurs during each mode of reflection qualitatively different in significant ways? For example, is proactive reflection less emotional than active reflection?

The ultimate outcome of active versus proactive reflection is also an important issue. Do the two modes lead to different insights in quantity, quality, or type? Since the two modes occur in very different ways, it is reasonable to assume they will produce different outcomes. The results of the research reported here suggest that active reflection results in more narrow, micro-level insights whereas proactive reflection produces lessons that are less task-oriented and at more of a macro level. However, the results are only suggestive of this difference, and there is some evidence that both modes produce outcomes at multiple levels of specificity. Much would be gained by more direct comparison of the outcomes of active and proactive reflection to Argyris's (1982) notion of double-loop learning, Senge's (1990) ideas about generative learning, and O'Neil and Marsick's (1994) work on critical reflection. Active and proactive reflection appear to occur not just at different levels of specificity (i.e., micro vs. macro) but also at varying levels of depth. These important aspects of both modes of reflection deserve more attention.

Individual differences among managers are another important issue. Are some managers predisposed toward one mode of reflection over the other? If so, why? Does their preference relate to personality or gender or learning style? Recent research at the Center for Creative Leadership has identified four "learning tactics" (Dalton, 1998), which refers to the preferred behavior managers exhibit when they encounter developmental challenges on the job. Four tactics have been identified: feeling, action, thinking, and accessing others. Much could be learned from examining the relationship of these tactics to active and proactive reflection.

It is also possible that different types of developmental experiences as well as different types of organizational cultures lead more readily to one mode of reflection than the other. Exploring any systematic tendencies here is important. A related question is whether proactive reflection could compensate for a lack of contextual conditions enabling of active reflection. That is, could proactive reflection be used to help promote active reflection?

Questions are key to both modes of reflection. This includes not just asking and answering questions but also casting questions. *Casting* refers to the way a question is framed before it is asked. The answers one gets to the questions one asks are determined by the questions with which one starts. Different questions or even the same question cast in a different light will produce different answers. Meaningful insight into experience is largely determined by the way managers cast questions about their experience. Even though questions are important to both modes of reflection, they seem to be important in different ways. The different ways that questions are cast, asked, and answered in active versus proactive reflection need to be explored.

Just as questions are important to both modes of reflection, so too are other people. There is increasing evidence that people grow and develop the most in the context of relationships (Hall and associates, 1996; Jordon, 1997). Three of the seven contextual conditions discovered in the theory-building study and two of the three interventions tested in the experimental study involved interactions with other people. What are the similarities and differences in the way interactions with others influence active and proactive reflection? Are different people needed to support each mode of reflection, or do different interpersonal roles need to be played to support each mode?

Finally, a very instructive line of research would be to follow learners throughout a challenging developmental experience to examine how both modes of reflection happen for the same person. It is conceivable that productive interactions will occur between active and proactive reflection such that they feed off of and support each other. A truly holistic investigation of managerial reflection requires this type of integrated approach.

If reflection really is important to learning from experience, and if managerial reflection really involves two different but complementary modes of reflection, then much more research needs to be devoted to the issues described here. Future research that balances both modes of reflection will be most productive.

SUMMARY

This chapter compared the research reported in this book to existing theory and research. The contributions and implications for future scholarly work of the theory-building study of active reflection and the experimental study of proactive reflection were thoroughly described. Consideration was also given to where fruitful future research could be conducted given a holistic perspective on managerial reflection. Work that looks at active and proactive reflection in combination has the potential to make the greatest contribution to the literature. It is our hope that this book stimulates just that kind of research.

Future research of managerial reflection also needs to view it inside out; that is, attention must be given to both the internal cognitive process of reflection and the outside forces that enable it. Such research will recognize both the active and proactive modes of reflection, paying particular attention to their differences and interactions. There is very little scholarly writing in both the management and education literatures on the nature of managerial reflection in learning from experience. This is not only unfortunate; it is intolerable. Continual learning at work is indispensable today, and reflection is unquestionably vital to such learning. There is still much to be learned in this area, and its importance to future scholarly inquiry cannot be overestimated

Chapter 14

Practical Implications: Enhancing Managerial Learning

One of the most important conclusions that can be drawn from this book is that managers do not learn from experience—at least not directly. The original research described here demonstrates that learning happens when managers reflect *in* (i.e., actively) and *on* (i.e., proactively) experience. These are significant findings based on research that addresses important gaps in the scholarly literature on managerial learning. But the original impetus for this research was as much interest in a critical business issue as it was the desire to make a scholarly contribution. Based on our experience as management development professionals, we have a personal interest in helping managers learn. It was our deliberate desire thus to conduct research that would make important contributions to both scholarship and practice. The purpose of this chapter is to present the practical implications of our work.

The chapter begins with suggestions for enhancing proactive reflection in business organizations. Suggestions for promoting active reflection are provided next, followed by recommendations for taking a holistic approach to enhancing managerial reflection at work. Finally, after a summary of the chapter, we will share some concluding thoughts on the issue of reflection in managerial learning.

SUGGESTIONS FOR ENHANCING PROACTIVE REFLECTION

The fundamental way to enhance proactive reflection is to require managers undergoing developmental experiences to schedule periodic structured reflection opportunities during and at the conclusion of their assignments. Time away from their normally hectic routines is critical to consolidate learning. Fortunately, this research demonstrates that all that is needed is a 1-hour reflection session. For a

3-month assignment, given a 45-hour work week, this amounts to 0.17 percent (or less than one-fifth of 1 percent) of a manager's time! The benefits produced by a proactive reflection session are well worth such a small investment of time. Indeed, if a manager and a company cannot commit to this, they are not really serious about promoting learning.

The materials used in the experimental study described earlier provide the content of an effective proactive reflection session. They include a four-step proactive reflection activity and a set of proactive reflection questions (which were summarized in Exhibit 10-1) as well as general guidelines for proactive reflection (see Exhibit 14-1). These steps, questions, and guidelines may be combined to design reflection sessions that meet the specific needs of managers. Daudelin (1996a) has used these tools to create handbooks and workshops that help managers reflect alone, with a tutor, and in a variety of group formats.

A company's management development function is in an important position to support proactive reflection. In addition to coordinating use of *The Reflection Handbook* (Daudelin, 1996b), it can ensure that the goals of proactive reflection interventions match the outcome desired. Proactive reflection that occurs individually or with a tutor is most conducive to reinforcing individual learning. If

Exhibit 14-1
General Guidelines for Proactive Reflection

Learners:

- Don't censor what you write—consider this a brainstorming exercise.

- Access feelings, dreams, memories, and metaphors to stimulate thinking.

- Dig below your immediate thoughts; push yourself beyond surface evaluation.

- Explore difficult issues and search uncomfortable reactions.

- Surface assumptions, values, or beliefs underlying your actions.

- Don't try to force ideas into meaningful patterns.

- Allow contradictions to occur and record them.

- Approach this as an opportunity to learn about yourself, not as a test.

Tutors (if appropriate):

- Assure participants that all information will be treated confidentially.

- Help learners make sense of their experience by asking questions, challenging observations, repeating what you hear them saying, and providing encouragement.

- Listen more than you talk.

---

the goal is to generate lessons learned of a team, then a peer group approach may be more useful.

Obviously, proactive reflection sessions should be scheduled for all managers following developmental experiences, including job assignments like those described by McCall et al. (1988) as well as on-the-job training exercises and even classroom training activities. Personal learning guides could also be developed and distributed to managers to use in uncovering learning from their own challenging work experiences and to assist managers in helping others surface the lessons embedded in their experiences. Proactive reflection activities could also be integrated into corporate succession planning systems. These activities offer another source of feedback to succession planning candidates to gauge their readiness for promotion, a source of feedback that should be readily accepted by managers since they generate it themselves. Firms that are the most committed to promoting managerial learning will include engagement in proactive reflection as an element of their performance appraisal system, because what gets measured usually gets accomplished.

Daudelin (1996b) has also developed an exercise called "community reflection" to provide a positive atmosphere for group-based proactive reflection. After agreeing to a set of ground rules, learners spend 20 minutes proactively reflecting in writing alone. This is followed by an hour of group reflection led by a facilitator. Learners share their individual lessons, discussion ensues, and the exercise ends with consideration of additional learning that emerged from the process.

Based on work with managers from a Fortune 500 firm, Daudelin found that managers who use this exercise surface significant amounts of personal learning that would otherwise not have been recognized. Additionally, some managers involved in an especially challenging new experience reported two unexpected benefits of the community reflection exercise. First, they reported that the session gave them a much-needed opportunity to slow down and catch their breath during an intense experience. Being able to reflect quietly on what they had learned provided relief from the rapid and ongoing assault of new learning that was a normal part of their developmental experience. Second, they discovered that the community reflection time created a sense of camaraderie, of "we're in this together." Feelings of trust and friendship, which had not previously existed, emerged through the process of disclosing what was being learned from positive and negative experiences alike.

SUGGESTIONS FOR ENHANCING ACTIVE REFLECTION

Management development personnel have a major role to play in promoting proactive reflection. They also have a role to play in facilitating active reflection, but here the primary responsibility lies with managers and their supervisors. Since proactive reflection occurs in real time as challenging assignments unfold, the role of management development is more limited. The key here is to help managers become consciously aware of the active reflection they are probably already doing naturally and to help them realize how their immediate work environment can make it easier or harder to engage in that reflection.

Helping managers become more intentional about the active mode of reflection is of the utmost importance; increased intentionality is the key. The theory-building study described active reflection as a dialogue of inquiry and interpretation, as though managers talk to themselves by formulating questions and then develop interpretations to answer them. Being curious and deliberate about the questions one asks is important to effective active reflection. If reflection involves an internal dialogue of inquiry and interpretation, then managers must become *intentional internal conversationalists*. This does not mean producing managers who run around their companies mumbling to themselves; rather it means helping managers gain control of the inquiring and interpreting they do naturally so that the most relevant questions are posed and multiple interpretations are formed and tested.

Question casting was described in the previous chapter as the way a question is originally formed in the mind. Question casting is probably more important than question asking and answering, since how a question is cast sets the direction for the information search that follows. Question casting is relevant to both proactive and active reflection, but it is especially important to the latter since it occurs in real time. Managers need to become skilled at formulating good questions on the fly, and it is not a simple skill.

Managers will also benefit from being made aware of the levels of questions that are typically considered during developmental experiences: questions of fact, function, approach, purpose, and self (arranged hierarchically from the least to the most significant). Building on McGregor's (1960) idea that agriculture provides the most useful metaphor for thinking about managerial learning, the questions formed during active reflection can be viewed as arranged along a trellis. Alerting managers to the "trellis of questions" and encouraging them to climb as high as their experience enables them should produce reflection that will lead to more profound learning. Such learning is associated with questions at the top of the trellis—questions of purpose and of self.

Greater intentionality is also needed concerning the interpreting that is done during active reflection. Recall that inquiry in active reflection leads to "interpretations," not "answers." During on-the-job developmental challenges, some interpretations certainly capture reality more accurately than others, but rarely is there one "correct" interpretation. Helping managers appreciate the interpretive nature of active reflection should make them better learners.

To actively reflect requires a high tolerance for ambiguity, which is also true of experiential learning in general. This makes learning stressful since learners, by definition, cannot draw on existing knowledge and skill to respond to situations. This produces strong incentives to gain the necessary knowledge/skill as quickly as possible so as to build competence and reduce feelings of inadequacy. But challenging, on-the-job learning experiences today are complex, ambiguous, and ever-changing. Learning is hindered in these situations when the learner strives for premature closure by trying to build understanding immediately. When managers are reassured that true learning takes time and that they should be striving for effective interpretations, not for the one correct answer, they will be more likely to learn.

Finally, with respect to interpretation, since active reflection occurs on the fly in the midst of challenging experiences, it is important that learners' emerging insights not be lost. Many of those insights will be immediately applicable to the situation, but others may require further examination and processing. Any number of simple techniques can serve as *idea cisterns* to capture these useful thoughts. Since these are usually thoughts that are in process, it is better not to overly formalize the means for capturing them. Examples of idea cisterns available to managers include jotting ideas down on a scrap of paper, calendar, napkin, or electronic notepad when they first occur; dictating them; or e-mailing them to someone. The point is to do something with the interpretation before it is lost in the urgency of the moment.

Active reflection occurs off-line as well as on-line, and managers should use brief moments alone as prime opportunities for this kind of active reflection. Waiting for a meeting to start (or even during an unproductive meeting), while on hold on the telephone, while waiting in line, and even while walking from a parking space to the office are all such opportunities. Even though these moments are brief in duration, they provide an opportunity for inquiry into and interpretation of relevant issues.

As important as brief moments alone are to active reflection, so is time spent with other people. Active reflection involves external as well as internal dialogue, and one of the most powerful tools for reflection appears to be meaningful discussion with a person a manager trusts. Thus managers must also become good *intentional external conversationalists*. They need to recognize interactions with other people as chances to inquire and interpret, which involves establishing connections with people with whom managers can talk openly about their experiences. Articulating their ideas to someone else forces managers to make those ideas clear to themselves. Another advantage to actively reflecting in relationships is the emotional support they provide, which is crucial for working through the tough, emotionally laden issues that are an inherent part of developmental experiences.

The influence of the work environment surrounding a developmental experience on active reflection has been repeatedly emphasized here. Contextual conditions in a manager's immediate work environment should be susceptible to deliberate manipulation. While it is not possible to perfectly control them, contextual conditions certainly can be influenced more readily than more macro-level forces like organizational culture or structure. Thus, managers and their bosses need to work together to cultivate working conditions that are conducive to active reflection. To the extent managers and bosses cultivate enabling conditions, they will reap active reflection that contributes to experiential learning.

Cultivating enabling conditions involves personalizing the list of contextual conditions described earlier (i.e., autonomy, feedback, interactions with others, and two types of pressure) by assessing their impact on managers' active reflection and then applying the list to their current assignment. Specific suggestions for cultivating all of the contextual conditions are described elsewhere by Seibert 1999; a few examples will be given here. If inadequate opportunities exist for interactions with people who will stimulate, inform, or support a managers' active reflection, then specific action needs to be taken to provide those opportunities, such as introducing the manager to relevant subject matter experts, customers, and executives.

Quality is more important than quantity in interpersonal interactions; rather than connecting with a lot of people, managers need to connect with people who are relevant to their assignment. A manager's boss should also recognize that straightforward activities like asking managers detailed questions after they have completed a business trip or an important piece of their assignment as well as requiring that they make formal presentations to senior management and/or customers are powerful techniques for promoting active reflection. Managers and their bosses would be well served by working down the list of contextual conditions together (see Figure 8-1) to come up with several specific suggestions for each condition that are relevant to a given developmental experience.

Ignoring contextual conditions is as harmful to active reflection as is ignoring the light, water, nutrients, and insects affecting a garden. In all of this a manager's boss and company must demonstrate their support for proactive reflection. McCall (1991), the lead researcher on the Center for Creative Leadership's lessons of experience project, has said that organizational support for learning from experience is the area where the most can be done to ensure that managers and their firms gain all they can from developmental experiences.

SUGGESTIONS FOR A HOLISTIC APPROACH TO ENHANCING REFLECTION

A view of managerial reflection that integrates its active and proactive modes implies much for practice. At the most basic level, it means that managers and their organizations need to realize that there are two different forms of reflection, each of which needs attention if managers are to learn all they can from experience. Greater intentionality is called for with respect to both dimensions of the integrated matrix presented in Figure 12-2: external forces—internal processes and natural—induced.

Reflection has historically not been an integral part of management practice because it has been inaccurately and narrowly stereotyped as an activity relevant only to scholars, monks, and the like. Our research shows that is clearly not the case. Instead, reflection is an essential element for learning from developmental experiences in today's dynamic marketplace.

Effectively learning from experience involves maintaining proper balance among the four elements of the reflection matrix. Emphasizing one mode over the other or focusing on internal processes to the exclusion of enabling external forces will impede learning. This is a delicate balance to strike, as is the need to provide enough structure to encourage reflection without oversystematizing it. Mandating a highly formalized program of reflection will likely attain compliance but not commitment to the value of reflection. The last thing busy managers and organizations need is yet another "program."

An effective approach is to try to build both modes of reflection into managers' normal work routines. Reflection activities that are a part of existing assignment management, succession planning, performance appraisal, and progress reporting will be more readily accepted by managers and ultimately more effective. On the other hand, some time set aside explicitly for proactive reflection can produce great dividends, especially since it need take only 1 hour. This provides an escape from the daily pressures that debilitate proactive reflection. But maintaining balance means managers will also simultaneously embrace promotive and directive pressure in the service of active reflection.

Both studies reported here demonstrate clearly the vital significance other people have on managers' reflection. Thus managers would do well to obtain the assistance of at least one other person (a boss, peer, or management development professional) if to do nothing else but hold them accountable for being more intentional about their active and proactive reflection. A solitary reflector is as much an oxymoron in a business context as is a reclusive manager.

A Time Line for Promoting Learning Through Reflection

Active reflection and proactive reflection are necessary but not sufficient conditions for learning from experience. Meaningful experiences, genuine challenge, and incentives for learning, among other things, are also needed. But the reflective piece of learning from experience is usually ignored in the business environment. Figure 14-1 provides a practical way to highlight the importance of reflection over the course of developmental experiences. The time line presents the minimal requirements for promoting reflection. While it is possible to do much more, completing the activities presented in Figure 14-1 should result in tangible benefits.

The elongated, horizontal triangles in the middle of the figure suggest that the relative emphasis given to active and proactive reflection changes over the course of an experience. Active reflection deserves the most attention at the beginning of an assignment as well as throughout the assignment. Its influence diminishes, however, with time, at least in relation to proactive reflection. Proactive reflection is most important at the end of the assignment as well as at periodic intervals during it. It is recommended that a 1-hour proactive reflection session be held every 3 months during a developmental experience, although this interval is admittedly not based on specific research findings. These sessions will allow the manager to momentarily disengage from the experience and participate in a structured debriefing activity. The particulars of this activity as well as the tactics used to engage in active reflection were described earlier in this chapter.

Figure 14-1
Time Line for Promoting Learning Through Reflection

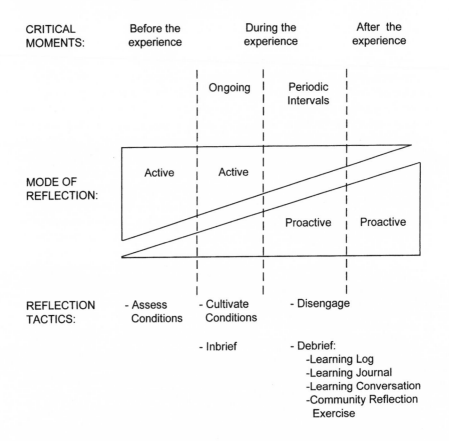

Jean's Line-to-Staff Switch Revisited

Chapter 12 presented a case example of a loan officer at a bank whose developmental experience involved moving to corporate human resources to undertake an important compensation project. Jean's situation was used to illustrate the integrated model of managerial reflection presented in Figure 12-2. Figure 14-1 is also relevant to her situation. Jean, her boss, and the bank's management development function could have used the time line to more intentionally manage her reflection over the course of her assignment.

Before her assignment began, Jean and her boss should have met to assess the contextual conditions surrounding her assignment. Do they appear to be enabling of active reflection and if not, what could be done to cultivate enabling conditions? Once the assignment began, Jean needed to be intentional about cultivating enabling conditions and inbriefing on an ongoing basis. Essentially this means remaining conscious not just about what she was learning during the assignment but also about how she was learning. Recall from chapter 12 that Jean received inadequate feedback from her boss during her assignment, which made her feel less informed than she would have liked and hindered her active reflection. Recognizing this during the experience should have led Jean to talk with her boss about the effect of this disabling condition on her reflection and her learning. Corrective action could then have been taken by Jean and her boss.

As described in chapter 12, Jean participated in a proactive reflection session at the conclusion of the 1-year compensation project. This helped her uncover, among other things, the anxiety she had felt during the assignment over its impact on her future career in commercial lending. A discussion at this time with the vice president of commercial lending eased her fears about this issue, which was good, but it would have been better if Jean had made this discovery earlier. A required proactive reflection session 3 months into the experience would have addressed this issue much earlier, thereby enabling Jean to focus even more of her attention on the assignment itself.

Jean did engage in active reflection because on balance her work environment was conducive to such reflection. She also participated in a proactive reflection activity at the conclusion of her compensation assignment. Engaging in both modes of reflection contributed significantly to the learning she acquired through her experience. It is likely, however, that she would have learned even more and deeper lessons had she been intentional about her active reflection and if she had had periodic opportunities for proactive reflection during the experience.

Convincing Managers and Organizations of the Importance of Reflection

Those who doubt the utility of reflection may be persuaded by the empirical evidence presented here. Indeed, a primary purpose of this book is to present hard data on the relevance of reflection to managerial learning. Managers and organizations may be uncomfortable with the notion of reflection, but it plays a central role in experiential learning.

Those in business who are not convinced by the empirical evidence presented here may be able to relate more readily to an athletic metaphor. As a dynamic and pressure-filled game, football shares much in common with today's marketplace. Likewise, managers in challenging learning situations share much in common with an effective quarterback. Like a good quarterback, a manager needs to know when and how to run a postgame review (i.e., proactively reflect), call a time-out during a game (i.e., actively reflect off-line), conduct a huddle, and—one of the most difficult skills—call an audible (i.e., actively reflect on-line). The best quarterbacks are physically and intellectually developed, and they are able to adapt their game plan on-the-fly as circumstances change. In similar fashion, the best managers are those who are technically and intellectually developed and who realize that learning and reflection are core competencies in today's dynamic world.

Finally, some managers and organizations may simply be hung up by all the baggage associated with the term *reflection*. Another important purpose of this book was to disabuse those in business of their stereotyping of reflection. Managers can and do reflect and, indeed, must do so to learn from experience. Active reflection is a natural part of functioning as a manager in a challenging situation, and proactive reflection is something that takes only a small fraction of a manager's time. If the term *reflection* is an obstacle to a business, then an alternative term—perhaps *processing* or *analyzing*—should be used that is more palatable to the company.

Years ago there were those who questioned the need for planning in business, who believed businesses should "just do it." Today no one questions the need for sound business planning, even if it does take time and even if it is removed from the actual conduct of business. We believe that reflection is in the same position today that planning was 50 years ago. Forward-looking companies will not scoff at reflection but will see it as an essential tool for managing in a world of constant change.

SUMMARY

Although the focus of discussion in this book has been business managers undergoing developmental experiences, the findings of the research studies described here are applicable to anyone who needs to learn from experience in a dynamic environment. The ability to continually learn is becoming a requirement of the postmodern world that most people cannot avoid.

This chapter introduced the implications for practice of the research described here. Suggestions for enhancing active and proactive reflection independently as well as in combination were presented. A practical time line was offered and applied to Jean, the manager whose experience was introduced in chapter 12. Our research is of direct relevance to practical attempts to enhance managers' experiential learning. There are many ways beyond what was presented here to apply this research to making managers better reflectors and better learners. The intent of this chapter was simply to illustrate several practical uses of this research.

CONCLUDING THOUGHTS ON MANAGERIAL REFLECTION

Previous work on reflection in the workplace, including our own individual research, has focused on only one or two aspects of reflection. The purpose of this book was to provide a holistic and integrated perspective of reflection by considering the two modes that are apparent in managerial learning and by examining those modes in relation to both their internal cognitive processes and the external forces that impact them. An attempt has been made to give balanced consideration to all of the important factors affecting managerial reflection.

Approaching managerial reflection in this balanced way has produced important theoretical and practical insights. Specifically, this book has made the following contributions: First, we have provided a comprehensive review of current scholarly thinking on the role of reflection in managerial learning. Second, we have used contrasting theory-building and experimental research approaches to produce (*a*) the first in-depth description of the active reflection of a substantial qualitative sample of managers, including the first identification of conditions in managers' work environments that enable reflection during developmental job experiences, and (*b*) the first experimental test of the relative effect of three types of proactive reflection interventions on a managerial sample. Third, we have proposed a new holistic model that integrates research findings on active and proactive reflection. Fourth, we have integrated theory, research, and practice as they relate to reflection in managerial learning.

Long ago Socrates claimed, "The unexamined life is not worth living." Reflection is a primary way to examine one's life. Such examination not only makes life worth living, but for today's overstretched manager, it makes life in business sustainable in an age when learning has become *the* central survival skill.

References

Allinson, C. W., & Hayes, J. 1988. The learning styles questionnaire: An alternative to Kolb's inventory? *Journal of Management Studies*, 25(3): 269–281.

Argyris, C. 1957. *Personality and organization*. New York: Harper.

Argyris, C. 1976. Theories of action that inhibit individual learning. *American Psychologist*, September: 638–654.

Argyris, C. 1982. The executive mind and double-loop learning. *Organizational Dynamics*, Autumn, 5–22.

Argyris, C. 1991. Teaching smart people how to learn. *Harvard Business Review*, May–June: 99–109.

Argyris, C., Putman, R., & Smith, D. M. 1985. *Action science*. San Francisco: Jossey-Bass.

Argyris, C., & Schön, D. 1978. *Organizational learning: A theory of action perspective*. Reading, MA: Addison-Wesley.

Arthur, M. B., Hall, D. T., & Lawrence, B. S. 1989. *Handbook of career theory*. Cambridge, England: Cambridge University Press.

Bandura, A. 1986. *Social foundations of thought and action: A social cognitive theory*. Englewood Cliffs, NJ: Prentice-Hall.

Barnett, B. G., & Brill, A. D. 1989. *Building reflection into administrative training programs*. Paper presented at the Convention of the University Council for Educational Administration, Cincinnati, OH.

Barrett, F. J. 1995. Creating appreciative learning cultures. *Organizational Dynamics*, 24(2): 36–49.

Bartunek, J. M., & Louis, M. R. 1988. The design of work environments to stretch managers' capacities for complex thinking. *Human Resource Planning*, 11(1): 13–22.

Belenky, M. F., Clinchy, B. M., Goldberger, N. R., & Tarule, J. 1986. *Women's ways of knowing: The development of self, voice, and mind*. New York: Basic Books.

Bennis, W. 1989. *On becoming a leader*. Reading, MA: Addison-Wesley.

Berlew, D. E., & Hall, D. T. 1966. The socialization of managers: Effects of expectations on performance. *Administrative Science Quarterly*, 11: 207–223.

Bogdan, R. C., & Biklen, S. K. 1982. *Qualitative research for education: An introduction to theory and methods*. Boston: Allyn and Bacon.

Bouchard, T. J. 1976. Field research methods: Interviewing, questionnaires, participant observation, systematic observation unobtrusive measures. In M. D. Dunnette (Ed.), *Handbook of industrial and organizational psychology* (363–414) Chicago: Rand McNally.

Boud, D., Keogh, R., & Walker, D. (Eds.) 1985. *Reflection: Turning experience into learning.* London: Kogan Page.

Boyd, E. M., & Fales, A. W. 1983. Reflective learning: The key to learning from experience. *Journal of Humanistic Psychology*, 23(2): 99–117.

Brockmann, E. N., & Simmonds, P. G. 1997. Strategic decision making: The influence of CEO experience and use of tacit knowledge. *Journal of Managerial Issues*, 9: 454–468.

Brookfield, S. D. 1987. *Developing critical thinkers: Challenging adults to explore alternative ways of thinking and acting.* San Francisco: Jossey-Bass.

Brooks, A. K. 1989. Critically reflective learning within a corporate context. (Doctoral dissertation, Columbia University Teachers College.) *Dissertation Abstracts International, 50–08A*, 2348.

Brown, D., & Brooks, L. 1990. Introduction to career development: Origins, evolution, and current approaches. In D. Brown, L. Brooks, & Associates (Eds.), *Career choice and development* (2d ed., 1–13). San Francisco: Jossey-Bass.

Bunker, K. A., & Webb, A. D. 1992. *Learning how to learn from experience: Impact of stress and coping* (Report No. 154). Greensboro, NC: Center for Creative Leadership.

Burgoyne, J. G., & Hodgson, V. E. 1983. Natural learning and managerial action: A phenomenological study in the field setting. *Journal of Management Studies*, 20(3): 387–399.

Burgoyne, J., & Reynolds, M. (Eds.) 1997. *Management learning: Integrating perspectives in theory and practice.* London: Sage.

Campbell, D. T., & Stanley, J. C. 1963. *Experimental and quasi-experimental designs for research.* Chicago: Rand McNally.

Campbell, J. P., Dunnette, M. D., Lawler, E. E., & Weick, K. E. 1970. *Managerial behavior, performance and effectiveness.* New York: McGraw-Hill.

Canning, C. 1991. What teachers say about reflection. *Educational Leadership*, 48(6): 18–21.

Clark, M. C., & Wilson, A. L. 1991. Context and rationality in Mezirow's theory of transformational learning. *Adult Education Quarterly*, 41(2): 75–91.

Dalton, M. A. 1998. *Becoming a more versatile leader.* Greensboro, NC: Center for Creative Leadership.

Daudelin, M. W. 1996a. Learning from experience through reflection. *Organizational Dynamics*, 24(3): 36–48.

Daudelin, M. W. 1996b. *The reflection handbook: Guidelines for leveraging learning from challenging work experiences.* Ayer, MA: Marilyn W. Daudelin.

Davies, J., & Easterby-Smith, M. 1984. Learning and developing from managerial work experiences. *Journal of Management Studies*, 21(2): 169–183.

de Rivera, J. (Ed.) 1981. *Conceptual encounter: A method for the exploration of human experience.* Washington, DC: University Press of America.

Dewey, J. 1910. *How we think.* Boston: D.C. Heath and Co.

Dotlich, D., & Noel, J. 1998. *Action learning: How the world's top companies are recreating their leaders and themselves.* San Francisco: Jossey-Bass.

Eichelberger, R. T. 1989. *Disciplined inquiry.* New York: Longman.

Eisenhardt, K. 1989. Building theories from case study research. *Academy of Management Review*, 14(4): 532–550.

Evered, R., & Louis, M. R. 1981. Alternative perspectives in the organizational sciences: Inquiry from the inside and inquiry from the outside. *Academy of Management Review*, 6(3): 385–395.

Flor, R. F. 1990. Integrating experiential education. In R. F. Flor (Ed.), *Proceedings manual of the annual conference of the Association for Experiential Education.* St. Paul, MN: Association for Experiential Education. (ERIC Document Reproduction Service No. ED 327 355)

Freedman, R. D., & Stumpf, S. A. 1980. Learning style theory: Less than meets the eye. *Academy of Management Review*, 5: 445–447.

Fritts, J. C. 1989. A reflective leader development model: An investigation into the current use and potentialities of reflective thinking activities (Doctoral dissertation, Seattle University). *Dissertation Abstracts International, 50–07A:* 1865.

Fulwiler, T. (Ed.) 1987. *The journal book.* Portsmouth, NH: Heinemann Educational Books.

Garvin, D. A. 1993. Building a learning organization. *Harvard Business Review*, 71(4): 78–92.

Geertz, C. 1983. Thick description: Toward an interpretive theory of culture. In R. M. Emerson (Ed.), *Contemporary field research* (37–59). Prospect Heights, IL: Waveland Press.

Gioia, D. A., & Poole, P. P. 1984. Scripts in organizational behavior. *Academy of Management Review*, 9(3): 449–459.

Glaser, B. G., & Strauss, A. L. 1967. *The discovery of grounded theory: Strategies for qualitative research.* New York: Aldine De Gruyter.

Glenn, H. S., & Nelson, J. 1989. *Raising self-reliant children in a self-indulgent world: Seven building blocks for developing capable young people.* Rocklin, CA: Prima Publishing and Communications.

Guba, E. G., & Lincoln, Y. S. 1994. Competing paradigms in qualitative research. In N. K. Denzin and Y. S. Lincoln (Eds.), *Handbook of qualitative research* (105–117). Thousand Oaks, CA: Sage.

Gummesson, E. 1991. *Qualitative methods in management research.* Newbury Park, CA: Sage.

Hackman, J. R. 1985. Doing research that makes a difference. In E. E. Lawler, A. M. Mohrman, S. A. Mohrman, G. E. Ledford, T. G. Cummings & Associates, (Eds.) *Doing research that is useful for theory and practice* (126–155). San Francisco: Jossey-Bass.

Hackman, J. R., & Oldham, G. R. 1980. *Work redesign.* Reading, MA: Addison-Wesley.

Hall, D. T. 1976. *Careers in organizations.* Pacific Palisades, CA: Goodyear Publishing Co.

Hall, D. T. 1986a. Dilemmas in linking succession planning to individual executive learning. *Human Resource Management*, 25(2): 235–265.

Hall, D. T. 1986b. Breaking career routines: Midcareer choice and identity development. In D. T. Hall & Associates (Eds.) *Career development in organizations* (120–159). San Francisco: Jossey-Bass.

Hall, D. T., & Associates. 1996. *The career is dead—long live the career: A relationship approach to careers.* San Francisco: Jossey-Bass.

Hall, D. T., & Fukami, C. V. 1979. Organization design and adult learning. *Research in Organizational Behavior*, 1: 125–167.

Hall, D. T., & Seibert, K. W. 1992. Strategic management development: Linking strategy, succession planning, and managerial learning. In D. H. Montross & C. J. Shinkman (Eds.), *Career development: Theory and practice* (255–278). Springfield, IL: Charles C. Thomas.

Hall, E. T. 1959. *The silent language.* Garden City, NY: Doubleday & Company.

Hammer, M., & Stanton, S. A. 1997. The power of reflection. *Fortune*, November 24: 291–296.

Hedlund, D. E. 1989. A dialogue with self: The journal as an educational tool. *Journal of Humanistic Education and Development*, 2(3): 105–113.

Hill, L. A. 1992. *Becoming a manager: Mastery of a new identity.* Cambridge, MA: Harvard Business School Press.

Hoberman, S., & Mailick, S. 1992. *Experiential management development: From learning to practice.* Westport, CT: Quorum Books.

Horwood, B. 1989. Reflections on reflection. *The Journal of Experiential Education*, 12(2): 5–6.

House, R. J. 1967. *Management development: Design, evaluation and implementation*. Ann Arbor, MI: University of Michigan Bureau of Industrial Relations.

Hullfish, H. G., & Smith, P. G. 1961. *Reflective thinking: The method of education*. New York: Dodd, Mead & Company.

Hutchings, P., & Wutzdorff, A. 1988. *Knowing and doing: Learning through experience*. San Francisco: Jossey-Bass.

Isaacs, W. N. 1992. *Dialogue project summary*. Unpublished manuscript, Massachusetts Institute of Technology, Organizational Learning Center, Cambridge, MA.

Isaacs, W. N. 1995. *Dialogue and a field theory of thought*. Unpublished manuscript, Massachusetts Institute of Technology, Cambridge, MA.

Jordon, J. 1997. *A relational theory of organizing*. Paper presented at Academy of Management, August 1997, Boston, MA.

Justice, D. O., & Marienau, C. 1988. Self-assessment: Essential skills for adult learners. In P. Hutchings & A. Wutzdorff (Eds.), *Knowing and doing: Learning through experience* (49–62). San Francisco: Jossey-Bass.

Kahn, W. A. 1990. Psychological conditions of personal engagement and disengagement at work. *Academy of Management Journal*, 33(4): 692–724.

Kanter, R. M. 1986. *Mastering change and innovation* (Report No. 5). Boston: The Forum Corporation.

Kaskowitz, G. 1995. Factor analysis of the model constructs suggested by Kolb's learning skills profile. *Perceptual and Motor Skills*, 80(2): 479–486.

Katz, R. L. 1974. Skills of an effective administrator. *Harvard Business Review*, September–October: 90–102.

Kelleher, D., Finestone, P., & Lowy, A. 1986. Managerial learning: First notes from an unstudied frontier. *Group and Organization Studies*, 11(3): 169–202.

Kerlinger, F. N. 1973. *Foundations of behavioral research* (2d ed.). New York: Holt, Rinehart and Winston.

Killian, J. P., & Todnem, G. R. 1991. A process for personal theory building. *Educational Leadership*, 48(6): 14–16.

Knapp, C. E. 1992. *Lasting lessons: A teacher's guide to reflecting on experience*. Charleston, WV: Applachia Educational Laboratory. (ERIC Document Reproduction Service No. ED 348 204)

Knights, S. 1985. Reflection and learning: The importance of a listener. In D. Bond, R. Keogh, & D. Walker (Eds.), *Reflection: Turning experience into language* (85–90). London: Kogan Page.

Kolb, D. A. 1976. *Learning style inventory: Technical manual*. Boston: McBer.

Kolb, D. A. 1984. *Experiential learning: Experience as the source of learning and development*. Englewood Cliffs, NJ: Prentice-Hall.

Kolb, D. A., & Lewis, L. H. 1986. Faciltating experiential learning: Observations and reflections. In L. H. Lewis (Ed.), *Experiential and simulation techniques for teaching adults* (99–107). San Francisco: Jossey-Bass.

Kottkamp, R. B. 1990. Means for facilitating reflection. *Education and Urban Society*, 22(2): 182–203.

Kram, K. E. 1985. On the researcher's group memberships. In D. N. Berg & K. K. Smith (Eds.), *Exploring clinical methods for social research* (247–266). Beverly Hills, CA: Sage.

Kram, K. E. 1988. *Mentoring at work: Developmental relationship in organizational life*. Lanham, MD: University Press of America.

Kram, K. E., & Isabella, L. 1985. Mentoring alternatives: The role of peer relationships in career development. *Academy of Management Journal*, 28: 110–132.

Kuhn, T. 1970. *The structure of scientific revolutions*. Chicago: University of Chicago Press.

Langer, E. J. 1989. *Mindfulness*. Reading, MA: Addison-Wesley.

Levinson, D. J., Darrow, C. N., Klein, E. B., Levinson, M. H., & McKee, B. 1978. *The seasons of a man's life*. New York: Ballantine Books.

Levitt, B., & March, J. G. 1988. Organizational learning. *Annual Review of Psychology*, 14: 319–339.

Lewin, K. 1947. *The research center for group dynamics*. New York: Beacon House.

Lewin, K. 1948. *Resolving social conflicts*. New York: Harper & Row.

Lewin, K. 1951. *Field research in social sciences*. New York: Harper & Row.

Lindholm, J. 1988. *Interaction patterns at work: The manager's role in developing subordinates*. Paper presented at the Academy of Management, August 1988, Anaheim, CA.

Louis, M. R. 1980. Surprise and sense making: What newcomers experience in entering unfamiliar organizational settings. *Administrative Science Quarterly*, 25: 226–251.

Louis, M. R., & Sutton, R. I. 1991. Shifting cognitive gears: From habits of mind to active thinking. *Human Relations*, 35: 55–76.

Mann, R. W., & Staudenmier, J. M. 1991. Strategic shifts in executive development. *Training and Development*, 45(7): 37–40.

March, J. G., & Olsen, J. P. 1979. *Ambiguity and choice in organizations*. Bergen, Norway: Universitetsforlaget.

March, J. G., & Simon, H. A. 1958. *Organizations*. New York: Wiley.

Marshall, C., & Rossman, G. B. 1989. *Designing qualitative research*. Newbury Park, CA: Sage.

Marsick, V. J. 1988. Learning in the workplace: The case for reflectivity and critical reflectivity. *Adult Education Quarterly*, 38(4): 187–198.

Marsick, V. J. 1990. Action learning and reflection in the workplace. In J. Mezirow & Associates (Eds.), *Fostering critical reflection in adulthood* (23–46). San Francisco: Jossey-Bass.

Marsick, V. J., & Watkins, K. E., 1997. Lessons from informal and incidental learning. In J. Burgoyne & M. Reynolds (Eds.), *Management learning: Integrating perspectives in theory and practice* (295–311). London: Sage.

McCall, M. W. 1991. Personal communication.

McCall, M. W. Jr., Lombardo, M. M., & Morrison, A. M. 1988. *The lessons of experience*. New York: Lexington Books.

McGregor, D. 1960. *The human side of enterprise*. New York: McGraw-Hill.

Merriam, S. B., & Caffarella, R. S. 1991. *Learning in adulthood*. San Francisco: Jossey-Bass.

Mezirow, J. 1978. *Education for perspective transformation: Re-entry programs in community colleges*. New York: Teacher's College, Columbia University.

Mezirow, J. 1985. A critical theory of self-directed learning. In S. Brookfield (Ed.), *Self-directed learning: From theory to practice* (New Directions for Continuing Education, #25). San Francisco: Jossey-Bass.

Mezirow, J. 1991. *Transformative dimensions in adult learning*. San Francisco: Jossey-Bass.

Mezirow, J., & Associates. 1990. *Fostering critical reflection in adulthood: A guide to transformative and emancipatory learning*. San Francisco: Jossey-Bass.

Miles, M. B., & Huberman, A. M. 1984. *Qualitative data analysis: A sourcebook of new methods*. Newbury Park, CA: Sage.

Mintzberg, H. 1973. *The nature of managerial work*. New York: Harper & Row.

Mintzberg, H. 1979. An emerging strategy of direct research. *Administrative Science Quartely*, 24: 580–589.

Mintzberg, H. 1990. The manager's job: Folklore and fact. *Harvard Business Review*, March–April: 163–176.

Mirvis, P. H., & Louis, M. R. 1985. Self-full research: Working through the self as instrument in organizational research. In D. N. Berg & K. K. Smith (Eds.), *Exploring clinical methods for social research* (229–246). Beverly Hills, CA: Sage.

Morgan, G. 1986. *Images of organization*. Beverly Hills, CA: Sage.

Mumford, A. 1990. The individual and learning opportunities. *Industrial and Commercial Training*, 22(1): 17–22.

Neugarten, B. L. 1984. Interpretive social science and research on aging. In A. Rossi (Ed.), *Gender and the life course* (291–300). Chicago: Aldine

O'Neil, J., & Marsick, V. J. 1994. Becoming critically reflective through action reflective learning™. *New Directions for Adult and Continuing Education*, 63: 17–30.

Osterman, K. F. 1990. Reflective practice: A new agenda for education. *Education and Urban Society*, 22(2): 133–152.

Passmore, D. L. 1990. Invited reaction: Pick a paradigm, any paradigm. *Human Resource Development Quarterly*, 1(1): 25–27.

Patton, M. Q. 1980. *Qualitative evaluation methods*. Beverly Hills, CA: Sage.

Paul, R., & Binker, A. J. A. 1990. Socratic questioning. In R. Paul (Ed.), *Critical thinking* (269–298). Rohnert Park, CA: Center for Critical Thinking and Moral Critique.

Pedhazur, E. J. 1982. *Multiple regression in behavioral research*. New York: Holt, Rinehart and Winston.

Permaul, J. S. 1982. Monitoring and supporting experiential learning (Panel Resource Paper #5). Raleigh, NC: National Society for Internships and Experiential Education. (ERIC Reproduction Service No. ED 260 633)

Peters, T. 1992. *Liberation management: Necessary disorganization for the nanosecond nineties*. New York: Alfred A. Knopf.

Piaget, J. 1968. *Structuralism*. New York: Harper Torchbooks.

Reimer, J. 1993. Research design: Experimental and quasi-experimental. In E. T. Nickerson (Ed.), *The dissertation handbook: A guide to successful dissertations* (2d ed., 48–58). Dubuque, IA: Kendall/Hunt Publishing Co.

Reinharz, S. 1979. *On becoming a social scientist*. San Francisco: Jossey-Bass.

Revans, R. W. 1982. *The origins and growth of action learning*. London: Chartwell-Bratt Ltd.

Robinson, G. S., & Wick, C. W. 1992. Executive development that makes a business difference. *Human Resource Planning*, 15(1): 63–76.

Roth, R. A. 1989. Preparing the reflective practitioner: Transforming the apprentice through the dialectic. *Journal of Teacher Education*, 40(2): 31–35.

Ruderman, M. N., Ohlott, P. J. & Kram, K. E. 1995. Promotion decisions as a diversity practice. *Journal of Management Development*, 14(2): 6–23.

Ryan, M. 1988. The teachable moment: The Washington Center Internship Program. In P. Hutchings & A. Wutzdorff (Eds.), *Knowing and doing: Learning from experience*. San Francisco: Jossey-Bass.

Saari, L. M., Johnson, T. R., Mclaughlin, S. D., & Zimmerle, D. M. 1988. A survey of management training and education practices in U. S. companies. *Personnel Psychology*, 41(4): 731–743.

Sanders, P. 1982. Phenomenology: A new way of viewing organizational research. *Academy of Management Review*, 7: 353–360.

Sayers, D. L. 1979. The lost tools of learning. *National Review*, January 19: 90–99.

Schön, D. A. 1983. *The reflective practitioner*. New York: Basic Books.

Schön, D. A. 1987. *Educating the reflective practitioner*. San Francisco: Jossey-Bass.

Seibert, K. W. Reflection-in-action: Tools for cultivating on-the-job learning conditions. *Organizational Dynamics*, 27(3): 54–65.

Seibert, K. W., Hall, D. T., & Kram, K. E. 1995. Strengthening the weak link in strategic executive development: Integrating individual development and global business strategy. *Human Resource Management*, 34(4): 549–567.

Seidel, J. V., Kjolseth, R., & Seymour, E. 1988. *The ethnograph: A program for the computer assisted analysis of text based data* (Version 3. 0). Amherst, MA: Qualis Research Associates.

Senge, P. M. 1990. *The fifth discipline: The art and practice of the learning organization.* New York: Doubleday/Currency.

Sherman, S. 1994. Leaders learn to heed the voice within. *Fortune*, August 22: 92–100.

Shuner, R. 1990. Reflection: At the heart of experiential learning. In R. F. Flor (Ed.), *Proceedings manual of the Annual Conference of the Association for Experiential Education.* St. Paul, MN: Association for Experiential Education. (ERIC Document Reproduction Service No. ED 327 355)

Sims, H. P., & Lorenzi, P. 1992. *The new leadership paradigm: Social learning and cognition in organizations.* Newbury Park, CA: Sage.

Sparks-Langer, G. M., & Colton, A. B. 1991. Synthesis of research on teachers' reflective thinking. *Educational Leadership*, 48(6): 37–44.

Stehno, J. J. 1986. The application and integration of experiential education in higher education. (ERIC Document Reproduction Service No. ED 285 465)

Strauss, A., & Corbin, J. 1990. *Basics of qualitative research: Grounded theory procedures and techniques.* Newbury Park, CA: Sage.

Thomas, L., & Harri-Augstein, S. 1977. Learning to learn. In M. J. A. Howe (Ed.), *Adult learning: psychological research and application* (85–102). London: Wiley.

Tichy, N. M., & Devanna, M. A. 1986. *The transformational leader.* New York: Wiley.

Tobin, D. 1996. *Transformational learning.* New York: Wiley.

Tyler, L. E. 1983. *Thinking creatively: A new approach to psychology and individual lives.* San Francisco: Jossey-Bass.

Vicere, A. A. 1996. Executive education: The leading edge. *Organizational Dynamics*, 25(2): 67–81.

Weick, K. E. 1979. Cognitive processes in organizations. *Research in Organizational Behavior*, 1: 41–74.

Wexley, K. N. 1984. Personnel training. *Annual Review of Psychology*, 35: 519–551.

Wutzdorff, A., & Hutchings, P. 1988. An integrating seminar: Bringing knowledge and experience together. In P. Hutchings & A. Wutzdorff (Eds.), *Knowing and doing: Learning through experience.* San Francisco: Jossey-Bass.

Zemke, R. 1985. The Honeywell studies: How managers learn how to manage. *Training*, August: 46–51.

Index

question casting, 200–201, 206
questionnaire. *See* posttest questionnaire
questions: active reflection, 78–79; case
   study, 188; inbriefing/debriefing, 179;
   integrated model of reflection, 185,
   200; posttest questionnaire, 151;
   proactive reflection, 29–30, 148, 168;
   spontaneous reflection, 68; types,
   80–82; use, 25–26, 65–66. *See also*
   inquiry; question casting
quick response, 135

real-time. *See* on-line reflection
recommendations: enhancing reflection,
   proactive, 203–5; active, 205–8; holistic approach, 208–12
reflection-in-action, 9, 25, 63, 90, 182,
   192. *See also* Schön
reflectivity, 20. *See also* critical reflectivity
regression analysis, 152
requirements, for proactive reflection, 26.
   See also conditions
re-reflecting, *See* off-line reflection
research approaches, 33–43
research design, proactive reflection, 149
research participants, demographics, 56
research participants: Food Corp., Bob,
   51, 73, 75, 81, 87, 89, 92, 101, 107,
   124, 137, 141; Christine, 51, 73, 97,
   127, 131; Cliff, 51, 73, 81, 89–90, 98,
   99, 135; Gill, 51, 72, 73, 120; James,
   51, 72, 73, 120; Jerry, 51, 67–70, 73,
   74, 75, 79–80, 82, 83, 89, 91, 93, 97,
   98, 104, 106, 111, 127–28, 130, 135,
   137–38, 181; Mark, 51, 73, 89, 92,
   107, 108, 111, 112, 132, 135–36;
   Patrick, 51, 72, 73, 100, 120, 136;
   Pete, 51, 73, 87, 97, 100, 103,
   111–12, 127, 129, 132, 181; Phyllis,
   73, 78, 97, 100; Rick, 51, 73, 91, 105,
   123, 124–26, 128–29, 131–32, 141;
   Ted, 51, 73, 74, 81, 83, 97, 99, 101,
   106, 111–12, 130, 133, 136–38, 140,
   181
research participants: Health Co., Brad,
   55, 73, 87–89, 105; Coleen, 55, 56,
   70–71, 72, 73, 120; Doug, 55, 73, 98,

107; Harry, 55, 73, 74, 89, 108–9,
   111, 132, 140; Loretta, 55, 56, 72, 73,
   120; Matt, 55, 73, 88–89, 105, 108,
   131; Meg, 55, 73, 86, 107, 108, 110,
   111; Paul, 55, 73, 103, 107, 138;
   Sarah, 55, 73, 87, 102, 118–19, 141;
   Steve, 55, 73, 84, 89, l08, 110–12,
   131, 136; Tim, 55, 73, 74, 85, 86, 89,
   96; Todd, 55, 73, 81
research participants, race and gender,
   193, 198
research questions: active reflection,
   47–48; proactive reflection, 145
Revans, R. W., 24
Robinson, G. S. and Wick, C. W., 5

sample: Food Corp., 50–52; Health Co.,
   54–56; limitations, active reflection,
   193; limitations, proactive reflection,
   198; Tech Inc., 147
satisficing, 82
"saturation," 61
Sayers, D. L., 18
Schön, D. A.: differences in research
   approaches, 35, 182; education literature, 25; off-line reflection, 101; professional practice, 8–12;
   reflection-in-action, 63, 98, 192. *See
   also* reflection-in-action
scientific procedures. *See* research
   approaches
self-analysis, 57, 62
Senge, P. M., 8, 81
setting, 147
Sherman, S., 5
Shuner, R., 18
Sims, H. P. and Lorenzi, P., 4
single-loop learning, 7–8
socio-emotional learning, 196
spontaneous reflection, 9, 68, 179
state of mind. *See* psychological states
steps of reflection, 21
stimulation by others, 118,133–36. *See
   also* contextual conditions
suggestions. *See* recommendations
support, lack of, 131–33
supported, 118–19, 129–33. *See also* psychological states

ABOUT THE AUTHORS

KENT W. SEIBERT is Assistant Professor of Business and Economics at Wheaton College (IL). He has twenty years of experience researching, writing, and working with employees and companies on issues of workplace learning.

MARILYN W. DAUDELIN is a writer and consultant specializing in helping people learn from their challenging work experiences using reflection strategies. She has over twenty years experience as an internal consultant and program manager at Polaroid Corporation.